Community Disaster Recovery

Disasters can serve as focusing events that increase agenda attention related to issues of disaster response, recovery, and preparedness. Increased agenda attention can lead to policy changes and organizational learning. The degree and type of learning that occurs within a government organization after a disaster may matter to policy outcomes related to individual, household, and community-level risks and resilience. Local governments are the first line of disaster response but also bear the burden of performing long-term disaster recovery and planning for future events. Crow and Albright present a framework for understanding if, how, and to what effect communities and local governments learn after a disaster strikes. Drawing from analyses conducted over a five-year period following extreme flooding in Colorado, USA, *Community Disaster Recovery: Moving from Vulnerability to Resilience* presents a framework of community-level learning after disaster and the factors that catalyze policy change toward resilience.

DR. DESERAI A. CROW is an associate professor at the School of Public Affairs at the University of Colorado, Denver and researches local- and state-level environmental policy, often focusing on crisis and disaster recovery and risk mitigation in local communities and natural resource agencies. Deserai's crisis and disaster work includes National Science Foundation funded work on disaster recovery, Covid-19 risk perceptions and behaviors as influenced by state-level policies, and environmental justice outcomes associated with local control of oil and gas regulations.

DR. ELIZABETH A. ALBRIGHT is an associate professor of the Practice at the Nicholas School of the Environment at Duke University and engages in research around questions of local-level resilience, and community learning in response to extreme events. Funded by the National Science Foundation, her work in Colorado was recognized for the Paul A. Sabatier Award for Best Paper in Environmental Politics at the American Political Science Association annual meeting.

Organizations and the Natural Environment

The increasing attention given to environmental protection issues has
resulted in a growing demand for high-quality, actionable research on
sustainability and business environmental management. This new
series, published in conjunction with the Group for Research on
Organizations and the Natural Environment (GRONEN), presents
students, academics, managers, and policy-makers with the latest
thinking on key topics influencing business practice today.

Community Disaster Recovery

Moving from Vulnerability to Resilience

DESERAI A. CROW
University of Colorado Denver

ELIZABETH A. ALBRIGHT
Duke University

Shaftesbury Road, Cambridge CB2 8EA, United Kingdom

One Liberty Plaza, 20th Floor, New York, NY 10006, USA

477 Williamstown Road, Port Melbourne, VIC 3207, Australia

314–321, 3rd Floor, Plot 3, Splendor Forum, Jasola District Centre, New Delhi – 110025, India

103 Penang Road, #05–06/07, Visioncrest Commercial, Singapore 238467

Cambridge University Press is part of Cambridge University Press & Assessment,
a department of the University of Cambridge.

We share the University's mission to contribute to society through the pursuit of
education, learning and research at the highest international levels of excellence.

www.cambridge.org
Information on this title: www.cambridge.org/9781009054379

DOI: 10.1017/9781009053457

First published 2021
First paperback edition 2024

A catalogue record for this publication is available from the British Library

Library of Congress Cataloging-in-Publication data
Names: Crow, Deserai A., 1975– author. | Albright, Elizabeth Ann, author.
Title: Community disaster recovery : moving from vulnerability to resilience /
    Deserai A. Crow, Elizabeth A. Albright.
Description: Cambridge, United Kingdom ; New York, NY : Cambridge University Press,
    2022. | Series: Organizations and the natural environment | Includes bibliographical
    references and index.
Identifiers: LCCN 2021017605 (print) | LCCN 2021017606 (ebook) |
    ISBN 9781316511640 (hardback) | ISBN 9781009054379 (paperback) |
    ISBN 9781009053457 (epub)
Subjects: LCSH: Community development–Environmental aspects–Colorado. | Sustainable
    urban development–Colorado. | Hazard mitigation–Colorado. | Sustainable development–
    Colorado. | BISAC: BUSINESS& ECONOMICS / Business Ethics
Classification: LCC HN79.C63 C637 2022 (print) | LCC HN79.C63 (ebook) |
    DDC 307.1/409788–dc23
LC record available at https://lccn.loc.gov/2021017605
LC ebook record available at https://lccn.loc.gov/2021017606

ISBN   978-1-316-51164-0   Hardback
ISBN   978-1-009-05437-9   Paperback

Contents

Part III   Review

Part IV   Individual and Group Engagement

Part IV   Review

Part V   Connections, Conclusions, and Recommendations

Figures

Tables

About the Authors

Elizabeth A. Albright is Associate Professor of the Practice at the Nicholas School of the Environment at Duke University. She engages in research around questions of local-level resilience and community learning in response to extreme events. She is currently working on projects studying response to disasters, including COVID-19 and hurricanes, in various regions across the United States. Funded by the National Science Foundation, her work in Colorado was awarded the Paul A. Sabatier Award for Best Paper in Environmental Politics at the American Political Science Association annual meeting. She has published on response to extreme events, perceptions of climate change, the advocacy coalition framework, and stakeholder participation in state-level regulatory processes. She earned her PhD from Nicholas School of the Environment, a master of public affairs and a master of science in environmental science from the School of Public and Environmental Affairs at Indiana University, and a BA in chemistry from the College of Wooster.

Deserai A. Crow is Associate Professor in the School of Public Affairs at the University of Colorado Denver. She researches local and state-level environmental policy, including stakeholder participation and influence, information sources used, and policy outcomes. Her work often focuses on crisis and disaster recovery and risk mitigation in local communities and natural resource agencies. Her crisis and disaster work includes National Science Foundation–funded work on disaster recovery, COVID-19 risk perceptions and behaviors as influenced by state-level policies, and environmental justice outcomes associated with local control of oil and gas regulations. She earned her PhD from Duke University's Nicholas School of the Environment. She also holds a master's in public administration from the University of Colorado Denver's School of Public Affairs and a BS in journalism from the University of Colorado Boulder.

Foreword

I am excited to provide the foreword to *Community Disaster Recovery*, because this book sets an important standard in studies of the policy process in general, and of disaster recovery in particular. While the title of the book may suggest that this is a book primarily about disaster policy, this book also makes an important contribution to public policy theory. It does this through the careful application, assessment, and refinement of policy theory to advance both our theories of the policy process and to apply those theories to a better understanding of how communities confront disasters, assess their vulnerability, and develop policies and practices that promote resilience.

This book is the result of eight years of intensive research. Those of us who have followed Crow and Albright's research will be pleased to see the results of their work compiled in one book; those who are novices to this research field are in for a treat, because you will find a very readable book on how communities can learn and become resilient after a disaster. This readability does not come at the cost of theoretical and empirical rigor. Instead, what Crow and Albright have done is draw upon an exceptionally large body of literature in the policy process, public administration, public participation, disaster studies, and related disciplines to not only illuminate how communities can learn from disaster but also what differentiates communities that are better able to learn from other communities that may have greater challenges to overcome to promote learning.

The theoretical contribution this book makes is straightforward. The theory is that sudden, shocking events – called *focusing events* in John Kingdon's seminal *Agendas, Alternatives, and Public Policy* (2011), and that in my work (1997, 1998, 2004, 2006) I amended to call *potential* focusing events – lead to greater attention to the problems revealed by these events. I argued that the attention sparked by these potential focusing events may trigger attempts to learn about policy failure, which in turn may yield efforts to improve policy based on this learning. The book you are about to read engages deeply with the link between focusing events and learning. My work has painted this learning process with a broad brush. By contrast, this book takes a very deep look at the processes of attention, perceptions of policy failure, and potential policy learning, at the very local level.

Unfortunately, in much of the literature on disasters and on the policy process, the term "focusing event" has become a catch-all term for "big event" or "crisis," but such superficial treatments of the term fail to take seriously my definition of *potential* focusing events. This definition is important because not all crises or big events yield much in the way of policy change or learning. Nor do such superficial treatments of the term explain *how* major events matter in the policy process beyond serving as important events, leaving the mechanisms of policy change either implicit or unspecified.

Certainly, big, shocking, and damaging events can gain a great deal of attention. But crises and disasters are *potential* focusing events – that is, they are only potentially consequential in the history of a body of public policy – because we can almost never know, *a priori*, whether and to what extent an event will gain broad and sustained attention. But does this attention translate to actual policy *learning* and change? This book tackles this seemingly simple yet deeply important question by relating the event to efforts in a community to learn from the event and to emerge from the event less vulnerable and more resilient in the face of ongoing risks than the community was before.

This book comes at an important time in the history of both policy studies and of disaster studies. Students of this field know that our societies – our communities, our economies, and our political systems and institutions – are being tested by events that, depending on their scope and scale, are called extreme events, disasters, or catastrophes. This characterization of an event in a particular community or unit of government is a matter of perspective: One house fire may not be a disaster to a community, but it can be catastrophic to a homeowner. The 2013 Colorado floods described in this book were, to some people, and some communities, a nuisance, or a challenge, but to other people and communities they were catastrophic. The same is true of communities: As you will learn in this book, the City of Boulder found that the 2013 floods were an important managerial and financial challenge, but the event was catastrophic in Lyons and Longmont, which continued to work on recovery *seven years* after the floods.

Clearly, these kinds of events test the resilience of a community. Resilience is a term that has become more common in the study and practice of disaster preparedness and recovery in the last two decades. Like the term it in many ways replaced in disaster studies, "sustainability," resilience runs the risk of becoming a buzzword, so broadly and carelessly applied that it loses most of its meaning. But resilience has at least two advantages as a term to help us to understand the long-term effects of disasters. First, resilience is a quality that we can understand intuitively, as an expression of the ability of a community to withstand a shock and then "bounce back" or even improve upon its pre-disaster state, or something close to it. Second, resilience is a quality that we can assess at various scales, from the micro – individuals who experience disasters – to the meso – the community level – to the macro, at the national level. Remarkable progress in understanding resilience at these scales has been made over the last two decades.

For students of the policy process, the degree to which a community is resilient can be considered in terms of its ability to withstand a shock and to *learn* from that shock so as to make policies that are likely to mitigate the effect of future events, and to develop the experience necessary to respond to future events should they occur. Put simply, more resilient communities are better able to learn from disaster experience and improve upon how they manage disasters in the future. Learning from events is important because extreme events, such as floods, are not new to the world generally, or to Colorado in particular. As Crow and Albright make clear, Colorado's hazard profile has long included floods, not least of which was the 1976 Big Thompson Flood, an event that led the pioneers in disaster studies, such as Dr. Gilbert White at the University of Colorado, to redouble their efforts to help communities understand how to work *with* nature to reduce the risks posed by floods. In this way, Colorado's experience has taught lessons that have been learned worldwide.

This is the underlying logic of the idea of *focusing events* in the literature. John Kingdon sought to help students of American politics understand the conditions under which policies can change. He argued that "windows of opportunity" for policy change are opened when policy problems gain attention. One way in which attention is drawn to problems is through focusing events. Kingdon's definition of the term was overly broad and includes sudden events that "bowl over" other issues on the agenda, as well as the life experiences of key policy makers and those times when symbols of problems suddenly take hold. In my work, starting with *After Disaster* (1997), I sought to more clearly specify the things that make focusing events *focal*. To be a focusing event is to gain *attention* to a problem. In my work I sought to explain the features of events that make them focus attention. In this and later work, I argued that *potential* focusing events reveal policy failure, thereby gaining attention and triggering efforts to learn what happened so that a similar event is less likely to happen again. Put more simply, the event *reveals* failure and triggers *learning*.

Formulating the function of focusing events in this way brings together several bodies of literature in the policy process. It draws on theories of agenda setting, both in terms of the "multiple streams" approach launched by Kingdon and built upon by others (Herweg, Zahariadis, & Zohlnhofer, 2017). It also draws upon the ideas of Frank Baumgartner and Bryan Jones, the originators of punctuated equilibrium theory in the policy process (2009). One of their many key insights is the idea that greater attention to an issue is usually greater *negative attention*. Drawing on the work of E. E. Schattschneider (1975), they argue that an event that reveals some sort of problem, including possible policy failure, will generally attract a great deal of attention to the problem, leading to some form of mobilization to address perceived shortcomings of policy. The idea of focusing events revealing failure and triggering learning relates to the advocacy coalition framework (ACF) most closely associated with Paul Sabatier and subsequent work by among others, Hank Jenkins-Smith and Chris Weible (Jenkins-Smith, Nohrstedt, Weible, & Ingold, 2018). The ACF describes how core and peripheral beliefs can change and evolve as coalitions of groups learn about policies and form to pursue change.

The idea of learning from disasters draws upon the insights of the policy learning literature. The link between failure and learning is made particularly clear in an article by Peter May (1992), in which he argues that policy failure can stimulate instrumental policy learning (learning about the nature and function of various policy instruments or tools), social policy learning (learning about the things that cause problems to arise to begin with), and political learning, which is learning about better ways to advocate for different policy positions. Focusing events can influence all of these aspects: For example, a focusing event might induce us to review whether existing regulations are the most effective way to achieve a policy goal. They can also cause us to completely revisit our understanding of a problem to ensure that our policy approaches are correct. For example, for decades people felt that the best ways to prevent floods were to build levees and dams in an often-futile effort to "conquer nature." In disaster studies, Gilbert White and his intellectual progeny have taught us that a better way to think about flood management is thinking about working *with* nature, attempting to accommodate our built environment to natural processes such as annual floods. And disasters as focusing events have provided opportunities for political learning, because dramatic events can be used by advocates for policy change as exemplars and as lessons to be learned about how current policies failed, and why they should change. In the broader sweep of all this theorizing about dealing with floods, what Crow and Albright have written may seem to address a small matter – how some small communities and a modestly large city in Colorado responded to – and learned from – damaging floods. While this may, on its face, seem consequential only for the communities that were challenged by these floods, Crow and Albright have shown that studying policy learning at the local level is a remarkably promising way to study event-driven policy learning. Indeed, this sort of research is fundamental to our understanding of how people and communities address the flood hazard.

A key insight of this book is that "disasters are fundamentally policy-related." This is true for at least two reasons: policies made before disasters help shape whether a disaster will be, in some way, a challenging disaster or a community-crippling catastrophe, and disasters can shape the follow-on policies that themselves shape the nature of the next disaster. Our governments often create the conditions under which disasters are worse than they might otherwise be – they damage more property and kill and injure more people than would have happened had government taken effective measures to mitigate the worst effects of a disaster. It is this problem about which learning is most important in communities threatened by disasters.

The results of Crow and Albright's years of research are well summarized in the "key lessons" boxes in each chapter. The results of their research are exciting, opening new avenues for scholarship and new insights for practitioners. Some of these lessons are not new, such as their finding that different communities have different resources and capacities that they can mobilize in the face of disasters. But this heterogeneity in disaster response is often missed in popular accounts of disaster, and puts the lie to the idea that major disasters are "equal opportunity disasters" that harm the rich and poor indiscriminately. And Crow and Albright document how disaster effects are heterogenous within communities.

What does this mean for theory and practice? Crow and Albright link together *capacity* and *resources*, arguing that communities mobilize these attributes to pursue recovery. This matters because communities with greater human capacities can often devote these resources to improve learning from a recent disaster, so as to mitigate the impact of future events. From a practice perspective, this means that local policy makers should seek to develop their human resources to learn from disasters, and state and national leaders should investigate how they can invest in human resources that promote learning.

How, then, can a community learn and work toward resilience? These processes are profoundly shaped by the nature of individual beliefs around disaster causes and risks. Crow and Albright's book digs deeply into the role of individual beliefs at a level not often seen in studies of public policy, because most studies of the policy process are meso-level studies that tend to focus on the actions of groups and institutions. Here, in this book, Crow and Albright tell the story about how individuals, working together in a community, learn about disasters not simply through their direct exposure to hazard impacts, but through a complex set of interactions involving individuals, their local elected and appointed officials, and the public participation processes in which residents are involved to shape their communities' recovery from disasters. Central to that relationship – and therefore learning – is residents' trust in their local officials, because higher levels of trust are, in the data shown in this book, positively associated with deeper engagement with participatory processes focused on disaster recovery. Put simply, people who trust their local governments are more likely to engage in the very sorts of activity that lead to social policy learning – that is, learning not just about how to do what we do better, but also learning about why we do what we do at all. This has significant implications for the development of policy adoptions in communities that would mitigate or reduce flood risks, such as changes to land use patterns or building codes.

I stress this aspect to draw your attention to the important link between individual perception, trust, and broad community participation in the development of disaster recovery plans and policies in their communities. Crow and Albright put it very clearly: "Participation by residents and other stakeholders leads to higher levels of learning by local governments." But for this learning to occur, the process must include a diversity of stakeholders – the process of engagement cannot simply be one-way – pro forma information sharing, and the process must promote long-term and sustained engagement. These features of engagement are well known to experts in community engagement across a range of disciplines and policy domains, but this study empirically validates what public-participation professionals have long known intuitively: that public engagement requires diversity of viewpoints, trust, shared information, and extended participation. These findings make good the book's promise to be useful to practitioners. The book does not seek to say precisely how any given community should undertake participatory processes to improve recovery planning and implementation. But it does note that the process is intensive and time-consuming and must therefore be taken seriously. This once again highlights the importance of the mobilization of resources after disasters to help communities not only recover from disasters, but to learn *how* and *why* some recovery policies are better, based both on local residents' preferences and on professional criteria, than other policies. Those resources include money, of course, but they also include the resources the community can bring to the discussion, both from the city or town government itself, but also among the people of the community in whose name policies are made. In the end, the process of harnessing of these resources and of effectively deliberating about how those resources are used will influence community resilience.

It is rare to see a book that is deeply grounded in both policy theory and of the substantive area of public policy that it studies. This book is one of them. This book shows how years of dedicated effort to understand the policy decisions made even by smaller communities can yield important insights about the policy process and can point the way to objectively better policy. And, like all good scholarship, this book is likely to inspire other scholars to take up this challenge in their communities and their particular fields. This book both teaches us important lessons and shows the way forward. It is one you will enjoy reading and will value for years to come.

Dr. Thomas A. Birkland, professor of public policy, School of Public and International Affairs, North Carolina State University

Preface

Humans are resilient beings. We face risk and overcome it, often, but not always. We build, we engineer, and we think our way out of problems – both those that nature sends and ones we create for ourselves. Over the coming decades, humans will face unprecedented levels of risk. The most common forms of risk faced by humans are those we create when we interact with nature, by building our houses in fire-prone mountain landscapes and on hurricane-prone shorelines, or by developing dense forested areas and unleashing disease, among many examples.

As we complete this manuscript, people worldwide are confronting a new challenge. Cities and towns have come to a standstill. Multinational corporations and mom-and-pop businesses are shuttered. The most powerful nations appear helpless to the global pandemic of the novel coronavirus and the disease it causes – COVID-19. The most powerful nation with the most unstoppable economy in history has shed millions of jobs in just months, greater than at any similar point in history. The effects of the crisis will be felt for many years to come and countless lessons may be – or may not be – learned from this event. But this pandemic is not the first, nor will it be the last crisis that humans face.

The risks humans face and the myriad factors that cause events such as pandemics, natural disasters, technological accidents, and other crises will increase in the twenty-first century. From climate change and human development, to overpopulation, resource exploitation, and nation-state conflicts, the foundations for future crises are laid everyday around the globe.

So, what are humans to do about these risks? Are we helpless in the face of growing risk and increasing likelihood of crises and disasters?

Having dedicated our attention to understanding these questions, we think people can be resilient, and if not now, we think they can become so.

We think communities can change, adapt, and learn from past mistakes to do better in the future.

This book is rooted in hopefulness about the possibility of change and progress and the importance of making change happen. Only through learning from our past mistakes, changing based on new information, and adapting to future scenarios can we become more resilient. Our communities are on the frontlines of crisis response and planning. The age-old mantra in emergency management that "all disasters are local" guides this book. It is communities, their local governments, and their residents that must make changes to become more resilient in the face of a changing world.

Daily, we are surrounded by images of human failings and government failure. From ignoring public health experts on risk mitigation efforts during a pandemic to intergovernmental strife that can lead to insufficient critical supplies during crises, it is easy to come away with the impression that governments and the people who constitute them are self-centered, inept, and lacking in the empathy necessary to keep people safe and provide for secure futures. In the midst of those same images, however, are also images of public servants and frontline workers leading with courage, risking their own health and well-being to protect their neighbors, and making difficult choices that may not be politically popular but that can keep people safe.

Building more resilient communities will take the fortitude of such government leaders who serve the public interest and know that the risks are simply too great to fail this time. It will also take community members, businesses, advocates, and the rest of us to engage and push for the changes we need.

This time, we must get it right. To keep our communities safe and adapt to risks we naturally face or that we have helped create, we must learn, we must adapt, and we must become more resilient to the risks we face.

This book tells the story of communities in Colorado that faced disaster in 2013. These communities responded in a variety of ways. Those responses shaped the changes – if any – that they made after disaster. Whether the communities and their governments learned after the disaster affected if and how they changed. And whether they change will affect if they are resilient to future risks that they will inevitably face. Observing these communities and learning from them over seven years, we have come to see the possibilities and hope that disaster-affected communities embody. But we have also witnessed failures and frustration. We hope that this book provides some insight so that other communities and governments can begin on the path to resilience through learning and toward change.

Acknowledgments

A project such as this includes people without whom this book would not be possible. Those who contributed to the research, the process, the ideas, and the product were invaluable to ensuring that this book saw the light of day.

First and most importantly, we thank the Colorado study communities for letting us in. When disaster strikes, communities are inundated with volunteers, media, researchers, and ne'er-do-wells. Among those who descend on communities are researchers like us who hope to understand complex, difficult, and sometimes hidden processes that can benefit society if we can understand them and shine light on them. Despite the predictable inundation many of our study communities experienced, they let us in. They welcomed us into small Town Halls in Lyons where they fed us Christmas cookies. They sat with us in conference rooms to tell their stories. They walked along rivers and through destroyed neighborhoods with us. They made sure that their stories were heard and recorded. We hope that we did justly by their stories and helped ensure that these stories matter and can help others. We thank the communities and the people who govern and comprise these communities. Without them this project would not exist.

We must also thank those who inspired us and our ideas and made this project possible. The three-year study this book describes was funded by the National Science Foundation. Before he retired, Dr. Dennis Wenger served as our program director in the Infrastructure Management and Extreme Events program where he guided us, encouraged our ideas to develop, and eventually funded our first major grants as junior scholars. We cannot thank him enough for that mentorship and support.

Readers will note that this book builds upon a rich literature in disaster policy and learning. One scholar you will read in the pages to come has provided mentorship, guidance, and the intellectual foundations for our work. Dr. Tom Birkland is a friend and a mentor to us and to countless other disaster policy scholars whom he has encouraged and supported over his career. This book would look very different if not for Tom's work and the foundations he laid in our field of study. Thank you, Tom, for paving the path for so many of us.

A group of people quite literally made this project into a robust, exciting, and enjoyable part of our professional lives for half of a decade. The research assistants who worked on this project were invaluable to the data collection and development of the project, including Dr. Jack Zhou and Dr. Corrie Hannah. Two of our former graduate students in particular became collaborators and invaluable colleagues during the course of the project. Dr. Lydia Lawhon and Dr. Elizabeth Koebele were as much a part of this endeavor as we were. Their dedication to the project, to our team, to good science, and to being amazing humans made this the most fulfilling project in our professional careers.

Our collaborators and friends who helped make portions of our work come to life include Dr. Todd Ely, who enriched the product presented in this book, and we thank him for sharing his expertise with us.

No book would be possible without the editorial team. Thank you to our editors – Dr. Jorge Rivera and Dr. J. Alberto Aragon Correa – for supporting this work. Thank you to the team at Cambridge University Press, including Valerie Appleby and Tobias Ginsberg, for your hard work to publish this book.

Deserai would like to thank her husband, Jason, who fights for a better world and future every day and makes sure they always do it together. Her resilient, incredible children, Anderson and Josephine, are her reasons to hope for a better future. Also, her parents – Paula, Rick, and Bart – who made her love the places we studied and understand the importance of community.

Elizabeth dedicates this book to her parents, Judy and Terry Albright, who through their support and love encouraged her to question and seek knowledge in the service of society. Elizabeth also thanks the many folks who agreed to share their lived experiences that helped shape this book, and also the many students, friends, family members, and colleagues who have offered their support, which made this book possible.

Studying disasters and writing a book during a pandemic – while juggling online teaching, isolation, homeschooling children, and feeling the weightiness of the topics we research – is not an easy task, but it is best done with someone you trust, respect, laugh with, and call a friend. We met in graduate school at Duke University and this collaboration is truly a labor of love. From this project, if we were to give a piece of advice to junior scholars it would be this: Study something that is important. Research things that can make our world better. And find good people to do it with who make your ideas better and make your life more enjoyable. That will make it all worthwhile.

Abbreviations

ACF	advocacy coalition framework
BCC	Boulder County Collaborative
CDBG-DR	Community Development Block Grant Disaster Recovery Program
CRO	Colorado Resiliency Office
CRS	Congressional Research Service
CWCB	Colorado Water Conservation Board
DHS	Department of Homeland Security
DOLA	Colorado Department of Local Affairs
FEMA	Federal Emergency Management Agency
HHS	Department of Health and Human Services
HSEM	Department of Homeland Security and Emergency Management
HUD	Department of Housing and Urban Development
IPCC	Intergovernmental Panel on Climate Change
NCA4	Fourth National Climate Assessment
NGO	nongovernmental organization
PET	punctuated equilibrium theory
SBA	small business administration
TABOR	Taxpayer Bill of Rights
USFS	U.S. Forest Service
WUI	wildland–urban interface

Introduction

The second week of September 2013 began as many late summers do in Colorado, with a baking sun and dry weather. Those "unseasonable" days are more common than they once were (Bianchi, 2019a). The *Denver Post* described a changing Colorado climate, saying, "Changes to the climate have potentially suppressed recent September snowfall and expanded summer later and later" (Bianchi, 2019b). The changing climate in Colorado and across much of the western United States makes drought a perennial hazard and wildfires an urgent concern for residents and policymakers (Merzdorf, 2019). Less discussed by journalists, elected officials, and Coloradans is the threat of flooding that has also grown under a changing climate (McMahon, 2018).

In 2013, communities nestled along Colorado's Rocky Mountain foothills and metropolitan corridor changed dramatically when struck by extreme floods. These floods caused loss of life and damaged infrastructure, residential and commercial buildings, and recreation and outdoor amenities. They also placed extreme pressure on the governments that had to cope with the disaster. As we look back on the floods and the recovery in their aftermath, a story emerges of lessons learned by local governments that allowed some of them to make changes that may help their communities become more resilient to future disasters.

Communities worldwide live with hazards – whether natural hazards they live with daily or human-made and technological hazards that are real but have not yet captured attention. When risks that stem from these hazards culminate in a crisis event, communities jump into emergency response to save lives and protect property. But in the months and years after the disaster passes and the influx of outside assistance recedes, communities must confront hard decisions about whether and how to rebuild. These decisions can be minor tweaks or they can involve radical changes to community planning. Whether such changes help build community-level resilience to future risks may be linked to whether or not a community learned various lessons while managing disaster recovery.

The Plan of the Book

This book presents the story of communities faced with difficult decisions in the aftermath of disaster. The story and empirical analyses presented provide insight into what factors make disaster-affected communities more likely to build resilience during their post-disaster decisions. At the core of this book is an understanding that communities respond in differing ways when faced with a crisis. The learning that takes place after such an event may influence the extent to which a community becomes more resilient after a disaster. This book investigates factors that help explain variation in learning and resilience-building across communities.

The book discusses critical characteristics in disaster recovery and resilience-building in Colorado's flood-affected communities – factors that local governments can work to develop prior to disaster events so that they can see better disaster-related outcomes. First, *resources available* to a community's local government after a disaster are critical to processes and outcomes of disaster recovery. These resources can be internal to a community or external, and may include significant inflows of new resources. Resources are closely associated with a second factor: *type and extent of disaster damage* incurred. Low-capacity governments or those that face significant disaster damage may be more reliant on external resources for successful disaster recovery and their processes may be dictated by higher governmental authorities. Additionally, *internal community characteristics* can influence disaster recovery outcomes. These include belief systems of members of a community, as well as the scale of the disaster and the size and demographic composition of a community. Also internal to a community, risk and disaster-related *information dissemination* to the public is important during disaster recovery. These various internal community factors may also influence the degree to which individuals are concerned about the disaster, and this in turn may influence community members' support of policy decisions of their local government during disaster recovery. The procedural dynamics during disaster recovery also matter, with *participatory processes established by local governments during disaster recovery* and *intergovernmental dynamics* and relationships with higher-level governmental authorities important to consider when applying our understanding of learning after a disaster to local governments. All of these factors combine to influence the learning and policy change we observe within disaster-affected local governments, as readers will learn in the following pages.

Part I (Chapters 1 and 2): Introduction

The book looks specifically at a set of communities affected by extreme flooding in Colorado, United States, in 2013. The chapters are structured to examine potential drivers of learning. The current part (Part I) lays out the theoretical underpinnings and potential drivers of local-level learning and resilience-building (Chapter 1). Chapter 2 then examines the case of Colorado's extreme floods of 2013, describing the event, damages, and the aftermath during the early weeks of disaster recovery. Readers learn about the event, the destruction it caused, and the massive undertaking of disaster recovery that took place once the floodwaters receded. It sets the stage for subsequent chapters that empirically assess the disaster recovery processes and outcomes.

Part II (Chapters 3 and 4): Damage and Resources

Following the discussion of a theoretical framework described in Chapter 1 and the introduction to the Colorado 2013 floods (Chapter 2, Part I), Part II details and investigates the role that variation in disaster damage and resources plays in disaster recovery. Resources, including existing capacity the local government had prior to the floods and inflow of external resources during and after emergency response, are dissected in detail. Readers learn about the capacity-building strategies that communities used and the importance of resources to successful disaster recovery.

Part III (Chapters 5 and 6): Individual Beliefs

Part III articulates the ways in which internal community characteristics influence the disaster recovery processes and decisions made by local governments. Experience with damage from the most recent disaster, along with perceptions of problem severity and future risk perceptions can influence the degree to which residents view disasters as an increasing and urgent problem for their local governments to manage. Finally, the nexus of local government information dissemination and participatory processes (covered in Part IV) established during disaster recovery can serve two important roles: (1) garnering support for local government action and trust in government decisions, along with (2) incorporating a range of views beyond only technocratic experts to build innovative policy solutions.

Part IV (Chapters 7 and 8): Individual and Group Engagement

Part IV discusses the importance of relationships – within a community and with other governments – that can encourage or limit learning and resilience during disaster recovery. Important to this discussion are concepts related to the autonomy that local governments enjoy over their fiscal and decision-making affairs, intergovernmental relationships with state and federal agencies that can influence disaster recovery, and the dynamics of groups that form in the aftermath of a disaster. The degree of collaboration and dependence involved in intergovernmental relationships shapes the extent to which these relationships aid communities during disaster recovery. Part IV similarly presents characteristics of groups of stakeholders that form within communities to advocate for policy changes, which can influence whether a disaster-affected community initiates changes in the wake of a disaster.

Part V (Chapters 9–11): Connections, Conclusions, and Recommendations

As this introductory part argues, disasters are fundamentally policy related. Disasters affect communities globally and those events are expected to increase in the future under current climate and human development scenarios. Local governments are the first line of disaster response, but also bear the burden of performing long-term disaster recovery and planning for future events. And yet, scholars do not have a clearly articulated framework for understanding if, how, and with what effect local governments learn after a disaster strikes their community. The framework of community-level learning after disaster presented in Chapter 9 synthesizes the previous chapters and the disaster scholarship to develop a picture of what characteristics are necessary for a community to navigate a disaster and come out of that experience with greater resilience. Chapter 10 builds upon the analyses presented in the prior chapters and applies those findings to other cases in the United States and globally. This chapter illustrates that the various community-level characteristics and intergovernmental dynamics detailed in Parts II–IV are important for disaster recovery and resilience-building at the community scale beyond the floods in Colorado. Rather, after disaster, emergency managers, scholars, and policy experts observe similar factors that aid in successful disaster recovery and resilience-building. This final part concludes the book by providing a set of recommendations for practitioners to plan for disaster recovery and build community-level resilience.

1 | *Introduction to Disasters, Change, and Community-Level Resilience*

1.1 A History of Extreme Flood Events

Diverse weather- and climate-related disasters have occurred over United States history, too often causing extensive damage to infrastructure and property and leading to loss of life. Of all types of weather-related disasters in the United States, floods have caused the greatest amount of damage and disruption to lives, livelihoods, and property (Brody, Highfield, & Kang, 2011). For example, the Great Flood of 1993 – typifying slow-moving Midwestern floods caused by extended periods of precipitation across a vast area – overtopped and destroyed levees as rivers swelled beyond capacity, with damages exceeding $15 billion. A different type of flood event can strike mountain regions, such as in Colorado in 2013, where flash floods scoured river corridors with 20-feet-high walls of water rushing down mountain canyons, destroying or damaging communities. Coastal inundations from hurricanes and tropical storms have dumped inches of rains, often within days, flooding cities of the southern and eastern coasts, such as during Hurricane Harvey in Texas, Hurricane Florence in North Carolina, and Superstorm Sandy as it travelled up the eastern seaboard.

These are just a few examples in the long history of flooding that have shocked and altered many communities in the United States. Disastrous floods and other extreme climatic events can motivate a variety of changes, including in household behaviors and revision of policies at the local, state, and federal levels of government. With the goal of reducing future risks, governments – and sometimes nongovernmental actors – can respond to, recover from, and plan for the future with a focus on reducing the vulnerability of their communities to future disasters. Some extreme events may motivate changes in policies, but disasters often do not lead to learning, particularly the types that require examination of past failures and changes in beliefs about a policy problem (Birkland, 1997, 2006). In the wake of disasters, the recovery of damaged or destroyed communities and neighborhoods is often slow, bureaucratic, and incomplete. Minor policy changes may occur in the aftermath of a disaster, but rarely are policies examined, much less the core of policies overhauled or new risk-mitigating solutions enacted.

Much of what is known about the drivers of policy changes in response to disasters, and specifically extreme flooding, has been learned from studies at the national level focused on changes in national policies, programs, and funding mechanisms. As the locus of flood management in the United States, and elsewhere, has shifted from the federal to the local level, communities increasingly face decisions about how to prepare for, recover from, and reduce future risks of extreme flood events (Brody, Zahran, Highfield, Bernhardt, & Vedlitz, 2009). After a disaster, actions at the local level can be encouraged or constrained by other levels of government. Furthermore, nongovernmental organizations often play a key role in disasters, providing resources and capacity during response and recovery. The public, through engaging in flood recovery processes and through their personal decisions about rebuilding, also affect whether or not a community moves toward resilience. Other community stakeholders, such as businesses, can also play important roles during disaster response and recovery, including providing resources in emergency response and participating in long-term recovery processes. As this book presents, all of these actors and organizations have a role in whether governments and communities learn from disasters and make changes to become more resilient to future disasters.

1.1.1 Deadly Floods in the United States: Federal Changes and Lessons Learned

America's expansion across the continent was defined by attempts to control the environment. Land was converted from forests, wetlands, and prairies to farmland, indelibly altering the landscape and Indigenous communities from East to West. From the time around the Civil War, the Mississippi River was managed by the Army Corps of Engineers ("Corps") through a system of levees, under the belief that this system could adequately control the river and prevent deadly flooding (Arnold, 1988).

The river management approach developed in the early 1920s focused on managing the rivers for transportation, with little emphasis on flood management. The Corps had decided that it was not necessary to design emergency floodways to release water, even though scientists suggested such approaches (Barry, 2007). The Great Flood of 1927 changed that. The system of levees failed, bringing extensive damage to the lower Mississippi Basin, killing more than 500 residents, affecting lives and livelihoods of approximately 1 percent of the U.S. population (Barry, 2007). Caused by many months of severe rains in the Mississippi River Basin, the river swelled, overtopping and damaging levees along the river, displacing hundreds of thousands of residents who lived near the bloated river, disproportionately affecting African American communities living and working near the river and its tributaries (Barry, 2007). The Red Cross served over 300,000 displaced flood survivors, and hundreds of thousands lived in temporary tents. The flood encouraged continuing migration of African Americans from flooded communities in the South to urban areas in the North. Disasters, such as flooding, continue to disproportionately affect communities of color and have led to the displacement of marginalized peoples (Adeola & Picou, 2017; Bolin & Kurtz, 2018).

In the aftermath of the 1927 flood, flood mitigation centered on reengineering rivers to control and manage the flow of water heading downstream (Birkland, Burby, Conrad, Cortner, & Michener, 2003; Brody, Kang, & Bernhardt, 2010). The 1927 flood appears to have helped shift how the Army Corps approached river management – a shift from a levee-only approach to one that incorporated other structural methods of managing rivers. The U.S. Congress later enacted the Flood Control Act of 1936, an embodiment of this new focus on structurally managing rivers to prevent flooding. These changes stemmed in part from the national politics of the time, with the New Deal era prioritizing federal funding of large projects to put people back to work after the Great Depression. The 1936 Act increased funding for a number of public works projects across the nation. The damaging floods in 1927 and the ensuing focus on large federal public works projects, which followed less severe flooding earlier in the century, brought about policy change and a change in the approaches to managing rivers.

During this same period – the 1920s and 1930s – on the plains, farmers tilled their fields and overplanted until prolonged drought pushed ecosystems to ruin. Dark storms of dust blanketed millions of acres of land and starved farmers and their families out. Lessons were learned from many of these disasters – illustrated by the formation of the Soil Conservation Service in the wake of the Dust Bowl and improved flood management and levee construction – but such learning is not guaranteed when humans face disasters. Learning is uncertain at all times, but especially when the disasters that catalyze such learning are – at least in part – caused by how humans live on and manage their lands. Humans resist changing beliefs and practices, particularly when they play a role in causing catastrophes. From personal relationships to national politics, it is difficult to admit when we are wrong.

1.1.2 Extreme Floods of the Late Twentieth Century

As floods from 1927 to 2013 illustrate, extreme, damaging, and deadly floods are not new to the United States. While not novel, evidence suggests that they are becoming more frequent and damaging, but also less deadly (Intergovernmental Panel on Climate Change, 2012; Milly, Wetherald, Dunne, & Delworth, 2002). Extensive floods – greater than 100-year floods that occur in large river basins – have increased in frequency in some regions of the United States (Collins, 2009). Due, at least in part, to growing development and the value of development in flood-prone areas, damage estimates are also increasing (Kundzewicz et al., 2014).

Flooding during the first two decades of the twenty-first century (2000–2020) continued, including deadly and destructive hurricanes. Most notoriously, Hurricane Katrina struck southern Louisiana in 2005, killing over 1,800 people, displacing hundreds of thousands of others, and causing billions of dollars in damages. The Federal Emergency Management Agency (FEMA) estimated that Hurricane Katrina damaged or destroyed more than 200,000 homes in Louisiana alone (DHS, 2006), with a total damage estimate of more than $100 billion (in 2020 dollars).

In 2012, Superstorm Sandy struck the Bahamas, Cuba, Jamaica, Puerto Rico, the Dominican Republic, and Haiti before tracking north where it left more than $70 billion dollars in damage. The storm damaged 24 states along the East Coast of the United States and caused more than 160 deaths (Diakakis, Deligiannakis, Katsetsiadou, & Lekkas, 2015). This is currently ranked the fourth most damaging

U.S. storm in terms of costs – after Hurricanes Katrina (1st), Harvey (2nd, Texas, 2018), Maria (3rd, Puerto Rico, 2017), and Irma (4th, Puerto Rico, 2017). Again, the damage of these hurricanes disproportionately affected communities of color and under-resourced communities, whether in New Orleans, Houston, or Puerto Rico.

But extreme, repetitive flooding has also occurred in other regions of the United States. Extensive flooding in the Mississippi River Basin has repeatedly exacted extreme levels of damage, with severe impacts in 1993, 2011, and 2019, affecting large swaths of agriculture and communities along the river and its tributaries with damages totaling billions of dollars. States that live with continual threat of floods – whether from coastal risk, Midwestern seasonal floods, or more sudden western flash floods – have dealt with the risk of floods to varying degrees. As readers will learn in this book, there are vastly different approaches that government decision-makers can take when confronted with flood risks and disaster recovery.

1.2 Disasters and the Disaster Cycle

As disasters like the ones described here strike, response to and recovery from the devastation often unfolds in an ongoing iterative process of preparing for, responding to, and recovering from disaster, followed importantly by longer-term planning and risk mitigation for the next disaster. These phases are often more formally delineated into disaster preparation, emergency response, long-term recovery, and hazard mitigation (Petak, 1985). This simplification of the trajectory of disaster management conceptualizes these four phases as distinct, but on the ground, communities will say that these activities often overlap and are frequently nonsequential. A variety of policy actors and organizations may participate to varying degrees throughout the disaster cycle. These actors may shift roles across the different phases or alter the type and intensity of their activities depending on their responsibilities. Community members, specific sectors (e.g., business versus residential), individual neighborhoods, and whole communities often experience trauma and grief during the disaster cycle (Bates, Fogleman, Parenton, Pittman, & Tracy, 1963; Kaniasty & Norris, 1999). Learning and change, at both the individual and community levels, may occur throughout the cycle.

Attention to any disaster varies throughout the cycle, with attention peaking just prior to, during, and after the disaster event. Media coverage and public attention typically peaks during disaster and declines as time elapses (Crow, Albright, & Koebele, 2017; B. Miles & Morse, 2007). In the immediate aftermath of a disaster, government leaders and agencies focus on actions to save lives and protect property. During long-term recovery, governments often widen their focus to a broader array of policies and practices with the aim of restoring the social, economic, and political functions of a community. Support for hazard mitigation is greatest after a disaster as windows of opportunity for policy change open briefly (Birkland, 1997; C. B. Rubin, Saperstein, & Berbee, 1985). Engaging the public during hazard mitigation, outside of an immediate disaster, is often challenging, as other non–disaster-related issues compete for public attention. The overwhelming desire is to get back to normalcy, and communities become fatigued from the ongoing disaster-related focus (Peek, 2012; G. P. Smith, 2012). A complex set of policies and programs across all levels of government determines management during immediate emergency response through long-term recovery from major disasters. Whether these policies and programs change in response to disaster experiences has a lot to do with timing – as it relates to time since a disaster, attention to disaster-related issues, and overall salience of risk and disasters within a community (e.g., seasonal variance).

1.3 Focusing Events and Disaster Policy Subsystems

Disasters *may* serve as focusing events: "an event that is sudden; relatively uncommon; can be reasonably defined as harmful or revealing the possibility of potentially greater future harms; has harms that are concentrated in a particular geographical area or community of interest; and that is known to policymakers and the public simultaneously" (Birkland, 1998, p. 54). A focusing event raises awareness of and attention to a problem, potentially creating opportunities for policy changes to emerge. In the aftermath of such an event, the actors and organizations that address the variety of problems that stem from disasters work in a domain that spans across governmental sectors and levels. The concept of *disaster policy subsystem* captures these actors and organizations (Crow, Albright, & Koebele, 2021). This concept is similar to the term "policy regime" posited by May and Jochim (2013), which describes "the constellation of ideas, institutional arrangements, and interests that are involved in addressing policy problems" (p. 426).

Policy regimes are not limited to an affected geography, whereas a policy subsystem is, which is necessary for conceptualizing local-level disaster policy actions. In the aftermath of a community-level disaster, a new policy subsystem may emerge consisting of a system of individuals, agencies, experts, and organizations (governmental and nongovernmental) who are all involved in addressing the milieu of policy problems and issues that stem from a disaster during recovery. Contrasting this, at the federal level in the United States, a more established disaster policy subsystem exists, in part dictated by the federal legislation enacted by Congress and embodied in several federal agencies and departments to help manage disaster response and recovery. The local-level disaster policy subsystem, then, is likely more nimble and malleable, emerging as a specific subsystem only when disaster-related issues are under discussion and then dissipating back into related longer-term subsystems (i.e., transportation, public works, etc.).

1.4 Federal Governance of Disasters in the United States

Within a disaster policy subsystem, engagement by a variety of government and nongovernmental actors varies across the disaster cycle. In the United States, issues of federalism, including specifying and clarifying the roles of federal, state, and local governments in emergency response and disaster recovery, permeate disaster policy (Moss, Schellhamer, & Berman, 2009). The Federal Emergency Management Agency (FEMA) was formed in 1979, through executive order of President Jimmy Carter, to manage federal disaster-related functions (FEMA, 2019). At its inception, FEMA's mission included funding and coordinating emergency preparedness, implementing immediate emergency response, funding post-disaster reconstruction, and supporting hazard mitigation. Amending the Disaster Relief Act of 1974, the U.S. Congress enacted the *Robert T. Stafford Disaster Relief and Emergency Assistance Act* (Stafford Act) in 1988 that clearly defined a major disaster and the federal disaster declaration process. The Stafford Act defines a major disaster as:

any natural catastrophe (including any hurricane, tornado, storm, high water, wind-driven water, tidal wave, tsunami, earthquake, volcanic eruption, landslide, mudslide, snowstorm, or drought), or, regardless of cause, any fire, flood, or explosion, in any part of the United States, which in the determination of the President causes damage of sufficient severity and magnitude to warrant major disaster assistance under this chapter to supplement the efforts and available resources of States, local governments, and disaster relief organizations in alleviating the damage, loss, hardship, or suffering caused thereby.[1]

The Stafford Act gave authority to FEMA to administer disaster relief and recovery programs. In the aftermath of the deadly terrorist attacks on September 11, 2001, Congress enacted the Homeland Security Act. This legislation created the Department of Homeland Security (DHS) and brought FEMA under its jurisdiction, reducing the direct lines of communication to the president that FEMA had previously enjoyed. In response to the policy failures of the federal government during and after Hurricane Katrina that devastated the Gulf Coast (Birkland & Waterman, 2008), the Senate Committee on Homeland Security and Government Affairs in the 109th Congress issued the Special Report titled "Hurricane Katrina: A Nation Still Unprepared." In their report, the Senate Committee concluded:

But the suffering that continued in the days and weeks after the storm passed did not happen in a vacuum; instead, it continued longer than it should have because of – and was in some cases exacerbated by – the failure of government at all levels to plan, prepare for, and respond aggressively to the storm. These failures were not just conspicuous; they were pervasive. (U.S. Senate, 2006, 109–322, p. 1)

Hurricane Katrina led to a number of policy changes as outlined in a 2007 Congressional Research Service report (Congressional Research Service, 2007). Six new pieces of legislation dealing with disasters and emergency management emerged from the failures of Hurricane Katrina, including Title VI of P.L. 109–295 (H.R. 5441), the *Post-Katrina Emergency Management Reform Act of 2006*. These policy changes restructured FEMA and clarified its roles and that of DHS in managing disasters.

Although several other federal, state, and local programs are involved in disaster recovery, the federal policies described here establish the framework for the federal approach to disaster recovery during the 2013 Colorado floods. Under the Stafford Act, once a governor of

---

[1] 42 U.S.C. § 5122(2).

a state requests a disaster declaration from the federal government, the president decides whether to make such a declaration. Rules promulgated by DHS and FEMA govern the allocation of disaster-related resources from the federal government to the states. These regulations stipulate how federally-provided funds can be spent, as well as cost-share allocation between federal, state, and local governments. Federal regulations dictate the types of costs that can (or cannot) be reimbursed through the Public and Individual Assistance programs managed by FEMA (Bea, 2010; Stafford Act, 2000). The regulations established to help manage the recovery process – particularly allocation of recovery funds through a reimbursement process – may constrain decisions by local and state governments because they have to pay for recovery costs while they wait for reimbursement and manage the complex reimbursement process in order to maximize their reimbursement (Becker, 2009). As climate-related disasters increase in number and severity, it is unclear if the current system of disaster management is prepared to fund, manage, and mitigate disasters moving forward.

1.5 Managing Climatic-Related Disasters in a Changing World

The increasing frequency and severity of disasters stem, at least in part, from changing climatic and human development patterns. Increasing risks also result from our collective lack of focus on risk and vulnerability reduction, at both the individual and community levels. In the United States and throughout the world, populations are growing in areas prone to climate risks, including areas at risk of flooding. As populations increase along rivers and in coastal areas, communities become more at risk of flooding. Along with this trend, humans are increasingly congregating in urban areas, underscoring the importance of addressing the connected challenges of growth, urbanization, and climate change. It is critical to understand how these disaster-related dynamics play out at the local level, and more specifically how communities experience, respond to, and recover from climate-driven disasters.

The combination of exposure and vulnerability to a hazard, such as an extreme flood, forms the overall risk of disaster. As such, the risks from flooding depend on both the environmental and human factors that drive the event, as well as the vulnerability of populations who experience the impacts stemming from the disaster. The United

Nations Intergovernmental Panel on Climate Change (IPCC), a consortium of scientists working in collaboration to more fully understand the drivers and effects of climate change, explains the dynamics of exposure and vulnerability that drive climate-related risks:

> Exposure and vulnerability are dynamic, varying across temporal and spatial scales, and depend on economic, social, geographic, demographic, cultural, institutional, governance, and environmental factors (high confidence). [2.2, 2.3, 2.5] Individuals and communities are differentially exposed and vulnerable based on inequalities expressed through levels of wealth and education, disability, and health status, as well as gender, age, class, and other social and cultural characteristics. [2.5] (IPCC, 2012)

The IPCC has found links between climate change and flooding (IPCC et al., 2001). In 2001, the IPCC predicted an increase in precipitation intensity in a number of regions due to increased greenhouse gas concentrations in the atmosphere (Durman, Gregory, Hassell, Jones, & Murphy, 2001; Hennessy, Gregory, & Mitchell, 1997; Kothavala, 1997; Yonetani & Gordon, 2001). The U.S. Global Change Research Program, in its Fourth National Climate Assessment report (NCA4), found increasing risks of climate change coupled with aging infrastructure as major threats in the United States. The report also pointed to significant changes in water quantity and quality across the United States. The processes that drive riverine flooding are complex and differ across regions. The limited knowledge of mechanisms driving regional differences limits our capacity to clearly predict future trends in flooding. That said, predicted increases in intensity of rainfall under a warming climate will result in increases in flood magnitude and frequency (Berghuijs, Woods, Hutton, & Sivapalan, 2016). In an analysis of flooding in the Western United States, particularly the effects of rain-on-snow flooding, Musselman et al. (2018) predict that 55 percent of basins in the North American West will experience increases in water availability. The risks of flooding stem from increased rain-on-snow runoff in conjunction with greater intensity of rainfall and more precipitation falling as rain (instead of snow), leading to predictions that flooding will increase from between 20 to 200 percent (Musselman et al., 2018). In snowy mountainous regions, such as Colorado, scientists also predict that the number of rain-caused winter floods will increase, with a shift away from springtime floods driven by snow melt.

As climate change causes less predictable, more variable, and increasingly extreme weather across the world, disasters will ensue. Coupled with growing populations in risk-prone areas like coastlines and wildland urban interface zones, local governments will deal with disaster-related issues more frequently. Questions about how to cope with and plan for these events will consume attention, time, and resources for governments in the future.

Because hazard exposure and vulnerabilities vary from community to community, it is critical to understand the local experiences of disasters and disaster recovery. The recovery process is driven by resources and constraints of communities (G. P. Smith & D. Wenger, 2007). The types and amounts of resources available to a community before, during, and after a disaster may influence how a community recovers and the extent to which the community learns and changes in response to the disaster.

1.6 Community-Level Policy Change and Learning

In the midst of the radical changes taking place due to climate change, human development, and other factors such as technology and globalization, it is easy to forget that disasters are inherently and necessarily socially constructed (K. Tierney, 2014). Disasters – by definition – are events that cause harm to humans, their property, and their communities. Furthermore, humans create the conditions for disasters and if not for humans developing in hazardous areas or placing vulnerable development in those areas, disasters would not occur. Public policy plays a critical role in this nexus of humans, the natural world, and disasters. How we govern the environment, develop our communities, use energy, and insure losses from disasters are all examples of policy playing a critical role in risk creation/reduction, disaster preparedness, response, and recovery. Policies and the processes that produce them have a vital role to play in how humans socially construct disasters, as Tierney argues they do.

Immediately following and sometimes for decades after a disaster, decision-makers face a number of decisions about if, how, and where to rebuild infrastructure, residences, and commercial areas. Community leaders must also consider how to interact and engage with the public and other stakeholders, including business and non governmental and faith-based organizations. Extreme flood events, like the flooding in 2013 in Colorado detailed in this book, offer a prism through which to examine local-level learning and change. Many other communities may experience a similar event in the future, whether a flood disaster or other type. As such, the floods examined in this book offer an opportunity for communities to learn from experience and alter policies, programs, and processes to mitigate risks and increase resilience moving forward.

The policy literature defines and operationalizes learning in a variety of ways, focusing both on what is learned and who is doing the learning. Birkland asserts that learning is "a process in which individuals apply new information and ideas or information and ideas elevated on the agenda by a recent event, to policy decisions" (Birkland, 2006, p. 22). Learning may take place at a variety of different levels, from the individual- (micro), the organization- (meso), and to system-level learning (macro) (Moyson, Scholten, & Weible, 2017). With a focus at the meso scale, this book examines the extent to which seven Colorado communities learned and changed after an extreme flood event. Learning, broadly conceptualized, includes a range of actions and processes that involve collection and analysis of information to produce knowledge. For example, existing or former government practices, processes, and policies may be examined to look for root causes of failures that led to disaster. Beliefs about the causes underlying a disaster may also be examined and perceptions about severity of the risk of future disasters may shift.

Learning from disasters may be critical to reducing future exposure and vulnerability to similar events, but the policy literature suggests that learning from disasters is rare (Birkland, 2006). The policy change and crisis literature proposes multiple processes and factors that may explain the occurrence of policy changes in the aftermath of a disaster (Nohrstedt & Weible, 2010; Sabatier & Weible, 2007b). Understanding the factors that lead (or do not lead) to learning and adaptive policy change in local governments may prove critical, since this can chart a community's path – whether toward ongoing vulnerability to extreme events or long-term resilience. As such, this book provides insight into what factors lead a community – with particular attention on local governments that govern those communities – to learn, make changes, and move toward greater resilience after disaster strikes.

After a disaster, the type and depth of learning that occurs may be propelled or limited by a variety of factors, such as resource

Table 1.1. *Operationalization of learning concepts*

Type of learning	Relevant learning framework
Reflection on past experiences	Policy-oriented learning, social learning (Birkland, 2004; May, 1992; Sabatier and Jenkins-Smith, 1999)
Goal redefinition	Social learning (Birkland, 2004; May, 1992; Sabatier and Jenkins-Smith, 1999)
Belief change	Policy-oriented learning, social learning (Birkland, 2004; May, 1992; Sabatier and Jenkins-Smith, 1999)
Changes in policy instruments	Instrumental learning; Lesson drawing (Birkland, 2004; May, 1992; Rose, 1991)
Learning from others' experiences	Lesson drawing (Rose, 1991)
Learning about governmental organizations	Government learning (Bennett and Howlett, 1992; Etheredge, 1981)
Learning about strategies and tactics	Political learning (Birkland, 2004; May, 1992)

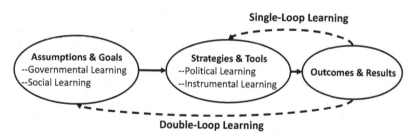

Figure 1.1 Single- and double-loop learning and learning concepts (Crow, Albright, Ely, Koebele, & Lawhon, 2018)

availability and public support. The extent or depth of learning observed can fall along a continuum, as depicted in Table 1.1, from simple lesson drawing on single-loop learning to more in-depth learning processes that include reflection on past events and policies or reexamination of goals and objectives. This latter type of learning is akin to double-loop learning (Figure 1.1), which includes modification of underlying goals and assumptions in addressing an issue (Argyris, 1977, 2001).

Double-loop learning may increase a community's ability to change and adapt to shocks and perturbations, such as disasters. A continuum of learning, as applied to communities after a disaster, may begin in a simple form such as copying or mimicking practices from other communities (lesson drawing), as discussed by R. Rose (1991) and others (Birkland, 2006; Heikkila & Gerlak, 2013). Policy-oriented learning, as conceptualized in the Advocacy Coalition Framework (Sabatier & Jenkins-Smith, 1993b; Sabatier & Weible, 2007a), is more robust learning and entails changes in beliefs about causes and the severity of a policy problem, whereas, similarly, social policy learning, as defined here by O'Donovan (2017), is "new understanding of a policy by a change in the social construction of the problem and the causal reasoning underlying the definition of the problem" (p. 543). As shown in Figure 1.1, social learning, the most in-depth type of learning, requires double-loop learning that involves a deeper analysis and discussion of past failures and a reconsideration of goals and objectives (Hall, 1993).

1.6.1 Stakeholders in Community-Level Learning

As communities potentially engage in learning after disasters, a number of stakeholders are key to disaster recovery, learning, and resilience-building. Community members and organizations as well as outside stakeholders can be part of the decision-making and corollary processes that make learning after disasters more likely. Depending on the disaster phase, various types of stakeholders may be more likely to engage in disaster-related activities. Some of these actions and stakeholders are more closely connected to learning processes than others. For example, during disaster response, actions such as evacuation and provision of temporary housing for residents are often provided by nongovernmental organizations, including the faith community and disaster response organizations such as the Red Cross, when local and state governments do not have adequate resources (Peacock, Dash, & Zhang, 2007). Many of these groups come from outside the disaster-affected community, which can cause problems with coordination and assistance based on differing approaches, cultures, or demographics of the outside assistance groups (Majchrzak,

Jarvenpaa, & Hollingshead, 2007; Quarantelli, 1988; Stallings & Quarentelli, 1985). Some groups that fall within this category may also work in disaster recovery phases. For example, some faith-based groups rebuild housing after disasters. Regardless of their activities, outside groups typically leave a disaster-affected community once their work has concluded. While these activities are vital to a community's recovery, they may not be linked to learning after a disaster.

Other stakeholders that live and work within a disaster-affected community will also engage in the work of response and recovery. During response to a disaster emergent groups within communities may arise that include residents, civil society nongovernmental organizations, and local businesses (P. Kennedy, Ressler, Rodriguez, Quarantelli, & Dynes, 2009; Majchrzak et al., 2007; G. P. Smith & D. E. Wenger, 2007; Stallings & Quarentelli, 1985). During disaster response, there are numerous examples of stakeholders beyond local governments playing important roles to assist their communities. For example, after Hurricane Katrina, Walmart assisted in bringing supplies into the hurricane-affected zone because their logistics chain was superior to the emergency management supply chains in place at the time (Cooper & Block, 2007). During disaster recovery, however, there is less known about the most appropriate role for various stakeholders in assisting their communities in recovery. Disaster scholarship indicates that collaboration and community engagement can lead to superior disaster recovery outcomes (G. P. Smith, 2012; G. P. Smith & D. E. Wenger, 2007), but less is known about how engagement in disaster recovery by a variety of stakeholders can lead to learning within a community or toward higher levels of community resilience.

A number of major categories of stakeholders are included when discussing the actors that may engage in disaster activities. Residents of local communities and their governments (local, state, and federal) are the focus of much discussion in this book. Beyond these actors, who readers will learn about, it is worth briefly noting the importance of several others that are also important as this book details disaster recovery processes. First, faith-based organizations are not formally delineated as actors in disaster response and recovery, but time and again disaster-affected communities will point to the importance of these groups in navigating the emergency and its aftermath (Adams, Prelip, Glik, Donatello, & Eisenman, 2018; J. D. Rivera, 2018; J. D. Rivera & Nickels, 2014). Many faith-based groups engage in disaster response through housing, feeding, and volunteering during this phase of a disaster. Others continue their work during disaster recovery, primarily in providing and rebuilding housing for disaster-affected residents.

Second, civil society organizations of various sorts engage in disaster activities. These stakeholders can take a variety of forms and are most often engaged in disaster response efforts and rebuilding, similar to faith-based organizations (Aldrich, 2008; Lein, Angel, Bell, & Beausoleil, 2009). Some, however, work on risk mitigation over the longer term, such as through education and resource provision in hazards reduction (Shaw & Izumi, 2016). Numerous studies demonstrate the importance of active civil society organizations to successful disaster response and recovery, particularly in the building of social capital after a disaster (Aldrich, 2008).

Third, the business community is a varied group of actors and organizations within most communities. They can be large multinational corporations or small local businesses or something in between. Businesses are well known for engaging in internal risk analysis, but a growing body of literature also focuses on nonmonetary risk calculations by businesses wherein they try to understand disaster risk or manage it before entering a new market (Oetzel & Oh, 2015; Oh & Oetzel, 2011; Oh, Oetzel, Rivera, & Lien, 2020). There is similarly a large area of scholarship focused on the effects of disasters on businesses (P. Kennedy et al., 2009; Runyan, 2006; K. J. Tierney, 2007; Webb, Tierney, & Dahlhamer, 2000). Less is known, however, about the role of businesses as members of a community during and after disasters. Due to the variety of businesses within disaster-affected communities, we may see business roles span a range, from those that look more like local civil society organizations to those that are disengaged outsiders to a community. As chapters throughout this book detail, the various stakeholders within a community that work to aid in disaster recovery may be critical to the learning that takes place and the eventual outcomes of recovery.

1.7 Flood Recovery in a Changing Climate, an Increasing Emphasis on Resilience

Although communities may learn and change policies after a disaster, higher-level learning rarely stems from disasters (Birkland, 2006).

Furthermore, it is often unclear what lessons communities learn and how they implement the lessons through changes in policies and programs. It may be the case that communities learn, but learning does not necessarily mean that communities have reduced future risks or become more resilient through major changes, such as building in a more adaptive manner to their existing hazards, building outside of hazard areas, planning future development with existing hazards in mind for vulnerable populations like the elderly, people living with disabilities, and children in school settings. Changes in policies may or may not lead to increased resilience. For example, in a study of local-level policy failures and learning, O'Donovan (2017) examined three cases of policy failure revealed by tornados in Greensburg, Kansas (2007); Joplin, Missouri (2011); and Moore, Oklahoma (2013). While Greensburg learned and changed after a tornado devastated the town, the lessons gleaned focused on sustainable building standards rather than about reducing the risk of damage from future tornados (O'Donovan, 2017). These findings suggest that it is critical to not only investigate the drivers and extent of learning that occurred, but also the content of these lessons and policy changes to see if such learning promotes risk mitigation, reduction in vulnerabilities, and increased resilience.

Resilience is defined, operationalized, and measured through a variety of theoretical and epistemological frames, including engineering, ecological, social, and socio-ecological lenses (Folke, 2006). Some scholars define resilience as the ability of a system to experience shocks and return to function as quickly as possible. Resilience is, however, also more than this. In a changing environment with many simultaneous and possibly compounding risks, a greater emphasis must be placed on resilience-building instead of the management of singular, isolated events or hazards. Returning a system to its previous functions may also be inadequate to withstand future shocks from a variety of sources, be they social, economic, or environmental risks.

Social-ecological resilience captures "the ability of groups or communities to cope with external stresses and disturbances as a result of social, political, and environmental change" (Adger, 2000, p. 347). Community resilience, as conceptualized by Cutter et al. (2008), stretches beyond the engineering and ecological conceptualizations of resilience to include multiple factors: ecological, social, economic, institutional (plans and standards), infrastructure, and community competence (health, understanding of risk, quality of life, etc.). Magis (2010) centers her definition of community resilience on the community members themselves and the extent of their capacity to respond to change, engage in community-level decisions about resource use, and thrive in a context of uncertainty (Magis, 2010).

Community resilience, as conceptualized in this book, encompasses the ability of a community – including the government and community members – to anticipate, learn from, and adapt to shocks by integrating new knowledge from past experiences to reduce the impacts of future risks. To build resilience, communities must build upon social connections, capacity, capacity-building strategies, and resources of natural and built capital to recover from a disaster while reducing the risks of future events. Communities that think about system-wide risks and vulnerabilities holistically, instead of individually, may be more successful in building resilience (Johansen, Horney, & Tien, 2017). Those that lack resources and therefore rely on financial or other support from outside of their community, such as FEMA and state funds, may be more limited in their ability to adapt and become more resilient. This book explores the various factors that make communities more likely to learn and make changes to policies that build resilience after a disaster. The lessons presented in this book matter to all communities – whether faced with risks from wildfires, floods, hurricanes, pandemics, industrial accidents, or economic decline. The various shocks that can alter a community all demand a similar set of community capacities, actions, and characteristics in response even though they may involve other factors that are unique (e.g., terrorist attacks involve law enforcement investigations while pandemics involve public health agencies and ongoing contagion, but both involve the aspects of resilience discussed here).

1.7.1 Drivers of Community Learning and Resilience

Disasters can increase and focus a community's attention on disaster-related concerns, including emergency response, recovery, and preparedness issues. A growing body of scholarship highlights potential drivers of post-disaster learning and policy change. While much of the literature addresses learning at the national or federal level (see, e.g., Birkland, 2006), an increasing number of studies have examined local-level recovery and learning (e.g., O'Donovan, 2017). One crucial missing piece of disaster recovery research is understanding the processes and arrangements that lead to learning and the adoption of policies to reduce community vulnerability to future events (Berke, Kartez, & Wenger, 1993). This book presents a framework of community-level learning after disasters, articulating a set of critical characteristics of communities that see more successful resilience-building in the aftermath of disasters.

First, resources available to a community's local government after a disaster are critical to processes and outcomes of disaster recovery. These resources can be internal to a community or external, and may include significant inflows of new resources. Access to diverse resources (including financial, public support, technical, and administrative capacity) may influence a community's ability to learn and recover from a disaster. Successful recovery is seen in communities where local empowerment, leadership, and planning for sustainability are all key components of the recovery process (Garnett & Moore, 2010). Personal and organizational linkages within a community, as well as the relationships to organizations outside of the community, may help increase resources (Berke et al., 1993). Relationships and trust between local and other levels of government may also affect recovery by either encouraging or discouraging learning and change.

Resources are closely associated with a second factor: type and extent of disaster damage incurred. Low-capacity governments or those that face significant disaster damage may be more reliant on external resources for successful disaster recovery and their processes may be dictated by higher governmental authorities. Damages caused by a disaster and access to resources in its aftermath, both internal and external, may dictate, in part, the extent to which a community can recover from a disaster.

Beyond resources and damage, *intergovernmental dynamics and relationships with higher governmental authorities are important to consider when applying our understanding of learning after a disaster to local governments.* Relatedly, the level of autonomy a local government enjoys is vital to consider with regard to the degree to which a local government can actually enact changes. The degree of autonomy a local government has is connected to its status as a Home Rule or Dillon's Rule community and is discussed further in Chapter 8.

Additionally, *internal community characteristics can influence disaster recovery outcomes.* These include the size and demographic composition of a community. Also internal to a community, participatory processes established during disaster recovery and planning are important, as is information dissemination of risk and disaster-related information to the public. These various internal community factors may also influence the degree to which individuals are concerned about the disaster, and this in turn may influence community member support of policy decisions made by their local government during disaster recovery. A community's history, beliefs, and culture may also influence how communities experience, learn from, and adapt to disasters. Communities with higher levels of social capital and a history of community participation – including by a variety of stakeholders across demographics and sectors of a community – can more effectively and quickly recover and move toward resilience when community leaders harness this social capital for collective decision-making (Nakagawa & Shaw, 2004). The stronger these ties within and outside a community, the more likely successful recovery will be in post-disaster contexts. Kweit and Kweit (2004) and others (Farquhar & Dobson, 2004; Stallings & Quarentelli, 1985; Wilson, 2009) have found that public engagement in recovery was key to long-term stability of communities. A community's ability to learn from disaster may depend on the extent to which decision-makers and community members perceive future risks of disaster as significant to call for policy change. The extent to which these individuals and organizations experience and perceive a disaster as severe may influence how they perceive future risks and their preferences toward policy solutions (Brilly & Polic, 2005; Wachinger, Renn, Begg, & Kuhlicke, 2013). All of these factors combine to influence the learning and policy change observed within disaster-affected local governments from Colorado's 2013 floods. Chapter 2 introduces the floods and the setting for understanding community-level learning toward resilience.

2 | Colorado's 2013 Floods
The Disaster That Primed Community-Level Learning

Colorado's changing climate – like in much of the western United States – means that drought and wildfires are perennial hazards and increasingly urgent concerns for residents and policymakers (Merzdorf, 2019). Less discussed by journalists, elected officials, and Coloradans is the threat of flooding, which has also grown under a changing climate (McMahon, 2018). These changing conditions are just the type discussed in Chapter 1 and mean that humans increasingly face greater risk. In Colorado, human development in risk-prone landscapes is commonplace, from wildfire-prone hillsides to flood-prone steep canyons. Wildfire, drought, and floods are hazards that settlements in Colorado have lived with for millennia. Now, however, human development is much more extensive and many more people and communities are at risk as a result of these hazards. In 2013, Colorado communities experienced the trauma that happens when living with natural hazards culminates in a disaster event.

After unseasonably warm weather during September 2013, between September 9 and 10, the hot late summer weather shifted. "After baking in unusually hot weather for days, the Front Range sees a dramatic weather shift. The temperature at the Loveland airport drop [ped] from 82 to 66 in one hour. The Denver area reports heavy rain, hail and street flooding" (Reporter-Herald Staff, 2018). What would happen in the days to come changed many Colorado communities and left them with years of recovery-focused decision-making and rebuilding.

2.1 The Setting

The Front Range of Colorado is a 200-mile corridor of the Rocky Mountains and abutting foothills and plains, stretching from the Wyoming border to the Arkansas River in the south. The geologic, economic, and demographic richness make it one of the most attractive

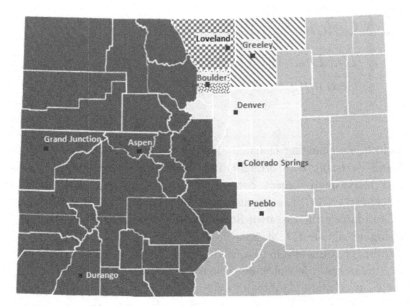

Figure 2.1 Map of Colorado, USA, with study locations highlighted in patterns

places to live in the United States, which has led to significant migration and development since the 1980s.

In Figure 2.1, the Front Range is shown in white with the three Front Range counties described in this book highlighted in patterns – Boulder County in dots, Larimer County in checkers, and Weld County in diagonal lines. The predominantly agricultural Eastern Plains portion of the state is shown in light gray and the Western Slope with its varied mountain terrain demarcated by the Continental Divide is shown in dark gray. The Front Range is not officially defined but is described by most Coloradans as reaching from the high peaks of Rocky Mountain National Park and Pikes Peak in the west to the arid agricultural plains in the east. It includes the major urban and suburban corridor in Colorado and much of the economic engine of the state. "The Front Range has a long history of human migration and habitation, as it offers access to the resources of both mountains and plains, as well as shelter from the extreme weather of both environments" (Tyler, 2017).

Colorado's early history involved significant struggle for European settlers who came West. Mining drew many people to the Colorado

Plateau, and difficult agricultural conditions due to the arid climate made permanent settlement tough until irrigation ditches and similar infrastructure were developed. As communities emerged on the plains, these settlements brought water resources from the mountains to their new communities ("Coffin v. Left Hand Ditch Co.," 1882; Dunbar, 1960; Hess, 1916; Knight, 1956). Agriculture and extractive resource industries such as mining were the prominent economic engines for Colorado into the late twentieth century, but that slowly gave way to industries such as recreation and professional industries, particularly as lifestyles and values shifted in the postwar years of the second half of the twentieth century (Colorado Office of Economic Development and International Trade, 2005).

Due in large part to the geography and climate of the state, the population grew rapidly at the end of the twentieth and early twenty-first centuries, ranking among the top ten fastest growing U.S. states (Tabachnik, 2018). Much of this growth comes from college-educated young people who relocate to Colorado for the quality of life and who work in service, technology, and business professions. These economic sectors are not uniform across the state, however. As Table 2.1 illustrates, the three counties that are the focus of this study show significant differences in the relative importance of various economic sectors, with much higher levels of service professions in the Denver–Boulder area, more government sector employment in Larimer County, and significant agricultural activity in Weld County (Colorado Department of Local Affairs, n.d.).

The seven Colorado study communities that are the focus of this book vary in terms of population size, socioeconomics, and size of their local governments' annual budget, as discussed in Chapter 3. Located in three counties in the Front Range region of Colorado (Table 2.2), the study communities are located on the eastern side of the Rocky Mountains and north of Denver, the capital of Colorado. These communities include Boulder, Lyons, and Longmont (Boulder County); Estes Park and Loveland (Larimer County); and Evans and Greeley (Weld County).

In Boulder County, the City of Boulder is a high-tech center and home to the University of Colorado, a public university with an undergraduate enrollment of approximately 30,000 students. Companies that focus on software development, aerospace technology, biological science, and clean/green technologies are also prominent

Table 2.1. *Economic sector employment by county*

Area	Industry group	Sector total employment	Sector % of local employment
Denver-Boulder	Traditional (Government 9.67%; Manufacturing 4.54%; Agribusiness 3.78%; Mining 1.06%)	234,960	19.06
	Services (Professional and Business 15.62%; Education and Health 9.46%; Trade and Transportation 4.42%; Finance, Insurance, Real Estate 3.96%; Construction 2.35%; Communications 1.46%)	472,070	38.3
	Tourism	100,191	8.13
	Retirees	129,845	10.53
Larimer	Traditional (Government 18.23%; Manufacturing 6.9%; Agribusiness 5.18%; Mining 0.35%)	43,993	30.66
	Services (Professional and Business 6.52%; Education and Health 7.94%; Trade and Transportation 2.68%; Finance, Insurance, Real Estate 0.66%; Construction 2.36%; Communications 0.75%)	30,215	21.06
	Tourism	12,689	8.84
	Retirees	16,595	11.57

Table 2.1. (*cont.*)

Area	Industry group	Sector total employment	Sector % of local employment
Weld	**Traditional** (Government 5.97%; Manufacturing 4.61%; Agribusiness 17.35%; Mining 8.76%)	37,724	36.7
	Services (Professional and Business 3.42%; Education and Health 5.82%; Trade and Transportation 2.13%; Finance, Insurance, Real Estate 0.88%; Construction 2.95%; Communications 0.15%)	15,793	15.36
	Tourism	4,932	4.8
	Retirees	8,418	8.19

industries in Boulder (Economic Development Council, n.d.). Many residents in Boulder are active outdoor enthusiasts, including elite athletes who use the miles of trails and open space for training. The City of Boulder maintains a complex of open space, trails, and mountain parks across the city, supporting hikers, runners, and ecosystems (Boulder County, 2020). Creekside open space also serves to mitigate the potential impacts of flooding. The City of Longmont, also located in Boulder County, sits at approximately 5,000 feet in elevation, at the base of the Rocky Mountains. The community includes a diverse population and a variety of economic sectors with roughly 3,400 licensed businesses. The community maintains more than 1,500 acres of parks and open space that provide amenities to both residents and natural ecosystems ("About Longmont," 2021). Longmont has been voted "Best Place to Live" multiple times over the past twenty years. The Town of Lyons, the third study community in Boulder County, is a

Table 2.2. *Study communities and demographic characteristics*

County (2014 pop.)	Community	Population before flood disaster (2010)	Median household income (2010–2014)	Race (White and Hispanic / Latino) (%)	Education: college degree or higher (25 years old +) (%)
Boulder (313,333)	Boulder	101,800	$58,062	83 8.7	71.5
	Longmont	88,600	$60,218	69.3 24.6	37.1
	Lyons	2,000	$93,844	90.9 5.7	57.8
Larimer (324,122)	Estes Park	6,000	$56,236	83.1 14	44.7
	Loveland	67,039	$55,580	84.8 11.7	34
Weld (277,670)	Evans	19,500	$47,798	53.4 43.1	16
	Greeley	95,300	$47,342	59.3 36	25.6

small (1.2 square miles), close-knit community of roughly 2,000 residents. The North St. Vrain River runs through the center of town – as it does in Longmont – and provides recreational opportunities for residents and visitors alike. Lyons' business community consists of small businesses that typically do not have the resources to withstand closures and weather disaster events that large businesses may have.

Loveland, located in Larimer County, sits at the base of the Rocky Mountains and is home to roughly 67,000 residents (2010). The city supports a variety of economic sectors, with no single sector propelling more than 15 percent of the economy. Several small lakes and water bodies dot the landscape in Loveland, which spans 25.5 square miles. The Town of Estes Park, a small mountain community in Larimer County (elevation 7,522 feet), sits at one of the eastern entrances to Rocky Mountain National Park, and pulls much of its economic revenue from the tourist industry and includes many second-home or part-time residents. Rocky Mountain National Park welcomes 3.1 million visitors annually, and approximately 400,000 of them visit the Estes Park Visitors Center each year (Persons, 2014). Situated along the Big Thompson River, Estes Park experiences spring runoff from winter snowfall that occurs typically from April to June.

Greeley and Evans are located in Weld County, a county to the east of Boulder and Larimer and located further away from the mountains, in the plains region of northern Colorado. Agriculture, manufacturing, the oil and gas industry, and the University of Northern Colorado are a few of the main economic drivers in Greeley, a community of roughly 95,000 (2010). The median household income in Greeley is below both Colorado and national medians. Evans, a smaller community of approximately 18,000 residents, borders Greeley to the south. Many of the residents in Evans work in Greeley and elsewhere in the region. Of all the study communities, Evans has the largest Hispanic/Latino population.

The population size and average median household income vary across these study communities. Comparing communities of similar sizes, the relatively small communities of Evans and Lyons differ in household income and education level. Approximately 45 percent of the population of Evans identifies as Hispanic or Latino, whereas Lyons residents are predominantly European American/White. Of the larger communities, Boulder has by far the highest level of educational attainment, but due in large part to the student population, does not have the highest median income, despite its reputation as highly affluent.

2.1.1 Colorado's Hazard Profile

Resilient communities are able to adapt and thrive no matter what disruptions they face, as discussed in Chapter 1. Most communities face some sort of ongoing or periodic risk or hazard. These risks can lead to disaster. Natural hazards may include wildfire, floods, drought, and others (Crow, 2019). The State of Colorado defines resiliency as follows:

The ability of communities to rebound, positively adapt to, or thrive amidst changing conditions or challenges—including human-caused and natural disasters—and to maintain quality of life, healthy growth, durable systems, economic vitality, and conservation of resources for present and future generations. (Colorado Department of Local Affairs, 2017)

This approach to thinking about risk and disasters underlies the central question of this book. If all communities face risks, what factors lead some communities to adapt and become more resilient than others? The case of Colorado's 2013 floods can provide some insight into this question.

Colorado's climate is famously sunny, dry, and variable. The state brags about its 300-days of sunshine a year in tourism promotional advertisements (Whipple 2011). The aridity and high altitude also mean that there are temperature swings between day and night and seasonally. The weather is also known to change rapidly, leading to flash floods, thunderstorms, and blizzards ("Colorado: An Overview," 2018). Floods, therefore, are not new to Colorado. Two historic floods provide lessons for policymakers, residents, and historians regarding the hazards that Colorado faces.

2.1.1.1 The Great Flood of 1894
In 1894, a flood came down the narrow mountain canyon above Boulder. Prior to the Great Flood, Boulder had more than 96 hours of rain starting on May 31 (Miller, 1959; Oaks, 1982). While no lives were lost in the flood according to contemporary accounts, it left significant damage and established early records of major flooding in the river basin.

The first storm for which there is much information occurred on May 29th–June 2nd, 1894, along the Front Range from Idaho Springs to the Wyoming State Line. The maximum recorded 24-hour rainfall was 5.80 inches and maximum 96-hour rainfall via 8.54 inches at Ward Center (elevation 9,230 ft.), west and north of Boulder, Colorado. This storm produced a disastrous flood at Boulder, Colorado, and flooding on the South Platte River throughout. The estimated peak discharges on the South Platte River at Denver and Fort Morgan, as a result of this storm, were 14,000 and 31,000 c.f.s. respectively, and 12,000 c.f.s. on Boulder Creek at Boulder (Miller, 1959).

The spring snowmelt combined to make this rainfall a flood event that was recorded as the first 100-year flood. It destroyed much of the downtown area of Boulder. Subsequent major floods also took place in 1919, 1938, and 1969 (About Boulder, 2015).

2.1.1.2 Big Thompson Flood of 1976
Colorado's deadliest recorded flood was the Big Thompson flood in 1976. Between 12 and 14 inches of rain fell over a four-hour period near Estes Park on July 31. The storm stalled over the mountains around Estes Park, leading to a huge flood down the Big Thompson River, which flows through a narrow canyon dotted by small villages and homes: 143 people died in the flood and another 150 were injured. Some bodies were never recovered in the flood waters that carried debris 25 miles. The 1976 flood caused $35 million in damage, destroyed 418 homes and 52 businesses, and resulted in numerous infrastructure losses such as roads, bridges, power lines, and communications networks (The Archive Blog, 2012). The Big Thompson Flood was a focusing event in flood management and rapid response in the United States beyond just its local effects, with local experts such as Gilbert White at the University of Colorado calling for better flood warning and response systems (Grundfest, White, & Downing, 1978). Flooding in Colorado is historically commonplace enough to have inspired White and others to study natural hazards and the risks that humans face through development and use patterns (White, Kates, & Burton, 2001).

Studies focused on disasters, learning, and adaptation toward resilience indicate that prior experience with disasters – particularly similar disasters – should increase the likelihood of learning in the aftermath of a disaster. Learning about factors such as ongoing risks, causes of disasters, increasing future risks, or even mundane aspects of organizational processes and personnel can lead governments to make various types of policy changes with the goal of improving future outcomes. Sometimes these changes can be substantive and lead to greater levels of community resilience. The history of flooding along Colorado's Front Range suggests that the study communities described in this book were primed to learn from the extreme flooding that inundated their towns in 2013. This book explores whether, when, and what they learned. Three years of community-level observation indicates that learning does happen in local governments and in the communities they serve. Such learning can lead to changes in policy, but significant changes that lead to more resilient future directions for communities are rare.

2.2 The 2013 Floods

Beginning September 11, 2013, "a slow-moving cold front stalled over Colorado, clashing with warm humid monsoonal air from the south" (McGhee, 2013). The stationary storm front dropped heavy rain and caused catastrophic flooding along Colorado's Front Range, with the worst coming on September 11 and 12. Boulder County saw 9.08 inches of rain on September 12 and up to 17 inches by September 15. In comparison, Boulder County's average annual precipitation is 20.7 inches (Freedman, 2013; M. Smith & Hennen, 2013). As the National Weather Service described,

A deep southerly flow over Colorado, ahead of a nearly stationary low pressure system over the Great Basin, pumped copious amounts of monsoonal moisture into the area. In addition, a weak stationary front stretched along the Front Range Foothills and Palmer Divide. This resulted in a prolonged period of moderate to heavy rain across the Front Range Foothills, Palmer Divide, Urban Corridor. By the 14th, storm totals ranged from 6 to 18 inches, highest in the foothills of Boulder County ... At Denver International Airport, the total precipitation for the month of September was 5.61 inches, which was 4.65 inches above the normal of 0.96 inches. This is the most precipitation ever recorded in Denver for the month of September. (National Weather Service, n.d.)

The enormous storm that stalled over the mountains along Colorado's Front Range led to a catastrophic disaster, due to which the state would spend most of the next decade engaged in disaster recovery.

The rivers along Colorado's Front Range swelled from the storm beginning September 9. Flash flooding soon occurred in the narrow mountain canyons leading from tourist communities like Estes Park located in the mountains down to Lyons, Boulder, Longmont, and Loveland, among others, that are located at the mouths of canyons. This floodwater then slowly moved east to the agricultural communities in the plains, including Evans. Seventeen Colorado counties across nearly 200 miles (north to south) were affected by the flood event, for a total of 4,500 square miles (9News, 2013). On September 12, Colorado's governor John Hickenlooper declared a disaster emergency focused on fourteen counties including Adams, Arapahoe, Broomfield, Boulder, Denver, El Paso, Fremont, Jefferson, Larimer, Logan, Morgan, Pueblo, Washington, and Weld. The situation was elevated to a federally declared emergency by September 15, for those same fourteen counties and Clear Creek County (Federal Emergency Management Agency, 2013b; McCarthy, 2010).

When the rain stopped and assessments began, experts determined that the rainfall and subsequent floods across the Front Range exceeded annual rainfall averages by extraordinary measures.

2.3 Flood Response: The First Minutes, Hours, and Days

The evacuation from Colorado's floods was reportedly the largest evacuation of people from a disaster in the United States since Hurricane Katrina (National Weather Service, n.d.). In Boulder, the University of Colorado and all government offices were closed and hundreds of students were displaced from the floods (Anas, 2013; Staff, 2013). The town of Lyons was almost completely abandoned as emergency responders and National Guard troops gave a final warning to leave Sunday, September 15, four days after the rains began. All told, in Colorado more than 11,000 people were evacuated and more than 550 people sought shelter in 24 shelters (Reporter-Herald Staff, 2018). A disaster recovery center opened in Lyons on October 7 but residents did not return home for many more weeks, finally coming home in December (Federal Emergency Management Agency, 2013a).

The stories from residents in flood-affected communities ranged from messy and inconvenient to catastrophic.

Flood damage leaves Boulder-area residents scrambling. Bob and Judy Rea are supposed to host 82 relatives this weekend for a family reunion at their south Boulder home, but 16 inches of basement floodwater say otherwise. (Anas, 2013; Brennan, 2013)

"I left here at 6 last night and everything was fine," he said Friday as a team of mud-splattered helpers shoveled muck from his corner office. "Then this morning, I turned the corner and I was in shock at how much debris there was in the road." (Aguilar, 2013)

In Longmont, some residents had to evacuate under quick orders to avoid rising flood waters:

The waters came quickly. One neighbor, Heidi Platt, said she had been coming home from a job at 7:30 a.m. and could still drive across Missouri [Avenue] then. Just two hours later, police were advising residents to start checking their escape routes.

"If you live in here, you might want to consider finding a place to stay," an officer shouted to watching neighbors on South Bross [Street]. "This is going to get worse."

Another officer on South Bowen [Street] was more succinct: "You need to leave, now!" (Kindelspire & Rochat, 2013)

In several communities, some of the hardest-hit areas also were areas occupied by the most vulnerable residents. In Evans, a mobile home park was the epicenter of the community's flood damage:

At Eastwood Village mobile home park, 200 37th St. in Evans, flood water swooped up the likes of trash cans, tires and a Fisher Price car and made diesel trucks look like they had been dropped in a bathtub.

Helpless residents clustered on street corners to watch as their homes were buried in water.

Jessica and Eugene Ortiz emerged from the virtual lake surrounding the park with their 3-year-old and 4-month-old daughters, with only the girls' birth certificates in hand.

Eugene works nights and the family was asleep during much of the melee, so they were taken by firefighters via raft to higher ground. (Romano, 2013)

The *Loveland Reporter-Herald* described the timeline of events in Larimer County beginning on September 9 and culminating during the days that followed when flood waters ravaged towns along the Front Range. The harrowing stories reported in Loveland were echoed in communities along the Front Range, with many of them even worse.

Friday, Sept. 13

Early morning. The fast-rising water tears through riverside homes in the canyon communities of Cedar Cove and Drake, causing two deaths. . .

By 9:30 a.m., I-25 is closed from Denver to Wyoming. . .

2 p.m. At a press conference, Larimer County Sheriff Justin Smith talks about his Friday morning helicopter surveillance of flood damage. He says he saw houses destroyed and houses still standing, "but there are no roads to them. . ."

7 p.m. Seven helicopters from the U.S. Army and Colorado National Guard and several privately owned helicopters have spent the day evacuating people stranded in flooded areas. The Sheriff's Office requests more air support.

Saturday, Sept. 14

7 a.m. The Sheriff's Office says critical medical rescues remain their top priority in the Big Thompson Canyon, and search-and-rescue teams are being dropped in flooded areas to look for survivors.

7 p.m. City crews spend the day working to redirect the river where it exposed a 36-inch waterline below the Loveland water treatment plant; they finish the job Sept. 17. . .

Night. President Barack Obama declares a major disaster for Larimer, Boulder and El Paso counties, releasing federal funding to help with recovery.

Monday, Sept. 16

11:45 a.m. Clearing weather allows helicopters to fly again. The Sheriff's Office says 1,000 people still need to be evacuated; 398 are unaccounted for, down from 643 at one point.

Loveland gets more rain, totaling 8.68 inches over seven days. . .

Tuesday, Sept. 17

1 p.m. The city releases most of the 1,000 evacuated addresses in the flooded area.

4 p.m. The town of Estes Park says it has restored power to all affected areas. . .

Wednesday, Sept. 18

8 a.m. The city's Disaster Assistance Center opens, offering flooded residents personal items, food and information. . .

Thursday, Sept. 19

12:25 p.m. The Sheriff's Office says 1,183 people have been rescued and 139 remain unaccounted for...

Friday, Sept. 20

10 a.m. CDOT representatives at a recovery meeting in Fort Collins tell the assembled local officials that their goal is to have at least temporary roads rebuilt all along the washed-out routes by Dec. 1...
Search-and-rescue teams have searched 7,724 structures, about 90 percent of the buildings in the flooded area.

Tuesday, Sept. 24

10:30 a.m. The last person listed as missing has been found alive, the Sheriff's Office says.

Wednesday, Sept. 25

Afternoon: Colorado Army and Air National Guard units turn road checkpoints over to the Larimer County Sheriff's Office and pull out of Larimer County.

Friday, Sept. 27

9 a.m. A countywide long-term flood recovery group meets in Loveland to coordinate efforts to help affected residents. (Reporter-Herald Staff, 2018)

The flood disaster left communities like Loveland with damage that the coming weeks and months would reveal. Federal government officials warned local recovery personnel that flood recovery would last for years to come.

2.3.1 Disaster Response and Community Stakeholder Actions

The 2013 floods created massive damage in most of the study communities across numerous sectors – described in more detail in Chapter 3. As the floodwaters inundated communities, stakeholders from within and beyond communities raced into action to help. As in many disasters, the faith-based community served vital needs for these Colorado communities from food and housing to fundraising efforts.

And there are some faith-based groups that have jumped in and done fundraisers. (EP-01[1])

So Samaritan's Purse, for example, came in here, two of the local churches were just incredible. They sheltered people, they brought food, they set up feeding stations, they found clothing. I mean, it was just incredible. And, quite frankly, that's what happens. All disasters are local. (EV-01)

But when we said we needed community volunteers for the disaster assistance center, also donated items, those kind of things, the community really came forward, not only faith-based organizations, non-profits, those kinds of things, all were mobilized and came forth and provided great service. (LV-01)

The local business communities in several towns, particularly the smaller study communities, were highlighted by local government officials as important during disaster response as well.

One of the issues we found is reality of it being a resort community with a lot of hospitality is these are a lot of folks that are undocumented [sic]. And they have a hard time getting help because they're not eligible for it and they're afraid to come to the officials because they're afraid of being reported and getting deported, losing their family or their jobs. So that's been an issue and we've had a couple of our business people concerned about that too and work with that population. (EP-01)

The business community [that] was much more affected was [sic] the small business owners, business owners who own property along the river, are close to the river that are more heavily impacted by the water and so what we had our staff do was I actually just asked them a survey, they ended up doing a door to door—which is I think even better—survey talking to everybody who as visibly taking water. (LG-03)

As is often the case in disaster response, the flood-affected communities had to rally together – across sectors, neighborhoods, and networks – to cope with the flood as it inundated them.

---

[1] As detailed in Appendix A, alpha-numeric identifiers are used to delineate segments of interviews from research participants. The alpha prefix identifies the community, while the numeric suffix identifies the individual within the community. Specific identifies are confidential to protect research participants.

2.4 Moving toward Resilience: Disaster-Related Changes

As Chapter 1 describes, local government personnel, academics, emergency professionals, and others increasingly focus on efforts to build community resilience. Colorado is no different. In fact, brought by wildfires in 2012 and 2013 and the floods in 2013, innovation in resilience planning won a mandate from the legislature in 2018.

After catastrophic wildfires and floods in 2012 and 2013, then-Governor Hickenlooper established the Colorado Resiliency and Recovery Office to coordinate disaster recovery efforts. In 2015, the office released the Colorado Resiliency Framework, the first-of-its-kind framework for how the state can better prepare for and recover from major shocks and stresses, including natural disasters and other disruptions. The Colorado Resiliency Framework is the road map and vision for a more resilient Colorado, outlining a holistic approach across six sectors for state agencies to address disruptions due to changing social, climate, and economic conditions. In 2017, the office moved to the Colorado Department of Local Affairs (DOLA) and was renamed the Colorado Resiliency Office (CRO). In 2018, the Colorado General Assembly passed HB 18-1394, which established the CRO and mandated the CRO create a Resiliency and Community Recovery Program in consultation with state, local, nonprofit, and business partners (Crow, 2019). The Colorado Resiliency Office describes the state's "Resiliency Story" as follows:

Coloradans are no strangers to significant disruptions. In recent years, wildfires and floods have impacted communities throughout the state. The 2012 and 2013 wildfires and floods alone caused more than $5 billion in damages, more than 3000 homes destroyed, and—tragically—17 lives lost.

We are, however, not defined by our losses, but rather by our collective strength and determination to recover and build back stronger in the face of known and unknown threats. By becoming more resilient today, Coloradans are not just prepared to survive another major event, but are poised to adapt to changing social, economic, and climate conditions in order to keep their community safe, healthy, and vibrant.

Through our interactive story map, you can explore Colorado's resiliency story in a multi-part series that examines the challenges we face in our path towards a more resilient future, what the State and communities across Colorado are doing to tackle these challenges head on, and what resources are available for communities to act on their resiliency today. (Colorado Resiliency Office, 2019)

The State of Colorado is not the only entity working toward building resilience in communities. Municipal and county governments are doing the work, as are a handful of groups composed of community members and local officials. In Boulder County, the Boulder County Collaborative (BCC) emerged in the wake of the 2013 floods. Its mission includes resilience at its core.

Resiliency is rising as a priority for government and nonprofit entities because the ability to bounce "forward" instead of "back" after natural hazard events and other shocks and stresses is imperative in the face of increased variability associated with the impacts of climate change. BCC communities have embraced the importance of incorporating resilient design features and processes into the projects and planning efforts funded through the CDBG-DR grant program, and continue to share their experiences to [sic] a national audience. (Boulder County Collaborative, n.d.)

Media and federal organizations describe this collaborative as innovative in structure and purpose. The *Colorado Sun* reported at the 5th anniversary of the floods:

Created in 2015 after the first round of block grant funding was already distributed, the Boulder County Collaborative was a group of officials from the county and each of its worst-hit communities that functioned as a middleman between the state—which was in charge of allocating the federal program's dollars—and the county's municipalities. Led by Longmont officials, the collaborative secured *$74.5 million from the feds via the state in the second and third rounds of block grant funding so the group could then decide on a more local level how to divvy up the money between the municipalities and the county.* It was a strategy that likely sped the recovery process for towns like Lyons and Jamestown, whose municipal government staffs were too small and lacked the expertise to secure federal funds as quickly as their larger counterparts like the cities of Boulder and Longmont immediately after the floods.

"During round one (of block grant distribution), communities essentially competed against each other for funding and operated individually with the state," Longmont officials Peter Gibbons, Molly O'Donnell and Kathy Fedler wrote collectively in an email. "(The collaborative) is an example of resilient governance in and of itself. It is a successful model of local governments making decisions together in crisis and being flexible enough to put resources where they are most lacking, regardless of jurisdictional boundary." (Lounsberry, 2018)

Innovative and collaborative intergovernmental relationships are one of the important factors that Chapter 8 presents as important to learning after disasters. Boulder County local governments saw more such learning than the other counties, as the following chapters discuss.

The reuse of materials during the Boulder County Transportation Department and City of Longmont flood recovery projects also demonstrated efforts toward building resilience in infrastructure and environmental sectors. Hundreds of thousands of tons of rock and dirt were reused in streambank remediation, hillside and erosion repair, or road base throughout Boulder County during disaster recovery (Lounsberry, 2018).

Five years post-flood, notions of resilience and strength were common themes when people in the disaster-stricken communities discussed their experiences, as reported by Colorado journalists (Aguilar, 2018).

"The summer of 2016 was a very busy season in flood recovery, as we saw many projects coming out of the ground with a lot of construction activity with housing, roads, bridges and watersheds," she said. "We saw activity begin to peak this year and will continue through 2017 as the process for various projects continues through engineering, environmental reviews and permitting at the local level." (Aguilar, 2016)

Long-term recovery efforts began to wind down in Boulder County nearly six years after the damage occurred (Boulder County, n.d.), although the hardest-hit communities such as Lyons and Longmont continued to work on flood recovery well into the seventh year post-disaster. During these years, the communities described in this book coped with the damage incurred from the 2013 floods, individually and collectively.

As communities see increasing risks from natural, human-caused, and other hazards, the onus is on government leaders, organizations, and the public to work toward resilience. By increasing resilience, a community will be better prepared to face a disaster should one occur. Beyond preparedness, the characteristics of community resilience suggest that there are numerous important co-benefits from building resilience. Because resilience-building requires developing trust with residents, encouraging community member engagement with local governments, increasing resources within a community, and improving resident–government and intergovernmental relationships, not only do these factors provide benefits during crisis but also to the health and well-being of the entire community. These factors also make a community more likely to learn from disasters and adapt when necessary. The coming chapters outline the factors that allow communities to learn from a disaster and work toward a more resilient future. Part II begins this discussion by presenting the type and extent of damage that the study communities experienced, along with the role of resources – both those local governments had prior to the floods and those that flowed in afterward – in disaster recovery and learning.

Damage and Resources

As Part I introduces, disasters can wreak havoc on communities, which can mean years of recovery and rebuilding. This recovery period is difficult and uncertain to navigate, but it also provides an opportunity for communities – specifically their governments and decision-makers – to learn and make changes that can increase community-level resilience to future disaster risks. In 2013, Colorado communities saw extreme floods that left significant but varied damage as described in Chapter 2. This part tackles the first pair of factors that are important to understanding what allows some communities to learn after a disaster and improve their resilience. In this part readers learn about the varying extents and types of damages incurred by the study communities as well as the resources they brought to bear on their recovery – both those that existed before the disaster and those they built afterward.

Extreme flood events are primarily local problems, both in terms of who experiences the effects and who manages the response and recovery. Disasters, like the extreme flooding Colorado saw in 2013, can disrupt everything involved in the day-to-day functioning of communities, including lives, livelihoods, homes, businesses, and the infrastructure on which all communities depend. When disaster strikes, the impacts and damage left in its wake are often felt unevenly across communities. And within each community, disasters often wreak disproportionate damage, leaving some neighborhoods devastated while others escape relatively untouched. Some communities or neighborhoods located closer to a hazard, such as a flood-prone river, may be more at risk because of increased exposure, while others may be less exposed or communities may vary according to vulnerability to these risks. Policy and disaster scholars have shown that disasters often affect under-resourced communities and residents the most (Fothergill & Peek, 2004; Hartman, Squires, & Squires, 2006; Myers, Slack, & Singelmann, 2008). These underserved communities and neighborhoods are often the same ones that had fewer resources available to them before the disaster and then suffer most afterward.

Financial resources are critical to disaster recovery, as infrastructure must be rebuilt, homes need to be repaired, and livelihoods require reestablishment. But financial resources are only part of the story. Research shows that civic and administrative capacity also matter in disaster recovery (Aldrich, 2012). Some individuals and families may have close ties with neighbors or the broader community and are involved in their community's decision-making processes, whereas others may be less engaged, less trustful, or marginalized. The capacity of local governments to manage recovery, seek outside funding, and handle bureaucratic procurement and reimbursement processes also influences successful recovery. Chapter 4 explores the resources that Colorado communities had available to them before the floods and how the disaster affected their resources afterward. Specifically, the preexisting capacity of communities to withstand such events, along with the type and severity of disaster damages are explored. In the wake of a disaster, a community's resources, including financial, technical, administrative, and civic capacity, may propel a community toward more resilient recovery or, alternatively, may constrain the actions taken to rebuild and recover from a disaster.

Policy process scholars posit that policy change and learning is often influenced by existing resources and changes in resources after a shock, such as a disaster (Nohrstedt & Weible, 2010; Sabatier & Jenkins-Smith, 1993b). Theoretical frameworks of the policy process, such as the Advocacy Coalition Framework (ACF) (Jenkins-Smith & Sabatier, 1999; Sabatier & Weible, 2007a), Multiple Streams (Kingdon, 2003), and Punctuated Equilibrium Theory (PET) (Baumgartner & Jones, 2010; Baumgartner, Jones, & Mortensen, 2014), suggest that shocks – abrupt changes to a policy subsystem – may alter the flow of resources and attention to policy issues. Disaster recovery scholars also argue that resources are key to recovery, but it is less clear how local governments actively build capacity through seeking resources in the aftermath of disaster, and, in turn, how these resources motivate or limit policy change and learning. In his model of learning after disaster, discussed further in Chapter 9, Birkland (2006) offers a framework that outlines the policy processes and mechanisms that may stem from disaster. Birkland's model focuses on national disaster policy processes and does not explicitly include resources and resource mobilization to

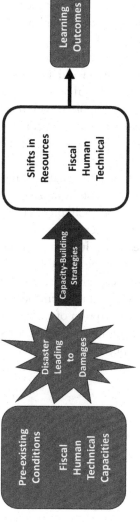

Figure II.1 Capacities, damages, and resources influencing post-disaster learning and recovery

understand how they may lead to or inhibit policy change and learning. This part of the book integrates and clarifies how resources and resource mobilization may influence post-disaster policy change and learning at the local level.

Before a disaster, communities have varied levels and mixes of resources, some of which they can bring to bear after a disaster. Resources that are critical after a disaster include financial resources, human capacities, civic capacity, and technical assets and skills, which are explored in detail in Chapter 4. Existing capacities prior to a disaster and inflow of resources from external sources may influence the adoption of new policies or changes in old policies related to long-term recovery and resilience-building. Local decision-making about long-term recovery may be limited by or supported with these resources. The mix of resources local governments can access before and after disaster may influence how a community approaches long-term disaster recovery and the extent of learning that occurs (Figure II.1).

Chapter 3 begins teasing apart the relationships illustrated in Figure II.1 by detailing the type and extent of damage caused by the floods in the Colorado study communities. Chapter 4 then focuses on the pre-disaster resources and post-disaster influx of resources and what these resources and damage meant for learning and policy change toward greater levels of resilience after the 2013 floods. These chapters draw from interview data, document analysis, and survey response data from the Colorado study communities introduced in Chapter 2 (see Appendix A for a detailed description of the research methods). Part II of the book focuses on community-level factors that can influence learning after a disaster, while the latter parts tackle individual- and group-level analyses.

3 | *Disaster Damage, Severity, and Extent*

The historic storm and Colorado flooding in September 2013 killed ten people and caused nearly $4 billion in damage across twenty-four counties (Colorado Resiliency Office, 2019). It remains Colorado's costliest natural disaster (Traylor, 2017). FEMA reports show that nearly $350 million in public assistance grant dollars flowed to Colorado (Federal Emergency Management Agency, 2017). Colorado residents received more than $62 million in individual disaster recovery assistance (16,551 applications were approved).

Broken down by sector, the following summaries illustrate the damage that Colorado sustained from the 2013 disaster. The resource inflows listed here are discussed further in Chapter 4, while this chapter focuses on the damage that warranted such significant flows of resources for recovery and rebuilding.

Housing: 28,363 homes were damaged and 1,852 were destroyed. $66 million in national flood insurance claims were paid (Aguilar, 2014), with total damage to housing of $676 million. And yet there were still unmet needs totaling approximately $364 million. In addition, FEMA's National Flood Insurance Program approved nearly $65.5 million on 2,093 claims, which is approximately 98 percent of all submitted claims (Federal Emergency Management Agency, 2017).

Businesses and Economic Development: Economic impacts were estimated at $556 million (Department of Local Affairs, 2015b), with approximately 200 businesses destroyed (Aguilar, 2016). Financial resources of about $103 million flowed in, leaving an unmet economic need of $453 million (Department of Local Affairs, 2015b). To promote tourism, $500,000 was provided to "promote tourism in and for one of Colorado's most highly traveled attractions, Rocky Mountain National Park, and the nearby community of Estes Park for applicants who meet the

unmet needs for Marketing/Tourism Dollars." The U.S. Small
Business Administration (SBA) provided more than $110 million
in low-interest loans to small businesses and homeowners for
recovery. Of this total, SBA loaned approximately $30 million to
small businesses and nonprofit organizations (FEMA, 2018). As a
part of the SBA loan process, SBA Business Recovery Centers were
established in Estes Park, Greeley, Longmont, and Loveland
(FEMA, 2020).

Infrastructure: Thirty state highway bridges were destroyed,
according to the Colorado Department of Transportation.
Twenty had severe damage (Colorado Division of Homeland
Security and Emergency Management, 2013). Infrastructure damages were estimated at $1.71 billion, while resources were
approximately $1.04 billion, leaving an unmet need of approxi-
mately $670 million (Department of Local Affairs, 2015b).

Ecosystems and Environment: Erosion and significant river bank
stability remained a significant concern for years after the floods,
potentially adding to structure/dwelling instability (Department of
Local Affairs, 2015a). Bank stability and riverine health was
especially concerning during spring river runoff during the two
years following the floods.

After the initial months of recovery funding from federal agencies,
nearly $200 million had been provided by March 2014, with nearly
80 percent of that going to Boulder, Larimer, and Weld counties. "This
additional money will fund a local vision to rebuild homes and businesses, repair badly damaged roads and bridges, and spur economic
development," HUD Secretary Donovan said (Staff, 2014). These
counties' experiences during flood recovery form the foundation of
the argument presented in this book – that certain factors can make
communities more likely to learn from disasters and build back more
resilient to future events.

3.1 Damages and Policy Subsystems

Communities are composed of a constellation of policy subsystems,
which consist of groups of individuals and organizations, such as local-
level agencies that address specific policy problems, from housing or
public health to emergency response. These individuals and

organizations may include government officials as well as nongovernmental organizations, such as business, advocacy, and faith-based organizations. Subsystems are often interdependent and interact across multiple levels of government (e.g., local, state, and federal government) and governance (e.g., cross-sector). Individuals active in a policy subsystem often have greater access to decision-makers and decision-making processes (Sabatier & Jenkins-Smith, 1993b).

The severity of a disaster in terms of its impacts on various policy subsystems may influence how a community recovers from a disaster. Disasters affect individual policy subsystems within a single community to varying degrees. For example, an extreme flood may devastate or destroy a portion of housing in a community, while leaving its park system relatively untouched. Greater geographic and policy proximity of a disaster – the similarity or connectedness between the disaster damage and the activities within a policy subsystem – may result in higher levels of resource mobilization for that subsystem (Nohrstedt & Weible, 2010). How disasters affect policy subsystems may directly affect resources within a community as well as a community's ability to mobilize resources for disaster recovery. Knowing how a disaster affects the policy subsystems within a community provides information about factors that may lead to changes in resources from before to after disaster. The scale of a disaster may also be critical to understanding changes in resources. Shifts in resources may encourage or constrain changes in policies after a disaster. The closer and more severe a disaster is to a community, the greater the likelihood that policy actors and the public will perceive pre-disaster policies as failures, potentially leading to increased resource mobilization directed toward making changes in those failed policies (Nohrstedt & Weible, 2010).

As discussed in Chapter 3, the Colorado floods of 2013 caused massive damage across Boulder, Larimer, and Weld Counties – and nearly a dozen other counties – in Colorado. Within each of these counties, damages varied across and within the specific communities included in this study. Greeley (Weld County) suffered relatively minor damages whereas the flood devastated multiple sectors in Lyons (Boulder County). Across the study communities, multiple policy subsystems were affected, including emergency management, public works, transportation, housing, economic development, and parks and recreation. Town officials from Boulder and Lyons described the extent of damage to their communities in the aftermath of the September floods:

The city itself had over $28 million of damage to city-owned infrastructure and that was pretty widespread ... ranging from our roads to our waterways, so our storm water infrastructure to parks and recreation and open space, and our facilities. Almost every piece of the city was touched. (BO-07)

When the water came through it ripped out all of the underground utilities with it. So we lost all connections to our wastewater plant, gas lines, electric lines, sewer lines, communication lines. We lost all access in and out of Lyons. In some cases, the roads and bridges were totally washed out ... no one in and no one out. (LY-01)

Indirect or secondary losses such as tourism revenue also limited resource availability in some communities, particularly in Estes Park. The federal government shutdown due to a congressional budget impasse, and the resulting closure of Rocky Mountain National Park and other federal lands in October 2013 also complicated some aspects of recovery, particularly local coordination with federal agencies in Estes Park.

3.1.1 Transportation

In the wake of the floods, a significant number of interstates, highways, roads, and bridges were impassable – or worse, destroyed. For example, sections of U.S. 36, a highway that connects Rocky Mountain National Park in Estes Park to Lyons, Boulder, and Denver was closed for months after the floods, making transportation between communities very difficult. Not only did road closures negatively impact tourism and associated revenue in Estes Park, a community that relies heavily on tourist dollars, but the closure of U.S. 36 also made it difficult for residents of multiple communities to get to work or to return home. Between Lyons and Estes Park, repairs of U.S. 36 mandated nightly closures in the spring of 2014, nine months after the disaster (Denver, 2014). An official in Estes Park described the challenges that their community faced due to damage to local road infrastructure, which intersected with issues of affordable housing:

A lot of the employees can't afford to live up here because it's kind of expensive so they live in Loveland or Longmont or Lyons or Boulder and commute. Well, it's fine when it was a 45-minute commute. It's not so fine when it's a 4-hour commute. Or in the beginning, when it was an 8-hour commute. Most of our police officers actually live in Loveland. To go to Loveland from Estes Park via Grand Lake [on the opposite side of Rocky Mountain National Park], that's a long drive. (EP-01)

In addition to U.S. 36, other highways, local roads, and bridges were damaged or destroyed. Bridges along one of the two major interstates across Colorado (I-25) were not passable for several days following the floods, halting transportation along the north-south corridor that connects all three counties to Denver (and Wyoming to the north). The floods also damaged local roads in communities across Colorado. The transportation policy subsystems were consumed with decisions about debris removal and road repair, all of which mandated coordination of funds, equipment, and personnel across multiple levels of government. Coordination among communities, counties, and the Colorado Department of Transportation, which is responsible for interstate and state highways, was required to repair transportation infrastructure across the region.

3.1.2 Utilities: Power, Water, Wastewater, and Stormwater

Following the floods, many households and businesses were without power, water, and wastewater services. Bank erosion of many creeks in the region directly damaged or made vulnerable water infrastructure systems. In Larimer County, Loveland experienced extensive damage to energy infrastructure, as one official described:

And, so, the flood took out probably a third of the poles up there. And so obviously, completely trashed our ability to transmit electricity. It also took out the Idylwilde Dam, which was a minor part of our infrastructure. But, you know, it had the potential to provide load shaving through the water accumulated by the dam, and if we needed to generate power, there's a penstock that went down to the Viestenz-Smith Mountain Park and there was a generating station there which was also destroyed. So, everything—the dam, the penstock, and the generating station—were completely destroyed. (LV-06)

Across Larimer County, the floods damaged or destroyed utility infrastructure and services. The electric utility in Estes Park provides power to a rural region beyond the Town's limits, for a total area of 400 square miles. In the immediate aftermath of the floods, the utility provided electricity with a temporary overground system that passed over U.S. Forest Service (USFS) land, requiring coordination with USFS to lay the cables necessary. Roughly 2,500 households in the Estes Park valley were without sewage service, mandating a no flush zone. In Weld County, Greeley saw minimal infrastructure damage from the storm, while the Evans wastewater treatment plant was essentially destroyed by the flood, requiring a no flush ordinance for a portion of the community.

The Boulder water infrastructure, while affected, fared much better compared to many other communities studied. A Boulder town official described their drinking water treatment system in the aftermath of the flood, noting the importance of the redundancy of their system:

> If we didn't have two water treatment plants at significant distances apart, if we didn't have lines to town that were in two totally different canyons, if we didn't have a lot of duct tape and creativity, we really could have been in a position much more similar to some other communities where they had a lot of water and they lost massive amounts of infrastructure, they had people that just didn't have water for an extended period. And we were really fortunate that there were people in town that experienced no impact at all. (BO-02)

3.1.3 Housing

Across most study communities, housing and issues of affordable housing became a central point of discussion during recovery. Lyons, with a relatively small housing stock, saw around 211 homes damaged of 960, or roughly 20 percent of homes. A significant portion of those homes were mobile homes, many of which were destroyed, making many lower-income families and individuals housing insecure. In many communities, the need for temporary and long-term affordable housing increased significantly after the floods. In Evans, neighborhoods that saw the most damage included approximately 200 mobile homes that typically house lower-income families (Burns, 2015), families that are already among the most economically vulnerable. The destruction of mobile homes decreased the availability of affordable housing in Evans, Lyons, and Longmont. This pattern of disasters disproportionately affecting neighborhoods with mobile homes and lower-income housing is not unique to the Colorado floods. In Vermont, where approximately a third of mobile home parks are located in flood zones, Hurricane Irene significantly damaged a number of mobile homes (Baker, Hamshaw, & Hamshaw, 2014; Rumbach, Sullivan, & Makarewicz, 2020). The lessons from disasters such as Vermont's were instructive for Colorado's communities, but demonstrate the central importance of state government dynamics for local-level disaster recovery.

So in Vermont with their major flood that they had … they had the state come in and do a blanket condemnation order on mobile home parks … so we went and got with the governor's office and asked for this and provided the documentation and the governor's attorneys said no, this won't work … our state constitution doesn't allow this. (LG-03)

3.1.4 Business Districts

In addition to damages affecting homes across the region, central business districts saw massive flood damage. Downtown Lyons, home to numerous small businesses that sit at the confluence of two rivers, was devastated, crippling the economy of the small community. Evans also experienced severe damage to its historic business area, as did Estes Park. The damage to these business districts was acutely felt by the small communities in this study. Officials in both Lyons and Estes Park highlighted the small businesses that form the foundation of their economy and that had difficulty weathering the disaster. One Lyons-based restaurant and brewery organized a benefit to assist other small businesses after the flood.

Oskar Blues did a benefit called "Canned Aid," and they were able to give every business in town between $10,000 and $20,000 to help with that month of no sales. Our local Lyons community foundation did something similar, $10,000 grants to help offset or pay employees. Because what happened is once people realized it was going to be a few months, you know, employees had to go find jobs. And so then they lost those folks. (LY-01)

3.1.5 Parks, Trails, Open Space, and River Corridors

Across all study communities, parks and river corridors provide green space, a place for community members to recreate, and multimodal transportation options. Beyond recreation, green and open space provide habitat and flood protection. In Colorado, these outdoor places

Table 3.1. *Extent of flood-related damage across sectors in each community (Albright & Crow, 2015b)*

Community	Public works & infrastructure	Housing	River corridor	Parks, trails & open space	Business[1]
Boulder	• 50 municipal facilities with major damage • Sewer and stormwater infrastructure and treatment facilities damaged • 60 miles of debris-covered road	• 50 housing units uninhabitable	• $500,000 to $1 million in debris/sediment removal	• 25 damaged areas of trail system • Hundreds of open space and mountain parks areas damaged	• $10.9 million in verified loss to business sector
Longmont	• Storm drainage $74 million • Street repair $17 million • Sewer $4.6 million	• Mobile home park area experienced most damage	• $48 million in damage	• Parks $21 million damage • Two park closures	• $7.5 million estimated in business loss
Lyons	• Significant damage to roads	• >20% of residences destroyed or severely damaged	• Significant damage, including shifting of river	• Total damage to the two major parks in town	• Small businesses greatly affected • Approximately $8.2 million in business losses

Loveland	• $20–30 million in infrastructure damage	• Minor, little development in the floodplain	• Shifting of river for some landowners	• Extensive damage to two city parks	• Commercial area damaged • Estimated business losses approximately $8.1 million
Estes Park	• $30–40 million in damage, mostly to roads, bridges, and sewers	• Minor, along two specific river corridors	• Moderate to significant debris deposits • River moved up to 50 feet in some locations	• Some park damage but not a central focus of damage	• Small businesses greatly affected • $7.3 million in business damages
Evans	• Significant damage to infrastructure • Sewer system down eight days	• Significant damage in specific mobile home parks	• River damage, requiring levee reconstruction	• Significant damage • Park closure	• $2.6 million in estimated damage to business sector
Greeley	• Minor	• Minor	• Moderate debris removal costs	• Minor	• $350,000 in estimated damages to business sector

[1] Small Business Administration, 2020. Open Data Sources: SBA Disaster Loan Data FY2013 and FY2014. Retrieved from www.sba.gov/about-sba/sba-performance/open-government/digital-sba/open-data/open-data-sources.

also form part of the economic base in many communities where tourism and recreation are important to local revenue. The extreme flows of the floods scoured and remade many of the rivers and creeks in the region, depositing rock and rubble downstream. In Boulder County, parks suffered significant damage, causing short- and long-term closures and significant repair costs, including more than $20 million in park damages in Longmont. A Lyons official described the impacts of the flood on their creeks, which are central to the economy and lifestyle:

The creeks through our community were the lifeblood. They are the artery. That is what drove people here was the kayaking, the tubing, the picnicking, the trout fishing. The rivers are decimated. We only have 1.2 miles of trails left out of nearly—probably 8.5 miles of trails. So everything is just—when you said—the parks are no longer—there's no green grass anywhere. It is now about six to eight feet of cobble. (LY-01)

Table 3.1 summarizes information from interviews and documents the types of damages and losses that each community experienced, as outlined earlier. As shown in the table, each community experienced an array of losses across the different local government policy subsystems.

The damages outlined in this chapter varied considerably among communities. Some experienced damage to public infrastructure while others saw greater damage to residential neighborhoods or business districts. Others, however – like Lyons – experienced massive cross-sector damage that shook the entire community. The difference in the extent and severity of damage will play out as the book explores the various factors – such as processes, individual beliefs and experiences, and group mobilization – that made learning more or less likely in these disaster-affected communities. Chapter 4 addresses one of the most significant of these factors, the resources communities had in place or had to develop to cope with the damage they experienced.

4 | Pre-disaster Capacity and Post-disaster Resources for Recovery

4.1 The Role of Resources in Learning and Policy Change

Understanding the mix of resources local governments can access before and after disaster may influence how a community approaches long-term disaster recovery and the extent of learning that occurs (see Figure II.1 at the beginning of Part II). As the introduction to this section describes, this chapter focuses on community-level resources rather than individual-level resources. That said, individual-level resources can be critical in recovery for people living through disasters. The focus here, however, is on community-level learning and change toward resilience. The resources explored in this chapter and their connections to learning are those that local governments have in place prior to a disaster or can mobilize after a disaster. The variety and level of resources necessary to recover are linked to the extent and severity of damage explored in Chapter 3.

Before a disaster unfolds, communities have their own unique composition of resources to bring to bear after that disaster. Resources that may prove critical after a disaster include financial resources such as budget reserves and new sources of revenue (e.g., taxes, fees, or grants), human capacities such as administrative capacities (e.g., local government staff, nongovernmental support) and civic capacity, and technical assets and skills (e.g., flood mapping). Existing capacities prior to a disaster and inflow of resources from external sources, such as FEMA during and after emergency response, may influence the adoption of new policies or changes in old policies related to long-term recovery and resilience-building. Local decision-making about long-term recovery may be limited by or supported with these resources.

After a disaster, local governments can mobilize resources from a variety of sources, including federal and state agencies and foundations. Communities may also rely on internal resources, such as budget reserves, when available. When a federal disaster is declared, FEMA

governs the allocation of federal resources for emergency management
and recovery. The Stafford Act dictates what local-level expenses can
and cannot be reimbursed (Bea, 2010; Robert T. Stafford Disaster Relief
and Emergency Assistance Act, P.L. 93-288 as amended, 2003). After a
disaster, almost all communities are limited to varying degrees by
budgets, staff or administrative capacity, and technical capacity. If a
federal disaster is declared, frequently communities will seek reimbursement from FEMA for recovery costs. As a general practice, FEMA
covers 75 percent of the amount of damage that is reimbursable but is
not covered by insurance. In the case of the 2013 floods, The State of
Colorado was expected to cover 12.5 percent of the remaining reimbursable costs, with communities covering the remaining 12.5 percent.[1]
Federal disaster funding is a reimbursement-based process, and local
governments, sometimes with the help of states, must cover the money
for repairs and recovery and wait for reimbursements. This
reimbursement-based process may place constraints on local government decisions on how to recover, what and how to rebuild, and the
timeline on which recovery can take place (Becker, 2009).

Communities may have internal resources from which they can pull
to finance disaster recovery, such as a rainy-day fund or a reserve
allocated for emergencies. Communities may also have latitude with
which to alter their budgets to enable them to maintain government
functions while waiting for reimbursements from federal government
or other external resources. However, state constitutions sometimes
limit the ability of communities to alter their budget, depending in part
on the authorities granted through mechanisms such as Home Rule or
Dillon's Rule as discussed further below. In the 1990s and 2000s,
many U.S. states enacted constraints on local governments' ability to
raise revenue, which can significantly affect local government fiscal
autonomy after a disaster.

Larger reserves may allow for greater discretion in spending during
recovery, making a local government less reliant on reimbursements
from federal sources and their complex rules. Having more flexible
budgeting may also enable communities to prioritize projects and
implement projects that may not qualify for federal reimbursement.
Communities without reserves may be forced to complete projects

---

[1] All of these coverage amounts apply after insurance has been paid on covered
properties or assets.

Table 4.1. *Study communities' budget expenditures*

County (2014 pop.)	Community	Average governmental expenditures (2011–2012)	Annual expenditure per capita
Boulder (313,333)	Boulder	$190,530,000	$1,871.61
	Longmont	$101,593,561	$11,466.54
	Lyons	$1,974,433	$987.22
Larimer (324,122)	Estes Park	$13,024,982	$2,170.83
	Loveland	$95,833,592	$1,429.52
Weld (277,670)	Evans	$13,547,280	$694.73
	Greeley	$86,097,858	$9,025.16

one-by-one while they wait for federal or state reimbursement monies to finance subsequent projects. These constraints may slow the process of recovery, frustrating government officials and community members. Federal reimbursement rules limit what qualifies for reimbursement, often only allowing for projects that replace or replicate pre-disaster conditions. These rules potentially limit the ability of communities to reduce vulnerabilities and increase resilience moving forward when such recovery requires innovation in design, materials, or planning. Furthermore, the federal procurement and reimbursement processes are often time- and administration-intensive, limiting a community's capacity to act immediately out of fear of losing potential reimbursements.

Prior to the 2013 floods, the seven Colorado study communities varied in terms of population size and socioeconomics, as shown in Table 2.2. Before the floods of 2013, the annual expenditures of these local governments also varied widely, from Boulder with $190 million/year (2011–2012, average) to Estes Park with an approximately $13 million annual budget. Per capita expenditures were also diverse, from Longmont with an estimated $11,466 spent per resident to Evans with approximately $695 spent per capita per year (Table 4.1). Colorado is a Home Rule state, in which the State grants budget authority to local governments for most issues. Colorado also has adopted a Taxpayer Bill of Rights amendment (TABOR) as many states did in the 1990s, which mandates that voters must approve any increase in taxes. In addition, local governments in Colorado must maintain a 3 percent emergency reserve, as mandated by law. This reserve level may be revised if approved by voters. As a result, communities in Colorado operate in a context of extreme budget constraints, which are amplified during the time of disaster and disaster recovery.

4.1.1 Shifts in Resources and Capacity-Building after the Floods

The ability of any community to withstand and recover from a disaster depends in part on its pre-disaster capacities, along with post-disaster capacity-building strategies pursued to increase resources. Resources such as financial, human, and technical often propel or limit disaster recovery (Brody et al., 2010; Handmer, 1996; G. P. Smith & D. Wenger, 2007). The capacity of local government to experience and recover from a disaster includes interdependent fiscal, technical, and human resources (Leavitt, 1965). In the aftermath of a disaster, local communities may pursue a variety of strategies to strengthen or build capacity for disaster recovery. Damages from a disaster, along with the pursuit of capacity-building strategies lead to redistributions in the types of resources available to guide recovery and support of community initiatives.

To capture local government capacity after the Colorado floods, a set of capacity-related questions were included in a survey of local officials in each of the communities (see Appendix A for a detailed discussion of research methods). Although the questions were asked of local officials, they measured community-level resources such as fiscal, technical, and human resources the local government had at its disposal after the disaster. The survey was distributed annually from 2014 to 2016 to local officials, staff, and stakeholders involved in flood recovery.

While the respondents represented diverse backgrounds, they all had a formal local-government-sanctioned position at the time of the survey and were therefore labeled "local officials" broadly. During this period, respondents were asked to rate the adequacy of financial, technical, and human resources available to their community to respond to and recover from the floods. On average, the survey respondents perceived financial resources to be the most inadequate (mean, 2.2 of 5) and technical resources the highest (mean 2.9 of 5). As shown in Figure 4.1, the community of Lyons reported the lowest average score for adequate financial, human, and technical resources

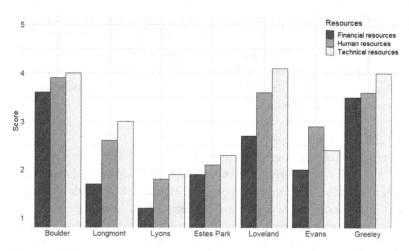

Figure 4.1 Mean responses to a series of Likert-scale questions about adequacy of financial, human, and technical resources needed for recovery in their community

for recovery, whereas Boulder reported the highest scores across all three resource types.

In addition to the survey results, the pre-flood budgets and flood-related expenditures also provide a picture of the financial capacities of each community to recover from the floods. A financial flood impact ratio was developed for each of the communities by dividing the expenses reported to FEMA four years after the floods by the pre-flood annual government expenditures (Crow et al., 2018). This financial flood impact ratio varied from 0.9 percent in Greeley to 1,802.7 percent in Lyons (average with Lyons, 286.7 percent; without Lyons, 34.0 percent). Evans had the second highest ratio (77.2 percent). The median ratio was Longmont with 54.3 percent. In other words, the fiscal impact of flood damage was extreme in every community except Greeley, where only debris removal was necessary. This degree of fiscal impact can spell long-term distress for any local government, which indicates the import-ance of understanding decision-making after disasters.

4.1.2 Capacity-Building Strategies

In response to the damages outlined in Chapter 3 and the inadequacy of local capacity to manage these costs for all study communities except Greeley, most communities pursued capacity-building strategies to increase resources to aid in recovery. After a disaster, as observed in Colorado after 2013, local governments may seek financial, administrative, civic, and technical resources, among other types of resources, and may seek resources from both internal and external sources, as outlined in Table 4.2.

4.1.2.1 Fiscal Capacity

Internal financial resources include making funds available for recovery through restructuring of annual budgets and/or levying taxes and fees to increase community revenue. For example, Estes Park increased fees for floodplain development permits, while Loveland increased rates for power customers. Longmont adopted a number of internal strategies to increase revenue for flood recovery, including a change in wastewater fee, passage of a bond ballot initiative, adoption of a Park Renewal Fee, and extension of a transportation sales tax. A Longmont official described their approaches to increase revenue for recovery:

Now we've added a parks fee and a storm drainage fee. And then we had to take that out for a bond, which means an election probably in April-ish to say, "Can we take, now, the money that we've raised from this increase in storm drainage fees and bond with it to try to create some capital to be able to put towards the projects?" Right now, we're looking at one bond issue for sure, but it could be two. It could have to raise [sic] rates again in two years, depending on how the finances start to work out at that point. I mean, we're trying really hard to be conservative around that. (LG-02)

Communities may seek external resources through reimbursements for disaster damages from federal agencies, and/or grants or loans from a variety of external sources. Local governments may increase internal resources through levying taxes and fees in their local communities (Muñoz & Tate, 2016; Spader & Turnham, 2014; Tate, Strong, Kraus, & Xiong, 2016). Typically, local governments seek additional resources after insurable losses are covered, leaving an expected gap in disaster recovery expenses that must be filled. These resources from external sources may increase a community's ability to recover from a disaster, but the sources of revenue and the corollary rules associated with the funds may also constrain or limit decisions that communities make during recovery such as where and how to rebuild. In addition, the management of these external resources and the

Table 4.2. *Overall capacity-building and resource shifts*[a]

	Fiscal capacity	Technical capacity	Administrative and civic capacity
Boulder	• Damages within capacity • Compared to other communities, self-reliant	High pre- and post-flood	New staff resources Limited development of civic capacity
Longmont	• Within capacity • Compared to other communities, self-reliant	Moderate	Limited development of civic capacity – circumscribed to park sector
Lyons	• Costs far exceed capacity • Influx of federal and state funds	Low but increased technical capacity by resources from external sources	Influx of new staff members/ human resources and high level of civic capacity development
Estes Park	• Moderate influx of federal and state funds	Moderate	Moderate/high development of civic capacity in long-term corridor planning process
Loveland	• Moderate influx of federal and state funds	High (but somewhat narrow focus) level of engineering/ technical capacity/focus	Limited development of civic or human capacity

Table 4.2. (*cont.*)

	Fiscal capacity	Technical capacity	Administrative and civic capacity
Evans	• Costs far exceed capacity • Influx of federal and state funds	Limited pre- and post-flood	Limited development of civic capacity through selected members of task force Increase and reorganization of staff members
Greeley	• Minimal damage • Little change in capacity	Little if any change in capacity	Little if any change in human or civic capacity

[a] Findings reported in this table are drawn from coding of interviews and municipal documents between 2013 and 2016.

associated procurement processes can significantly increase administrative and organizational workload.

Each flood-affected community studied sought reimbursement for debris removal and damages to public infrastructure. The *Robert T. Stafford Disaster Relief and Emergency Act* states that once the President of the United States declares a federal emergency, FEMA may supply finances to support debris removal and public infrastructure repair (FEMA, n.d.). The funds supplied by FEMA's Public Assistance Grant Program work through a reimbursement process and require federal, state, and local governments to share the costs. It is important to note that FEMA reimbursements only cover uninsured and approved expenses, not all costs incurred by the disaster. Furthermore, in order to be reimbursed, expenses have to be directly tied to damage caused by the disaster. In the case of extreme flooding, costs of restoration to river corridors or parks, for example, may only be reimbursed if the expenditures can be linked to flood risk mitigation. This can be a significant setback for communities that established economic development or recreation around river corridor amenities. Officials from Boulder and Longmont described the challenges of the reimbursement process for their communities:

The harder part is the rebuilding because what we're trying to do is, one, comply with FEMA to ensure that we maximize our reimbursement. And there are very strict guidelines about what you can do and what you should do, like you need every permit possible to get reimbursement. If you do work on a tributary or anything without a permit, it compromises and probably kills any chance of FEMA reimbursement, which is about 75%. (BO-01)

Now the problem that you deal with when you look at the $148 million-dollar number is that not all projects are going to be eligible for reimbursement. So when you talk about the greenway for example, they may pay for bank stabilization, they may pay for the walking paths but they're probably not going to pay for benches, tables, trees, sod, things like that. So we're estimating, and we're moving through this number trying to figure it out and we're trying to tell people don't think that we're only going to be responsible for 12.5% of the dollars. It's probably going to be more in the neighborhood of 17-20 when you calculate that some of those costs aren't reimbursed. And you don't know about it until you submit and you go through the worksheet progress and you get approval but you really don't get a final answer on it until the OIG [Office of Inspector General] comes in at the end of the event and goes through all of your documentation. (LG-01)

Due to relative size of local government budgets, limited emergency reserves, and more extreme recovery costs, not all communities could cover their 12.5 percent cost share of damages. Lyons, for example, requested that the State of Colorado cover more than the state's 12.5 percent cost share. Furthermore, because of the reimbursement process, communities like Lyons had to tackle recovery one project at a time to help minimize budgetary outlays prior to reimbursement, which means that disaster recovery takes much longer to achieve.

Based on their own internal capacity and the extent of damages outlined above, all study communities sought additional financial resources beyond reimbursements from FEMA. Depending on the community, these financial resources included a mix of (internal) restructuring of local government budgets, assessing new fees and taxes, (external) seeking funds from external grants, and formalized relationships with partners through intergovernmental agreements or memoranda of understanding.

Resources beyond FEMA. Most of the study communities found FEMA reimbursements inadequate to recover from the floods or to mitigate risks and build resilience for potential similar disasters in the future. The federal Department of Housing and Urban Development (HUD) provided the State of Colorado an initial grant of roughly $262 million through the Community Development Block Grant Disaster Recovery (CDBG-DR) program. These funds were allocated to county and local governments to support recovery and resilience-building. Additional CDBG-DR funds were provided in 2014 and 2015, totaling approximately $320 million. These funds supported a variety of programs, including household assistance, infrastructure repair and rebuilding, economic development (including small business recovery), agricultural relief, and resiliency planning and capacity-building. The CDBG-DR funds in Colorado also included $29.1 million to help fulfill unmet needs in housing and watershed restoration from wildfires that occurred in 2012–2013. Evans, which struggled to meet its 12.5 percent cost share of FEMA reimbursements, used CDBG-DR funds to offset these costs.

The State of Colorado provided CDBG-DR funds through an application process for local governments and provided grants as either direct grants or loans. Many communities sought funding for infrastructure repairs that were not covered by FEMA. In fact, this was an unmet need for so many communities that the State of Colorado received approximately five times the number of grant applications than funds could support (State of Colorado, 2020).

As described in Chapter 3, after the floods, the availability of affordable housing significantly decreased in several of the study communities. Recognizing this challenge, multiple communities applied for low-interest loans and/or grants through CDBG-DR to help address the shortage of affordable housing. For example, the Longmont Housing Development Corporation received a CDBG-DR loan to develop sixty affordable housing units. Communities in Weld and Larimer Counties sought funds for home repair, down payment assistance, and temporary rental assistance. Loveland successfully sought roughly $1.5 million for a single-family, owner-occupied rehabilitation program. To address the shortage of affordable housing, Estes Park sought $1.8 million to develop a new apartment complex after the flood. In addition to specific community projects, the CDBG-DR funds also supported Habitat for Humanity, a nongovernmental organization that focuses on building affordable housing. The State of Colorado also allocated $2 million to support the ReBuild Colorado Flood Recovery Program to help provide housing needs to 200 families in Colorado. An official from Longmont described the importance of the CDBG-DR program for housing recovery:

> Because of the background we have with the community development block grant program; [before the flood] that was the primary source of funding to Longmont for housing, individual housing assistance programs and then eventually the [Boulder County] Collaborative [discussed in Chapter 2]. But it started out that it really was around the individual housing assistance and stuff that we already do. So we applied to the state for the funding since the funding came directly from them. (LG-07)

In 2014, HUD allocated $199 million to the State of Colorado to allocate funds for resilience-building. The State of Colorado Department of Local Affairs (DOLA) received fourteen grant applications (eleven of which were funded) from counties and communities to build capacity and address long-term recovery and resilience in the aftermath of the disaster. These grants funded a Watershed Resiliency Pilot Program that was administered by DOLA, as well as initiatives in individual communities to build capacity for resilience. Evans used a $91,000 grant to conduct long-range planning. Estes Park used its grant funds to support a visioning and strategic planning process for one sector of town, which was supplemented by a community foundation.

Communities in Boulder County also received funds to support resiliency planning. For example, Boulder was awarded funds to support a participatory process focused on potential annexations of nearby neighborhoods. Longmont allocated CDBG-DR funds to support its comprehensive planning process to incorporate hazard mitigation and resilience-building into its river corridor master plan. In addition to CDBG-DR funds, these communities sought funds from other sources, including loans from the Small Business Administration (SBA), the Colorado Water Conservation Board, and the Colorado Department of Public Health and Environment, among other sources. The SBA approved loans to businesses in Estes Park of approximately $5.7 million and in Evans roughly $267,000 to help cover business losses (SBA, 2015). Evans secured approximately $41 million through the Colorado Water Resources and Power Development Authority to rebuild water infrastructure. This discussion demonstrates the importance of communities looking beyond FEMA to fill unmet disaster recovery expenses.

4.1.3 Building Administrative Capacities

Beyond fiscal capacity for disaster recovery, building organizational and administrative capacity can support local-level recovery efforts. In particular, these types of resources can provide the leadership a local government may need to deliberate, evaluate existing policies, and create new policies focused on resilience and risk mitigation. Local staff and leadership can influence the delivery and allocation of government services and can engage most directly with their community members, meaning that supplementing this aspect of local government capacity can pay dividends for communities (Andrews & Boyne, 2010; Brody et al., 2010; Ingraham, Joyce, & Donahue, 2003). Government staff and local-level leaders who encourage collaboration in government decision-making can play a crucial role in encouraging flood risk mitigation (Brody et al., 2010). These officials may encourage greater reflection on underlying causes of disasters and ongoing risks, existing policies, and identify policy failures, potentially leading to increased learning and policy change over time (Beck & Plowman, 2009). Such leadership may influence the outcomes of recovery and preparation for similar future events through resilience-building activities (Andrews, Boyne, & Enticott, 2006).

In the aftermath of a disaster, local government staff may be overwhelmed with the increased responsibility of managing disaster response and coordination with federal and state governments, nongovernmental organizations, and the residents. Local government staff capacity may be inadequate in size and expertise, requiring governments to hire new personnel. New staff may bring new perspectives, expertise, and experiences to the disaster recovery process, but may also require training, an additional administrative task. Communities may rely on established and new relationships among staff or between staff and the community or external stakeholders to facilitate successful recovery.

Out of necessity, local government staff may shift or increase their roles after a disaster, roles for which they may or may not have sufficient training or experience. Lack of training and experience in disaster recovery, along with changes in job responsibilities, may slow or hamper recovery from the disaster (G. P. Smith, 2012; Wolensky & Miller, 1981). A local official from Evans described his own background and why he pushed for more staff training:

> I was one of the assistant city managers in Oklahoma City when the Murrah Building was bombed, and so I was one of the rotating directors of the multi-agency coordination center there. We tell people, you know, "We earned a PhD in emergency response in 17 days." I had that background, and one of the things I did when I came here was really, really pushed hard for the employees—everybody to have the minimum Incident Command certifications, to go through the training. (EV-01)

The study communities employed diverse strategies to increase their human and administrative capacity to manage disaster recovery. All communities except Loveland and Greeley augmented their human resource capacity through the addition of staff members. The City of Boulder hired new staff to help manage recovery and work on issues related to increasing long-term resilience. Longmont and Lyons used external grant funds for temporary staff positions to work on flood recovery. Hiring additional staff can also create new challenges. In Lyons, new staff pushed the limits of available office space that was already limited because of flood damages and required training for new staff members (taxing existing staff capacity even more), some of whom were new to the area and less acquainted with the tight-knit community.

4.1.4 Building Civic Capacity

In addition to a community's fiscal and personnel capacity, successful recovery may also depend on civic capacity in flood recovery – or the extent to which the public participates in flood recovery decision-making (Berke & Campanella, 2006; Garnett & Moore, 2010; G. P. Smith, 2012), which is explored further in Parts III and IV, where individuals and groups are the focus. Before, during, and after disasters, communities may develop venues and public participatory processes to discuss issues related to disaster recovery. These venues and processes may look different across communities based on the damages they experienced, the local history and culture of civic engagement, and the relationships between local governments and community members.

The presence of strong social capital – the strength of ties, bonds, networks, and reciprocity among individuals – may enable deeper and more meaningful discussions after disaster (Aldrich, 2012). Encouraging public engagement in solving challenging and complex problems, such as how to rebuild after a disaster, often involves having conversations over time to develop a common understanding of the problem, its causes, and an agenda to address the issue (Page, 2016; Saegert, 2006). Developing strong relationships built on trust among community members, government officials, and other stakeholders may lead to more effective disaster recovery (Aldrich, 2012; Berke & Beatley, 1997; Chaskin, 2001; Kweit & Kweit, 2004). Stronger relationships and trust between community members and local officials may also strengthen support for recovery efforts and help mitigate potential conflict that can occur during recovery decision-making processes (Aldrich, 2012). These factors are explored in Part III. The diversity of community participants in participatory processes, such as broad representation across racial and ethnic identities, socioeconomic and educational backgrounds, abilities, perspectives, and experiences may help broaden the ideas discussed and help create a participatory process viewed as legitimate (Ansell & Gash, 2008; Fung, 2006; Page, 2016). These processes are analyzed in Part IV. These factors can shape the civic capacity a community has and can also be built, similar to financial or human capacity-building strategies.

4.1.5 Building Technical Capacity

Finally, in the aftermath of a disaster, local governments may deploy an array of technical tools to collect new information that can inform recovery decision-making processes. Tools such as floodplain mapping, economic modeling, and social science surveys of community members' concerns can help guide the allocation of resources during recovery. Studies may be conducted by the local government or contracted to outside experts, such as with floodplain mapping or hydrological modeling (Heikkila & Gerlak, 2013; Huber, 1991). Relying on technical experts, however, has the potential to constrain openness of policy discussions and the formation of novel ideas because this tends to marginalize the role of residents and lay stakeholders (Birkland, 2006; Crow, 2010a; Schneider & Teske, 1992). It may also be the case that when a community relies heavily on technical expertise, the opportunity to build local knowledge and capacity that fits with local contexts may be more limited (Berke & Campanella, 2006; Burby, 2003).

In the aftermath of the Colorado 2013 floods, all study communities – to varying degrees – conducted or contracted technical studies. Boulder, the home to the University of Colorado Boulder, demonstrated the greatest activity conducting technical studies to assess damages, model floodplains, and collect social science surveys of residents in the community. An official from Boulder described their relationships with engineers and project managers on the studies:

That's the thing where we have the skills and abilities and the resources. We have engineering project managers who, and we [sic] have contracts that exist that we do competitive bid processes and we have people who are under contract to be able to respond to emergencies as well as do projects and so we can contact our contractor and say and the engineer would know, okay, here's where we have a problem can you do this work? And that happened for pathways and the streets. And so a lot of it is contracted out. (BO-03)

The other communities engaged in studies and experts, but to a lesser degree. Evans, for example, with its high level of damages and limited resources, had demonstrated much less technical capacity to manage flood recovery, either internal or external.

4.1.6 Policy Changes as a Measure of Learning

The extent of policy change that occurs after a disaster often depends on the type of learning that motivated the change (Birkland, 2006; Crow et al., 2018). Policy change can be thought of as one measure or outcome of learning (Heikkila & Gerlak, 2013). Policy scholarship is somewhat ambiguous about the relationship between policy change and learning (Moyson et al., 2017) in that policy change may occur as an outcome of learning, but this is not always the case. Changes in policies may also arise in the absence of learning through processes such as mimicking changes from other jurisdictions or adopting changes only when mandated by other levels of government.

After a disaster, changes in policies may vary from instrumental changes in policies related to procurement and grant management practices to broader alterations in comprehensive planning focused on risk reduction. During the three years following the floods in

Colorado, all study communities revised or adopted new policies. These changes varied from instrumental changes to much more comprehensive changes, such as the development of a comprehensive recovery plan as seen in Lyons. A variety of individual projects across a number of sectors stemmed from the recovery plan.

The changes in policies detailed in Table 4.3 allowed for the capacity-building described in Table 4.2 to happen in many instances. For example, raising water rates or fees, as some communities did after the 2013 floods, allowed for fiscal capacity to be built beyond relying on FEMA or the State of Colorado for disaster assistance. These policy changes, therefore, are not only important to understand for the variety of lessons they depict, but also for the outcomes related to capacity that they allowed to occur. They also present a key insight from the study communities – that learning to navigate governmental processes and policies is one of the key functions a local government must understand in order to recover successfully from a disaster. Most of these policy changes depicted in Table 4.3 indicate types of learning along the instrumental, government, or political categories. The most common lessons across communities are listed in bold in the table.

4.1.7 Disaster-Related Learning: Resources and Capacity-Building

In the wake of a disaster or shock to policy subsystems, communities may mobilize resources to build capacity and this mobilization may lead to learning. As discussed in Chapter 1, learning after a disaster is rare, and when it does occur it varies in depth, from relatively thin learning – learning about instruments or tactics to accomplish a specific goal such as disaster reimbursement – to deeper, system-wide learning, such as social learning, that requires the acquisition and analysis of new information, examination of policy failures, redefinition of problems, and reconsideration of goals and objectives. Such learning may lead to alterations to existing policies or adoption of new policies.

Instrumental and government learning may occur after a disaster – for example, lessons about recovery processes for procurement, reimbursement, and grant management processes. This relatively thin learning may be coupled with seeking financial resources. To manage these tasks and the resources that a local government may receive after

... policy changes and studies in seven study communities

Community	Total documents coded	Flood recovery policy changes	Types of human (administrative and civic) changes related to flood recovery	Types of technical changes related to flood recovery	Types of financial changes related to flood recovery
Boulder	526	185	• Lessons about personnel turnover • Increase personnel for flood recovery	• Storm event modeling and floodplain mapping • Ecological health study	• **Lessons about FEMA rules and navigating the reimbursement process** • Increase fund for open space • Issue bonds for future capital projects • Increase sales and use tax • Budget reserve increase
Longmont	292	108	• Lessons about personnel turnover	• Floodplain mapping and engineering study of flood hazard • Housing needs assessment	• **Lessons about FEMA rules, and navigating the reimbursement process** • Wastewater fee change • Approval of bond ballot initiative • Park fee for flood recovery • Extended transportation sales tax for ten years • Acceptance of grants and approval of grant proposals for recovery funding

Table 4.3. (*cont.*)

Community	Total documents coded	Flood recovery policy changes	Types of human (administrative and civic) changes related to flood recovery	Types of technical changes related to flood recovery	Types of financial changes related to flood recovery
Lyons	408	278	• **Lessons about personnel turnover** • Hired personnel for recovery finance • New recovery planning process • Resident survey	• Public works infrastructure studies • Wastewater collection system study	• **Lessons about FEMA rules, personnel turnover, and navigating the reimbursement process** • Approve grant applications and acceptance of grant funding • Budget reserve increase
Estes Park	159	53	• **Lessons about personnel turnover** • Training of personnel on trauma • Development of civic capacity in corridor planning process	• Hydrological and floodplain mapping • Soil and environmental surveys • Ecosystem assessment	• **Lessons about FEMA rules and navigating the reimbursement process** • Suspend normal procurement/contracting rules to expedite recovery projects • Fee increase for floodplain permits • Accepting of grants and MOU adoption for grants and collaborations • Budget reserve decrease

Loveland	268	94	• Lessons about personnel turnover • Funding for flood recovery finance position • Annual survey of community households	• Storm event modeling and floodplain mapping • Site assessment for park redesign • Environmental assessment for hydroelectric and solar power	• Lessons about FEMA rules, and navigating the reimbursement process • Rate increase for power customers
Evans	134	95	• Hired personnel for recovery finance Consolidated staff working on recovery under the Deputy City Manager	• Park redesign study • Infrastructure feasibility study • Benefit-cost analysis of diversion project6	• Lessons about FEMA rules, personnel turnover, and navigating the reimbursement process • Wastewater fee change
Greeley	38	14		• Funding for rain gauge monitoring system • Adopted FEMA's digital floodplain maps	
Totals	1,825	827			

disaster, local governments may shift staffing and adopt new protocols to manage grant funds and other resources. Structural changes in the governance of a community, such as the formation of new governing bodies or stakeholder processes, may suggest government learning – a deeper level of learning. Lyons developed the flood task forces described earlier to help vision and plan for recovery across several community sectors, suggesting that some level of government learning occurred, as Chapter 7 describes in detail. Along with the various changes presented in Table 4.3 that suggest learning of various types, the role of damage and resources was linked to some of the most critical lessons that local governments in Colorado learned after the 2013 floods.

Across the seven communities studied, local governments that developed human resources (such as Boulder) showed more extensive learning, as demonstrated by more in-depth discussions of goals, past failures, and lessons learned after the floods. Although Boulder did not experience the extent of damage that Lyons did, Boulder did have high levels of administrative capacity in the local government to identify past failures and support recovery processes. Greeley and Loveland, communities that did not adopt human capacity-building strategies to the same extent, did not see the same level of learning compared to other communities.

Part III builds upon several of the themes introduced in this chapter. Individual beliefs – particularly about the disaster, its causes, and the appropriate course of action by local governments – and trust in government action may be crucial to understand in order to assess why some communities learn and make modifications to improve resilience after a disaster, while others do not. Part III also shifts the focus of analysis away from community-level characteristics, such as disaster damage and resources, to individual-level characteristics.

Review

Box II.1 Key lessons from Part II

1. Prior to a disaster, communities differ across types of resources and capacities that can be mobilized after a disaster.
2. Disasters inflict damages heterogeneously across and within communities. Type and extent of damage can vary widely, even in nearby communities and neighborhoods.
3. In the wake of a disaster, affected communities mobilize resources to build capacity for recovery. Strategies communities use to mobilize resources can influence the type and depth of learning that occurs post-disaster.
   a. Communities that develop human capacities may be able to leverage these resources to encourage more in-depth learning.
   b. Communities that have greater internal resources are less constrained by the timing and the administrative burdens of managing external funds, which often are reimbursement based (FEMA).

Individual Beliefs

To this point, the book has focused on community-level discussions – about damage, resources, histories – but this part turns our attention to the individuals who live and work within those communities. Their experiences, beliefs, and other characteristics are critical to understand so that we can explore the many facets that make learning after disaster within communities more likely.

Communities across the globe differ in history, culture, and beliefs; and these differences may help drive how communities process, learn from, and recover after a disaster. When struck by a natural disaster, communities can respond in many different ways, with processes that reflect the type and extent of damage incurred, their local needs and histories, and the resources available to the community. As discussed in Chapters 2 and 3, even communities in adjacent counties in the same state in the United States can have starkly different demographics, such as age cohort characteristics, racial and ethnic composition, and household economic status. Differences in economic status may also vary widely within a community. Community members across and within communities also hold differing beliefs about the world and the relationship between humans and the environment. Worldviews are how one sees and interprets the world. These worldviews are formed through social processes and can be passed down across generations. They range from individualist perspectives, in which competition is the focus, to an ethos of solidarity or communitarianism, where cooperation and collective benefits are valued over individuals (Douglas, 1970, 1982; Kahan, 2012). Under Douglas' schema (1970, 1982), worldviews may also vary from preferences toward hierarchical to egalitarian systems that can influence the way individuals view authority and the role of government. Worldviews vary among individuals in a community, but also differ in aggregate across communities. How one perceives the world serves as the foundation on which beliefs about risks, disasters, and policy preferences are built (Kahan, 2012).

Individual worldviews may help determine how individuals respond to disasters and disaster recovery, such as their willingness to engage in collective decision-making processes (Adger, 2003). The social capital formed through close ties among community members and a sense of trust and good will for others within a community is one key driver of successful disaster recovery (Aldrich, 2012; Aldrich & Meyer, 2015). In the aftermath of a disaster, networked neighbors and other community members serve as sources of information, resources, and as first responders to disaster in coming to the aid of others. The importance of these social ties has been observed in numerous disasters, including the 2005 Kobe earthquake and the 2011 earthquake and tsunami in Japan (Aldrich, 2012, 2019), the deadly heatwaves in Chicago (Klinenberg, 2003), and in the Vietnamese community in New Orleans after Hurricane Katrina (Chamlee-Wright & Storr, 2009). Social capital is also an important driver of collective decision-making processes after disaster due to the existing trust, networks, and relationships that exist in communities with high social capital (Adger, 2003). Worldviews, social capital, trust, and beliefs about the role humans play in causing disasters may all influence how individuals perceive future risks of the occurrence of a similar disaster, which in turn may help form and inform preferences toward policy solutions and whether they support actions taken by their local government during disaster recovery.

In September 2013, when much of Colorado's Front Range was inundated by floods, many communities were left dealing with a range of damages to housing, infrastructure, and other community sectors, as discussed in Chapter 3. Part III examines how beliefs, trust, and characteristics of the public and local officials in the study communities may influence risk perceptions, beliefs about recovery success, and policy preferences during disaster recovery decision-making.

A key component of a community's ability to learn from disasters is whether decision-makers and community members perceive risks of future disasters to be significant enough to push for changes in policies and programs that attempt to decrease risk exposure and vulnerabilities. Perceptions of future risks may shift in response to experiencing a disaster, as may preferences for various policies under consideration during disaster recovery. When disaster strikes, the public and

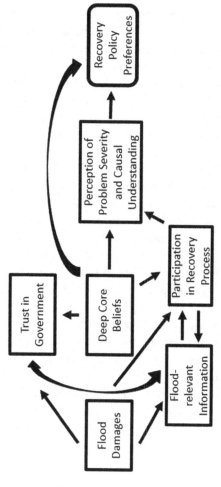

Figure III.1 A conceptual model illustrating the expected relationships between experience, flood damages, information, trust, participation, deep core beliefs, perceptions about problem severity and causes, and preferences toward policy preferences

stakeholders may become more acutely aware of and concerned about the risk of similar future events.

The ways individuals interpret their flood experiences may also affect their risk perceptions and how communities respond to and recover from disasters. Community- and individual-level experiences with flooding, community members' trust in government officials to manage disasters, and participation in disaster recovery processes may help explain preferences related to recovery in disaster-affected communities. A community's ability to manage hazards may depend on whether community members support changes in disaster-related policies. In response to disasters, communities may engage the public in disaster recovery processes and associated collective learning. In turn, these processes may influence community support for policy change. It is therefore important to understand what factors increase community support of flood-related policies and how perceptions of risks, trust of officials, access to information, and participation in recovery processes affect support for government action. Figure III.1 depicts a conceptual model that captures these individual-level relationships.

This part of the book delves into the individual-level experiences, beliefs, and perceptions that combine to determine what individuals want out of their local governments and their vision of their post-disaster communities. This part of the puzzle of learning is critical to understand in order to form a complete picture of learning after disasters that can aid in increasing community-level resilience to future disaster events. Chapter 5 begins by examining the perceptions and beliefs held by individuals, while Chapter 6 then explores what these beliefs mean for trust, policy support, and other collective forms of action after disasters. These chapters draw from survey data of the public and local officials, but also include some data from documents and in-depth interviews conducted in the study communities (see Appendix A for a detailed description of the research methods).

5 | Worldviews, Risk Perceptions, and Causal Beliefs

How Individuals Experience Disasters

Chapter 5 articulates how individuals – both residents and local government officials – perceive flooding, its causes, and future risks. These beliefs about causes and risks of disaster may be influenced by how an individual views humans' place in the world as well as deeply held normative beliefs about how humans should relate to each other and be governed – in essence, worldviews. As such, the focus of this chapter is the individual – individuals who live in each community (residents) and local officials who are key decision-makers in disaster recovery. These individually held beliefs may be influenced by direct experience with disasters, as well as through information acquisition. This chapter examines the relationships among these factors that are all held at the individual level.

5.1 Culture and Deeply Held Beliefs

Frameworks developed to explain the policy process, such as the Advocacy Coalition Framework, often assume that individuals are boundedly rational, self-interested, and hold deep core beliefs (Sabatier & Jenkins-Smith, 1999; Weible & Sabatier, 2007). Deep core beliefs, similar to cultural worldviews, are basic normative beliefs regarding concerns such as equity and individual freedom that cross multiple policy fields, as well as beliefs about humans' relationship with nature and concern for future generations (Sabatier & Jenkins-Smith, 1999). Deep core beliefs can influence preferences toward policy issues, including mechanisms that influence how individuals collect, filter, and interpret information (Quattrone & Tversky, 1988; Sabatier & Jenkins-Smith, 1999). While deep core beliefs are often slow to change, preferences toward specific policies are more prone to evolve. Studies show that deeply held egalitarian and collectivist worldviews may be associated with increased support for risk mitigation and resilience policies (Greenberg et al., 2014). Worldviews, as measured by the new ecological paradigm, can also be significant predictors of beliefs about ecological risks (Slimak & Dietz, 2006).

Table 5.1 provides some insight into the demographic and belief-related differences in each of the six study communities surveyed in a resident survey.[1] The socioeconomics, demographics, and political ideologies vary significantly across the study communities. The percent of individuals who hold a four-year undergraduate college degree ranged from 91.3 percent in Boulder (home to the University of Colorado Boulder) to 42.0 percent in Evans, a lower-resourced, more blue-collar community surrounded by agriculture, oil and gas development, and similar industrial economic sectors. Boulder has the lowest home ownership rate, however, which is one predictor of social capital because long-term residents are more likely to know their neighbors and participate in community organizations (DiPasquale & Glaeser, 1998).

Political affiliation – as one measure of ideology – also varies widely across study communities, with 2.5 percent of those surveyed in Boulder affiliated with the Republican Party, to approximately a third of respondents in Evans. In the United States, political party affiliation may serve as a proxy measure for core environmental beliefs, with Democrats more likely to report higher concern for the environment and support environmental policy action (Carman, 1998; E. Elliott, Seldon, & Regens, 1997; Konisky, Hughes, & Kaylor, 2016; Konisky, Milyo, & Richardson, 2008). The City of Boulder is often on the forefront of community environmental initiatives across the United States, while communities in Weld County draw their economic base from agriculture and oil and gas extraction. Estes Park is home to many second-home owners and welcomes tourists to neighboring Rocky Mountain National Park. In doing so, the businesses in Estes Park employ many immigrant workers, individuals who may be more vulnerable after a disaster, as one Estes Park official described:

Reality of it being a resort community with a lot of hospitality is these are a lot of folks that are undocumented. And they have a hard time getting help because they're not eligible for it and they're afraid to come to the officials because they're afraid of being reported and getting deported, losing their family or their jobs. So that's been an issue and we've had a couple of our business people concerned about that too and work with that population. (EP-01)

---

[1] Greeley was not included in the resident survey due to limited/minor flood damage in the community and corollary limited public awareness about the floods.

Table 5.1. *Demographics and environment-related deep core beliefs of survey of residents across six study communities*

Measure	Boulder	Longmont	Lyons	Estes Park	Loveland	Evans
# Respondents	191	123	200	160	120	109
% of respondents who own homes	82.2	95.9	92.0	97.5	94.2	93.4
% owned homes with pre-flood home value < $200,000	10.5	18.8	4.20	12.4	23.6	85.1
% of respondents with <$25,000 annual income	4.2	5.7	4.5	2.5	4.2	8.3
% College graduates	91.3	71.8	84.1	78.5	73.9	42.0
% Republican Party affiliation as reported in survey	2.5	18.4	9.7	25.0	32.0	33.3
Deep core belief, Control: Humans will eventually learn enough about how nature works to be able to control it. (Strongly Agree = 5, Strongly Disagree = 1)	2.15 (0.95)	2.32 (0.96)	2.03 (0.91)	2.12 (0.84)	2.13 (0.91)	2.45 (1.13)
Deep core belief, Modify: Humans have the right to modify the natural environment to suit their needs. (Strongly Agree = 5, Strongly Disagree = 1)	2.71 (1.13)	2.70 (1.02)	2.61 (1.03)	2.69 (1.12)	2.49 (1.1)	2.76 (1.07)
Deep core belief, Interfere: When humans interfere with nature it often produces disastrous consequences. (Strongly Agree = 5, Strongly Disagree = 1)	3.93 (0.89)	3.69 (1.00)	3.82 (1.01)	3.66 (1.08)	3.75 (0.99)	3.57 (1.06)
% of community that identifies as Hispanic/Latina/Latino/ Latinx (U.S. Census Bureau)	9.8	25.2	3	11.6	11.4	44.1

The resident survey included a set of questions designed to capture the deeply held beliefs of residents as measured by questions from the new ecological paradigm (Dunlap, van Liere, Mertig, & Jones, 2000). These questions measure how individuals perceive the relationship between humans and the environment. The extent to which an individual perceives human ability to control the environment, as measured by agreement with the statement "Humans will eventually learn enough about how nature works to be able to control it" was higher on average in Evans, the most Republican-affiliated of the study communities. The same held true for agreement with the statement "Humans have the right to modify the natural environment to suit their needs." Residents in Evans reported the lowest average agreement with the statement "When humans interfere with nature it often produces disastrous consequences." The resident survey responses to these questions, along with reported political party affiliation, suggest that residents of Evans, on average, may hold underlying beliefs that differ from the other communities. This belief system may privilege human use of the earth's resources over its protection. These differences in belief systems, both individually and collectively in communities, may be part of a complex set of dynamics that influence how individuals perceive future risks of flooding as well as policy preferences. For example, someone who holds beliefs that humans can safely interfere with nature may be more likely to support policies that focus on strengthening infrastructure rather than broader resilience-building to mitigate flood risks in their community.

5.2 Hazards, Risks, and Vulnerability

A hazard, as defined by the United Nations Office for Disaster Risk Reduction (UNDRR), is a "process, phenomenon or human activity that may cause loss of life, injury or other health impacts, property damage, social and economic disruption, or environmental degradation" (United Nations General Assembly, 2016). Natural hazards are those that stem from earth processes, such as climatic or geological processes (e.g., typhoons and earthquakes, respectively). The line between nature-driven and human-driven hazards continues to blur as human interference with climatic and other earth systems escalates and humans develop in risk-prone areas such as wildfire landscapes (Calkin, Cohen, Finney, & Thompson, 2014; Hammer, Stewart, & Radeloff, 2009; S. E. Jensen,

2006). Disasters may occur rapidly, such as a tornado or the quick spread of an infectious disease agent such as COVID-19, or they may involve slower processes, such as sea level rise, droughts that span years, and desertification (Linnerooth-Bayer & Sjostedt, 2010). The hazards humans face continue to evolve (Boin & Lodge, 2016), with new or altered hazards surfacing or worsening, including climate change-driven hazards.

Risk is a function of the hazard, along with exposure and vulnerability to the hazard. Exposure to a hazard is a function of development and assets located near the hazard, including human and nonhuman populations, public and private infrastructure, homes, businesses, government buildings, and the natural environment. In the case of flooding, a combination of history of development in floodplains and in river basins, along with climatological and meteorological processes (e.g., extreme precipitation events), are factors that drive exposure to an extreme flood hazard. The legacy of regulations, policies, and practices influences development in these hazardous areas. The type and extent of exposure to a single hazard can vary within a single community and across communities.

Vulnerability to a hazard is caused by social, political, economic, environmental, or physical drivers that increase the susceptibility of individuals, neighborhoods, and whole communities – including their built environment – to the impacts of a disaster (United Nations General Assembly, 2016). Potential vulnerabilities to an extreme flood event include poor public infrastructure or housing insecurity and inadequacies, such as housing located in a floodplain that is not elevated or flood-protected. Lack of home ownership may also directly or indirectly influence an individual's vulnerability to flood events, independent of income level.[2] This increase in vulnerability may affect how flood risks are perceived by individuals living with risks.

5.2.1 Risk Perceptions in Colorado Communities

As described in Chapter 3, the floods of 2013 left varied damages across communities in Colorado, including the seven study

---

[2] Home ownership may be capturing a number of dimensions, including, but not limited to, greater sense of individual agency in recovery process, economic security, stability (R. I. Palm, 2019; L. A. Russell, Goltz, & Bourque, 1995), or generational wealth, whereas self-reported income likely represents current financial resources.

communities. Exposure to the floods differed across communities because the amount and type of development in floodplains and other hazardous regions were different across communities prior to the floods. In the interviews with local government officials, several staff and community leaders described exposure and vulnerabilities to the flood in their communities. Discussions of exposure and vulnerabilities ranged from weaknesses in water infrastructure to inadequacies in housing. For example, a Greeley city official discussed a mobile home park that he considered particularly vulnerable to flooding:

I think the challenge is that we know we have one exceedingly vulnerable location. We probably have another. We have another mobile home court. The thing about that mobile home court is it's going to flood, but it's on the plain. What I mean, is it's on the flood plain ... This mobile home court is, like, right—it's in a hole. And so that one I'm talking about, the most vulnerable, is in a hole. So once the water ever gets there, it's going to fill that hole up. Does that make sense? And probably push the mobile homes down the road, unfortunately. (GR-03)

A Loveland official pointed to weaknesses in their water infrastructure system:

Then we had a number of water lines—three water lines underneath the city right out here behind us that had crossed underneath the river ... those three were actually washed away.... And those were smaller lines, like 8-inch and 12-inch. Then, between where our plant is in town, there were three other areas that had bigger lines; our 34-inch one line and a 22-inch one line that were damaged. And we turned those off as precautions during the storm event and had to go back on each of those and redo them because they showed to be vulnerable to flooding damage. (LV-03)

An official from Evans described the variation in damage across their community:

This was an interesting event. If you were north of 23rd street, you probably never knew anything happened except we got a lot of rain because once you got beyond—well, actually once you got beyond 35th, you weren't in the no-flush zone; you're in another basin, and so that goes to a different plant. And so we have a community that about almost 2/3rds of the community was initially affected by the no-flush, but once that was done, the event was over for them. And then, of course, we have the folks on the east side, who some of whom lost everything. Certainly many homes with a lot of damage. (EV-01)

The same official described the vulnerability of their infrastructure to manage the river:

Part of the problem that Evans had, and the reason that we sustained so much damage is, there was an old berm system. The folks that live that there, that have been there forever, like to call it a levee. It is not. In fact, it was built on compacted trash. So all those things we discovered later. (EV-01)

How people experience a disaster may influence how they perceive the risk of future events. Directly or indirectly experiencing a flood may increase community members' awareness of and attention to flooding as an issue that needs to be addressed. These often-devastating experiences may also alter how the public understands the causes of a flood or flood damage and their preferences toward policy options that could reduce future flood risks (Brilly & Polic, 2005; Wachinger et al., 2013). How individuals perceive the future likelihood of extreme events may be a function of their memories of similar past events. People often employ the availability heuristic when making assessments about future probabilities and draw on their most recent or salient memories to think about future risks (Tversky & Kahneman, 1974). Individuals tend to base their subjective probability judgment on the ease of retrieving similar events from their memory. As such, risk perceptions may depend on characteristics of the event remembered, such as the intensity, recency, frequency, and proximity of the event (Lindell & Hwang, 2008; Lindell & Prater, 2000).

Individuals who experience flooding often are more knowledgeable and aware of the underlying impacts of such events (Kellens, Terpstra, & de Maeyer, 2013; Pagneux, Gisladottir, & Jonsdottir, 2011). Study findings vary, however, as to whether direct or indirect personal experience with floods influences flood risk perception among individuals (Wachinger et al., 2013). Individuals may underestimate the risk of flooding if they lack direct flood experience, while individuals who have direct experience with flooding may overestimate the risk (Ruin, Gaillard, & Lutoff, 2007). Individuals whose communities are flooded but do not experience flooding on their own property can perceive that they escaped the risk and may underestimate flood hazards overall (Meletti & O'Brien, 1992; Wachinger et al., 2013). Individuals who were unaware of the causes of flooding may also tend to underestimate flood risks (Botzen, Aerts, & van den Bergh, 2009). Emotions also have been shown to affect risk perceptions in the aftermath of a disaster, with increased fear and dread potentially leading to perception of greater future flood risks and risks of severe flooding (Botzen, Kunreuther, & Michel-Kerjan, 2015).

In making judgments about the severity of risks such as an extreme flood, humans are prone to systematic biases – particularly when these events are rare. Studies point to differences in how experts (based on their risk-relevant knowledge) and the general public conceptualize disaster risks (Shrader-Frechette, 1991), with the public often relying more heavily on direct personal experience. Attributes of the individuals (Slovic, 1987), their past flood experiences, and social processes within flood-affected communities can all influence how individuals perceive risk (Ho, Shaw, Lin, & Chiu, 2008; Lin, Shaw, & Ho, 2008; Rogers & Prentice-Dunn, 1997). When individuals assess flood risks, they may select from their memory of prior experiences with floods to confirm their already held beliefs or they may ignore information that runs counter to their understanding of flooding (Lord, Ross, & Lepper, 1979; Nohrstedt & Weible, 2010).

Personal characteristics, such as gender, age, and socioeconomic status may also influence how an individual perceives a disaster event (Wachinger et al., 2013). Along with past flood experiences, the perceived level of control over an event, extent of preparedness, and expert knowledge about floods may also be important factors shaping risk perception (Siegrist & Gutscher, 2006; Wachinger et al., 2013). These characteristics may be associated with homeownership, length of time in the home, and levels of formal education. Levels of trust in officials and experts may also affect how individuals perceive future risks (Heitz, Spaeter, Auzet, & Glatron, 2009; Wachinger et al., 2013). Past flood experiences may directly or indirectly influence trust in officials, which may impact risk perceptions.

5.2.2 Risk Perceptions of Local Officials

Expertise and knowledge about a hazard often influence the extent to which individuals perceive risks of future disaster (Sjöberg, 1999; Wildavsky & Dake, 1990). Experts, as compared to the general public, often view risks from hazards more narrowly through the evaluation of probabilities and estimates of potential future consequences of an event. The public often views these same risks more broadly, through social, psychological, and cultural interpretations of risks (Dessai &

Hulme, 2004; Leiserowitz, 2005). Even though their processes of risk perception formation differ, both experts and the public often fall into systematic biases when thinking about risks (Slovic, 1987). Biases often occur through the systematic use of heuristics or shortcuts (Kahneman, 2011; Kahneman, Slovic, Slovic, & Tversky, 1982; Slovic, 1987).

Differences in the definitions of risk or how risk is conceptualized may, at least in part, explain different risk perceptions between the public and experts (Sjöberg, 1999). Experts tend to focus on the probability that an event occurs while the public may emphasize the consequence of the event such as the damage caused. This difference in emphasis may lead to differing risk perception depending on how risk characteristics are weighed (probability vs. consequence). A perceived sense of control may also influence how risks are perceived, with risks from hazards that can be controlled, such as choosing to smoke, viewed differently compared to a hazard out of one's control (e.g., a nuclear accident). Two local government officials and official documents in Boulder discussed perceptions of risks of flooding, communicating a sense of complacency regarding the risks.

I think there's a great resistance to recognizing risk. You know, that it hasn't happened before, or it's not going to happen here, or it's not going to be as bad, or we've had this before. . ... Well, no, we have actually [*sic*] newspaper clippings of when it's happened before. You know, it happened in 1960-something. It happened in 1920-something. And even this flood that we've had out here, we've got old maps of the city around, and you can see where it's flooded the same places before. So I think we have, you know, that complacency, "It's not going to happen." (EV-02)

Our lifespan is so short and our knowledge is so short, and be the Earth four billion years old, like some people think it is, we don't have a clue. We set up shop here at Greeley or wherever. ... And then we get a 17-inch rain, and everyone freaks out. Well, this is probably the way things work. I mean, this is the way things work. If you look at the mountains, you look at the floodplain, the erosion that's gone on here over millennia or however. (GR-01)

As reflected in the City Council's key objectives, the community's experience with the recent flood event and the likelihood that similar events or larger events will occur in the future, may trigger a broader discussion of what scale of event the city should use for its design standards. (BO-DOC-13)

The local official and resident surveys both presented a series of questions about risks. Figure 5.1 summarizes these results across communities.

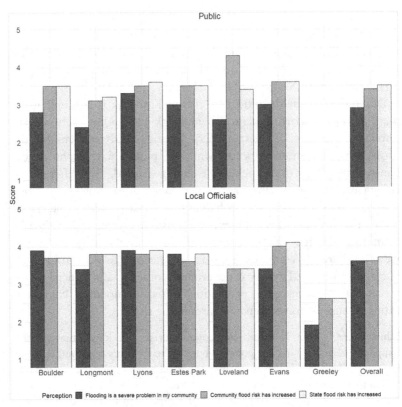

Figure 5.1 Risk perceptions: average of responses of public and local officials across seven communities

When asked if flooding is a severe problem in their community, local officials[3] in all communities perceived flooding as more severe, compared to residents. The same held true for perception that the risks of flooding have increased in their community and in Colorado. Unsurprisingly, perception of problem severity was greatest in Lyons, which experienced the most extreme devastation of the study communities, and in Estes Park, the tourism-based community that suffered significant damage along its river corridors.

---

[3] The survey was distributed annually from 2014 to 2016 to local officials, staff, and stakeholders involved in flood recovery (see Appendix A for details). The respondents represent diverse backgrounds, but they all had a formal local-government-sanctioned position at the time of the survey and are therefore labeled "local officials" broadly.

5.2.3 Public Risk Perceptions

In interviews with local government officials, they discussed how their residents perceive the risks of future flooding. Staff mentioned how many residents were traumatized from the experience several months after the event.

There's kind of a PTSD about that. I've seen that in the summertime. It starts raining hard—people get nervous. It's not, "Oh, it's a nice rainy afternoon," it's like, "Oh my god, are we going to do this again?" So I think people are gun-shy, and I think they're going to be that way for a while—there are still people that are pretty traumatized by it, and they're afraid about it. (EP-01)

The effects of the floods were not felt equally across each of the communities, and the distribution of damage may influence how different residents perceive future risks, as discussed by a Loveland official:

I think the average citizen doesn't think about flooding that often. Especially like I said before, if you [sic] part of the probably 90% of our population that wasn't even impacted by the flood. Those people that were impacted by the river and are by the river and could get impacted again, I think every time it rains for more than one day, I think they think about it a lot, what might happen again. (LV-02)

The risk perception literature suggests that those who directly experience a disaster may perceive elevated future risk of a disaster occurring again. Alternatively, some studies suggest that individuals who experience a disaster may think that they have "had their turn" and therefore discount the chance that a similar disaster will occur again. To try to capture the relationship between direct and indirect flood experiences and risk perceptions, the surveys of residents included a set of measures about the extent of damage experienced in their household, neighborhood, and community (Appendix A, Table A.5). Residents in Lyons reported the greatest community-level damage. The reported damages align with the home damages estimated by FEMA in each community and as described in Chapter 3.

The resident survey in six of the study communities included several questions to capture respondents' perceptions of the severity of the 2013 flooding in their community and whether they believe flood risks are increasing (Figure 5.1). The survey also presented residents a slider with which they could rate their perceived risk of an extreme flood occurring over the next twenty years. Residents in Lyons perceived flooding as a more severe problem for their community, compared to residents in the other surveyed communities. Residents in Loveland held the strongest belief that flood risks have increased over the past two decades, and their beliefs were greater, on average, than the flood officials in Loveland (n = 7), but this belief in increased flooding in their community did not extend to a similar belief about increasing flooding in Colorado as a whole (Figure 5.1). This is an interesting finding, given that Loveland was most recently affected by another devastating flood – the Big Thompson Flood in 1976 discussed in Chapter 2 – compared with the other study communities.

Similar to several studies on the effect of disaster experience on risk perceptions, the modeling of survey data across six study communities suggests that community-level damages, information acquisition, and deeply held beliefs were significantly associated with residents' perception of risk of future flooding in Colorado (Appendix B). Interestingly, household-level damage was a significant *negative* predictor of perceptions of future flood risks – all else constant, the more household damage a resident reported, perceptions of future flood risk decreased (Appendix B, Table B.2).

How individuals interpret their flood experiences may influence their perceptions about future risks and severity of flooding. These experiences, whether direct or indirect, may be refracted through the lens of deeply held worldviews and political ideology. Chapter 4, along with the literature on risk perceptions, suggests that deeply held beliefs, individual characteristics, and experiences with disasters intertwine to influence residents' perceptions about the future risks of disasters.

Experiences with flooding, whether at the individual, neighborhood, or at the community level, may affect residents' trust in government officials in managing flood risks, as well as their preferences toward policy solutions to mitigate future flood risks. A community's capacity to manage risks may be influenced by whether residents support changes in and adoption of disaster-related policies. Furthermore, how community members experience and perceive risks may influence the extent to which they engage with and participate in participatory decision-making processes about disaster recovery. Participation in such processes may further influence public support of risk-mitigating policies. For a better understanding of community-level policy change and learning after disaster, it is critical to examine individual-level factors that influence community support for flood mitigation policies. Chapter 6 explores how these factors may affect trust in government and support for disaster-related policy solutions.

6 | *Trust in Government and Support for Policy Action*

As discussed in Chapter 5, risk perceptions may be influenced by personal experiences, deeply held beliefs, and political ideology. But individual risk perceptions may also be affected by engagement in social processes, such as information seeking and participation in disaster-related discussions. Information sought and consumed after a disaster and trust in these sources of information may influence how individuals think about a disaster, its causes, and support (or not) of policy solutions (see Figure III.1). Furthermore, experiencing a disaster may erode trust in officials that are charged with managing disaster-related risks. Levels of trust in government officials may in turn influence information seeking and support for policy action. This chapter investigates the relationships among individual experiences, information seeking, participation in flood recovery processes, and attitudes toward risk mitigation actions.

6.1 Information Sources and Trust in Government Officials

Individuals seek information from various sources and interpret or discuss the information through social processes. After experiencing a disaster, changes in public perceptions of risk may lead to increased public participation in decision-making processes where future risks may be discussed. The risk perceptions that form in the wake of flood events and beliefs about the causes of flooding potentially help groups of individuals coalesce to push for policy changes that can make communities more resilient (Nohrstedt & Weible, 2010; Sabatier & Weible, 2007a). These same processes of information uptake and belief formation can also widen the gap between municipal officials and the public, potentially impeding policy change.

Individuals form subjective beliefs about risks, problem severity, and policy preferences though dynamic social processes, including consuming media and other sources of information (Ho et al., 2008; Lin et al., 2008; Rogers & Prentice-Dunn, 1997). The public most often does not synthesize or evaluate risk-based information on disasters themselves, but rather seeks synthesized and integrated information from other sources (McCallum, Hammond, & Covello, 1991; Steelman, McCaffrey, Velez, & Briefel, 2015). In the aftermath of a disaster, such as an extreme flood, the public may seek information from a diversity of sources (e.g., local government, FEMA, the media, friends, and neighbors) and from a variety of venues (e.g., local government websites, local television news). Local governments, the public, media, and nongovernmental organizations also leverage social media to disseminate information during and after a disaster. Peer-to-peer information dissemination about disasters and risks is occurring more and more frequently through social media (Steelman et al., 2015).

Disaster-related information may influence beliefs about a disaster (Steelman et al., 2015), such as the causes and severity of the disaster and attitudes toward risk mitigation (Wachinger et al., 2013). How individuals view risks may be modified by information they consume and the level of trust they place in the sources of information (Heitz et al., 2009; Wachinger et al., 2013). Individuals are likely to seek information from sources they trust, and often this information confirms their previously formed beliefs about an issue (called confirmation bias) (Nickerson, 1998), which may further entrench their prior views on flooding.

In addition to information dissemination, local governments may convene public meetings (discussed further in Chapter 7) to discuss disaster recovery and potential government action, including policy changes (Nickerson, 1998; Wachinger et al., 2013). Through these public engagement processes, local government officials communicate about risk among themselves, with external experts, and with the general public. While initially conceptualized as a flow of information from "the expert" to "the public," the risk communication process is now more often viewed as a dialogue between policy actors and the public, with an emphasis on social learning (Kellens et al., 2013). Community member participation in recovery discussions and perception of these discussions may influence policy preferences in recovery processes; however, the direction of influence between participation and policy support is unclear. The relationships between participation and policy preferences may be mediated by residents' level of trust in local government. For example, it may be that people who participate in recovery processes and trust local government for flood management report greater levels of support for flood mitigation policies. Alternatively, it could be that individuals who already support flood mitigation policies participate more and are more likely to trust government as a legitimate source of policy solutions to flood risk.

6.1.1 Information Sources in Colorado Communities

Local governments in Colorado used a variety of tools to inform their publics about emergency management and long-term disaster recovery. Local governments in the study frequently updated their websites during flood response and recovery with a variety of flood-related information. Local government websites served as a source of information for a majority of residents surveyed (roughly 60 percent), whereas roughly a fifth of residents surveyed accessed flood-related information from the State of Colorado's website and a fifth from FEMA. The type of information provided varied across communities, often including updates on roadwork, park and trail closures, and the flood recovery process. Local officials described their approach to information dissemination after the floods:

I think the town has tried to do education. They've had public hearings and public meetings. I think they've done a good job. They actually took—and I don't know if it's still on the website—but they actually had a preliminary map, and it showed these red. And it red and then pink. And it was bright red in pretty significant corridor, including this building. And it was like, "Whoa." And I think that did get some attention, and then I think it kind of dies down. (EP-05)

We did a press release and updated our website on a daily basis. So, I mean we were opening trails on a daily basis. And you know, we weren't doing it haphazardly, we had a very specific concept. We know where use is and the Chautauqua area gets the highest visitation so our first, it's very simple. We did Chautauqua, then something in the North and something in the South. The mountain back trail, the western part of the system is where people go because it surrounds the Boulder neighborhoods. (BO-04)

I was blown away by the number of people that were responding to tweets and asking via Facebook and via Twitter and all of that social media stuff, versus—I mean, they don't call on the phone anymore. They tweet you a question, and it's, like, "Oh, my goodness." (GR-01)

And just to that, with elected officials, really important role is ahead of time [sic], have the elected officials also go through disaster training, have them understand what their role is, and then implement that, but whether it's your elected officials, mayor and councilors, whether it's the public: communicate, communicate, communicate. Push information out. We used traditional sources and non-traditional—well, it's becoming traditional now, but social media—we were pushing lots of information out social media. We had a team of three people that were doing that constantly during this time. (LV-02)

The disaster literature shows that mainstream and social media activity often increases after a disaster (Crow, Berggren, et al., 2017; Pantti, Wahl-Jorgensen, & Cottle, 2012). Media and social media activity peaked in the direct aftermath of the floods and then steadily declined (Albright, Crow, & Koebele, 2019). Social media became popular tools of communication for policymakers and the public throughout recovery. A large number of tweets and newspaper articles were published in the direct aftermath of the Colorado floods, which then declined through the long-term recovery period (Albright et al., 2019). The public tweeted most frequently immediately after the floods, while policymakers and other elites tweeted (proportionally) later in the recovery period.

6.1.2 *Trust in Government Officials to Manage Flood-Related Issues*

The degree to which residents trust each other, local officials, and other stakeholders to deal with issues surrounding disaster management is critical to disaster recovery and building resilience to future risks. The public's trust in government and government officials may be especially critical for post-disaster policy adoption and effective governance of hazards. The dynamics of trust in a post-disaster context are complex (Han, Hu, & Nigg, 2011), in which both direct and indirect impacts of disaster and recovery may affect levels of trust (Cooper & Block, 2007; Han et al., 2011). Trust (or distrust) may influence where residents collect information about recovery and the extent to which they support disaster-related policy changes in their communities (Wachinger et al., 2013). Three years after the disaster, a local official in Lyons described the importance of establishing trust between community members and local officials before a disaster:

That—having the relationship and trust with the community beforehand, of course, so that when you told them things that we had to do, they just did it. You know, they weren't fighting with you about leaving and trusting you that you're going to keep their homes, when they were empty, safe, and those kinds of things. (LY-01)

The occurrence of a catastrophic event may transform the complex dynamics of trust in a community (Han et al., 2011). The role and importance of trust in disaster recovery, particularly as a component of social capital, is critical, although few studies have examined the causal link between disaster occurrence and the resulting levels of trust (Cassar, Healy, & von Kessler, 2017). Community members may change the extent to which they trust other community members, organizations (government or nongovernmental), or specific policy actions as a result of experiencing a disaster. Experiencing a disaster may also erode trust in government (Cooper & Block, 2007; Han et al., 2011). These corrosive effects on trust may occur at multiple levels of governance, including federal, state, and local (Haddow, Bullock, & Coppola, 2010). Post-disaster levels of trust in government may influence where community members turn to for information about the disaster, and, in turn, how much they trust the information gathered (Wachinger et al., 2013), as well as what policies they support or oppose. Trust in local-level government officials may encourage deeper engagement with the disaster recovery participatory processes discussed in Chapter 7, where distrust may discourage it. And in turn, more in-depth participation in recovery processes may affect trust that community members have for their local government. As such, the extent that community members trust their local government in disaster-related matters may influence their policy preferences in recovery in a number of ways.

In Boulder, trust issues arose in Open Space Board of Trustees meetings and caused difficulty during the recovery period, as described by meeting minutes:

Molly Davis said the Open Space Board of Trustees (OSBT) are tasked with a difficult job trying to balance interests. She said some interests are competitive in nature and proceedings need to be transparent; the Board needs to make sure Board actions take place during Board meetings. There needs to be a set foundation and effort to gain back the public trust. (Open Space Board of Trustees Minutes, March 9, 2016)

Local officials across communities discussed the importance of building trust in local government. Officials in Longmont described the process of building trust with their community and the importance of honesty and transparency in information dissemination:

…being honest with people and transparent in what you're doing. It's the best way, I think, to maintain the trust of the public and your elected officials, and of your staff. (LG-04)

But what we saw when we would give people this accurate source of information is it allowed the community to take over. So when we could tell people, "This is what the water did. We're not expecting it to happen again, and if it does, here's what we're going to do." You see what happened, like, in Southmoor Park when the residents came out with their snow shovels and they started clearing off the mud with their shovels. And they went door to door, feeding each other, and they had a big barbeque. And it's this magical sort of community thing that happens when they trust the information we're giving them. (LG-02)

The literature on the role of trust in risk perceptions is quite varied, with often contradictory results (Kellens et al., 2013). The impact trust has on risk perceptions depends on the type of trust – whether it is trust in government, institutions, disaster warnings, or government policy actions after a disaster (Kellens et al., 2013).

The resident survey across six of the study communities measured residents' trust in government officials at multiple levels of government (Figure 6.1). On a scale of one (no trust) to four (high levels of trust), residents reported greater levels in trust in local government staff to manage the flood issues compared to federal officials and local elected officials. Residents in the low-capacity and heavily damaged communities of Lyons and Evans reported the lowest levels of trust in local government officials (city staff, county staff, and mayors). Residents of Longmont and Loveland reported comparatively higher levels of trust in local staff to manage flood-related issues.

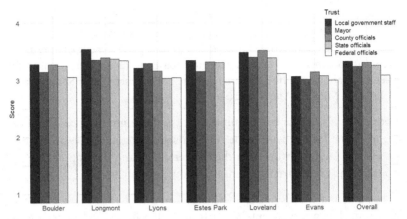

Figure 6.1 Trust in government officials: measures of trust across levels of government

6.2 Causal Understanding of Flooding and Support for Government Policy

To better understand the potential drivers of trust residents have in government officials, the resident survey included measures of flood damage (personal, neighborhood, and community damage), worldviews, information acquisition about floods, and participation in flood recovery processes. These factors were regressed against the level of trust in (1) local government staff and (2) resident's town mayor focused on how they manage floods. The results suggest that perceptions of higher damage in residents' neighborhoods is associated with lower levels of trust (see Appendix B, Table B.2). In short, controlling for other factors in the model, individuals who reported higher levels of flood damages in their neighborhoods reported lower levels of trust in local government management of the floods. Models also suggest that individuals who are more informed about floods trust their government officials more to deal with floods.

The public's perceptions of future flood risks are important beyond influencing the extent to which individuals and households adopt flood-mitigating behaviors, such as acquiring flood insurance or making basements more water resistant. Experiencing floods may also affect how communities interpret and conceptualize flooding and its causes, as well as influencing preferences toward policy alternatives

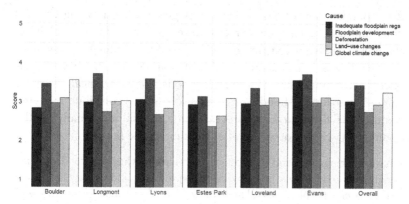

Figure 6.2 Residents' perceptions about the cause of the Colorado 2013 extreme flood

that could reduce future flood risks (Brilly & Polic, 2005; Wachinger et al., 2013). Past studies suggest that individual risk perceptions of greater flood risk do not necessarily correlate with increased personal mitigation efforts (Bubeck, Botzen, & Aerts, 2012). In this regard, individuals who are aware of flood risks, but less prepared to address impacts on their own, may "assume the responsibility for preparing the population for a hazard lays [sic] in the hands of authorities, instead of taking individual action" (Raaijmakers, Krywkow, & van der Veen, 2008).

Whether individuals perceive failures of pre-flood policies (or lack of policies) may also influence post-flood policy preferences held by the public. Disasters often involve failures in policies and therefore blame-placing can be central to post-disaster discussions (Bovens, Hart, & Gray, 1996). Studies suggest that the public often views flooding through a causal lens, frequently focusing on human error (Green, Tunstall, & Fordham, 1991). Wachinger et al. (2013) contend that if disastrous floods are caused by human actions, the public may place blame on governing authorities, and this, in turn, may affect future risk management through the erosion of trust in these government organizations.

6.2.1 *Causal Understanding of Colorado's Floods*

The resident survey asked respondents to rate the importance of potential causes that may have contributed to the severity of the Colorado

2013 floods, on a scale of one to five (Figure 6.2). On average, across communities, respondents perceive development in the floodplain as the most significant contributor to the 2013 floods. Interestingly, residents in Evans, which is more politically conservative but also experienced significant damage in neighborhoods and a park near the river, ranked inadequate floodplain regulations as a contributor to the floods. The flood in Evans revealed the landfill that many in the community where not aware of at the time of the flood.

One of the things we found was that our park complex which was flooded, which is right out by the mobile home parks, sits on top of an old sanitary landfill, so that uncovered the old sanitary landfill, so we can't do anything in that area until we figure out what's going on with the landfill. So the EPA has been here using their really cool whatever equipment that they have to map it underground to how big, how deep, all that kind of stuff. And they've got to make a determination of what we—so we can't do anything with the park complex until we figure out what's going on with the landfill. Then we can't do anything with the landfill until we figure out what's going on with the levee. (EV-02)

In Evans, perception of a failure in floodplain regulations may have been driven in part by the flood revealing the old landfill. Unsurprisingly, more politically conservative residents were less likely to see global climate change as a contributing factor the flood (as seen in Evans, Loveland, and Estes Park) while the more liberal communities of Lyons and Boulder perceived climate change as a more important contributor to the floods. This result aligns with the climate change public opinion literature (Egan & Mullin, 2017).

6.2.2 Policy Preferences in the Aftermath of the Floods

In the aftermath of disaster, local governments may consider adopting new policies or altering existing policies with the aim of mitigating future risks. The impact of extreme events on the public's beliefs about problem severity and the causes of disaster could potentially bring groups of individuals together to push for new policies (Albright, 2011; Nohrstedt & Weible, 2010; Sabatier & Weible, 2007a). Through these same processes, gaps between the public and town officials can widen, or between groups of the public, potentially limiting the opportunity for policy change.

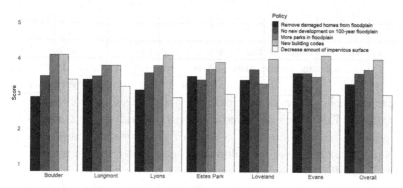

Figure 6.3 Policy preferences of the public

Policy preferences of residents were captured by a series of questions about policies that communities may adopt to mitigate the risk of future flooding. These questions are summarized for each community in Figure 6.3. The weakest level of support was for a policy calling for decreasing the amount of impervious surface, but the placement of parks in floodplains received relatively high support, especially in the City of Boulder. Policy preferences varied across communities and policies, with the greatest overall level of support for new building codes. Individual preferences toward policies were driven, at least in part, by worldviews, and perceptions of risk and problem severity (Appendix B, Table B.3).

The survey responses suggest that individuals' deeply held beliefs are significantly related to preferences toward potential risk-mitigating policies (Appendix B, Table B.3). The extent to which an individual perceives that humans have the ability to control the environment, along with beliefs about negative consequences of human interference with nature, was related to preferences toward risk-mitigating policies. These findings suggest that beliefs about human relationships with the earth are associated with beliefs about more specific flood-related policies, a finding that meshes with the belief hierarchy underpinning policy process frameworks, such as the Advocacy Coalition Framework, as well as the work of Greenberg et al. (2014), who studied policy support in the aftermath of Hurricane Sandy.

6.3 Conclusions

This chapter focused attention on various individual-level factors that may influence the degree to which residents trust their local governments, which in turn can influence support for government actions and potential policy changes and learning that can lead to more resilient outcomes. The factors discussed include: (1) worldviews, (2) risk perceptions, (3) trust in information and local governments, and (4) beliefs about causes and severity of floods. When disaster strikes, the public and local officials may become more acutely aware of and concerned about the risk of similar future events. The public and local officials view risks through their own lens of values, beliefs, and experiences. Disaster occurrence may lead the public to acquire additional information about the event, in this case an extreme flood, and perhaps participate in local-level disaster recovery processes. In turn, information collection and participation in the processes presented in Chapter 7 may alter beliefs about the severity of the disaster and support for risk mitigation policies. Trust in local officials may also play a key role in driving information collection, participation, perceptions about the event, and support for policy solutions.

Human perceptions of risks from hazards form through direct and indirect experiences with disaster. Risk perception formation is a social process in which information is collected and discussed, and through these discussions risks are interpreted. The evidence this chapter presents suggests that neither direct damage to personal property nor information acquisition by residents was a predictor of perceptions of problem severity, whereas participation in flood recovery processes was positively associated with perceptions of problem severity (see Appendix B and Chapter 7). Perceptions about problem severity may be driven, at least in part, through the social process of formal flood recovery discussions. These findings align with the risk literature that indicates that risk perceptions are often formed through social processes (Ho et al., 2008; Lin et al., 2008), and public engagement processes led by local governments may be an effective tool to increase risk awareness (Wachinger et al., 2013). However, it is unclear if resident participation in recovery processes drives perception of problem severity or vice versa (or both).

The public's trust in government and government officials may be critical for post-disaster policy adoption and effective governance of hazards. Greater levels of trust between residents and local officials may allow for greater depth of interaction and greater willingness to listen to each other's experiences, perceptions, and preferences toward policy solutions. More in-depth interaction between local officials and residents may, in turn, spur greater levels of trust. But the dynamics of trust in a post-disaster context are complex (Han et al., 2011), in which both direct or indirect impacts of a disaster and recovery may affect levels of trust (Cooper & Block, 2007; Han et al., 2011). Trust (or distrust) may influence where community members collect information about recovery and the extent to which they support disaster-related policies (Wachinger et al., 2013). In this study of individual responses to flooding in their own community, residents who experienced greater flood damage in their neighborhood reported lower levels of trust in their mayor and local government staff. Residents more informed about the flood reported greater trust in local staff. In turn, trust in local government officials and participation in recovery processes were moderately significant drivers of perceptions of problem severity, but not support of flood mitigation policies. Support for policies to address flood mitigation seems to be most strongly related to deeply held beliefs and ideologies. These factors – trust, beliefs about problem severity, and beliefs about causes of disasters – likely all contribute to learning after a disaster within communities.

Part III presents the complex individual-level factors that combine to influence the level of trust individuals have in their government and support for government's actions during post-disaster recovery. These are critical to understand in order to complete the picture of community-level disaster recovery decision-making and learning that can help some communities move toward greater resilience after a disaster. Next, Part IV further explores the participatory processes introduced in this part. It delves into the group dynamics and local government processes that further help explain learning after disasters in communities.

Review

Box III.1 Key lessons from Part III

1. Greater levels of disaster damage are associated with
   a. Individuals seeking disaster-related information and participating in disaster recovery processes
   b. Lower levels of trusts in local officials in managing disasters
2. Community members with lower levels of trust in government perceive the problems associated with a disaster as more severe.
3. Community members who participate in disaster recovery processes
   a. Perceive the problems associated with the disaster as more severe
   b. Tend to perceive greater risks of future similar disasters
4. Support for disaster recovery policies is predominantly driven by deeply held beliefs and ideologies.

Individual and Group Engagement

The Role of Relationships and Collaboration on Disaster Recovery and Resilience

To this point in the book, community-level characteristics such as history, disaster damage, and capacity of local governments were explored in detail in Parts I and II. Part III examined individual-level factors such as beliefs, perceptions, and disaster experiences that may influence collective processes within communities after a disaster. Part IV now builds upon those analyses to understand the group-level factors and government processes that were instituted after the 2013 floods that may contribute to community-level resilience-building through learning and change after a disaster strikes.

After the Colorado floods, local governments drew on the variety of resources detailed in Chapter 4 to recover, but were also helped – and sometimes hindered – by various stakeholders from inside and outside their communities. Lyons saw a huge influx of volunteers, NGOs, and federal government personnel who deployed to help the small town navigate complex federal government processes associated with disaster response and recovery. At times, these extra personnel were essential to accomplishing the seemingly insurmountable challenges that lay ahead. At other times, the numerous new faces in town made post-disaster processes difficult in a small town that thrives on relationships and sense of belonging. Additionally, the internal processes established by local governments during flood recovery engaged residents and other stakeholders in decisions made in the months after the floods, but these participatory processes varied and were associated with differing learning outcomes. Similarly, the relationships that towns like Lyons previously enjoyed or developed with personnel from other communities, state agencies, and the federal government would prove to influence long-term disaster recovery. Perhaps most importantly, the

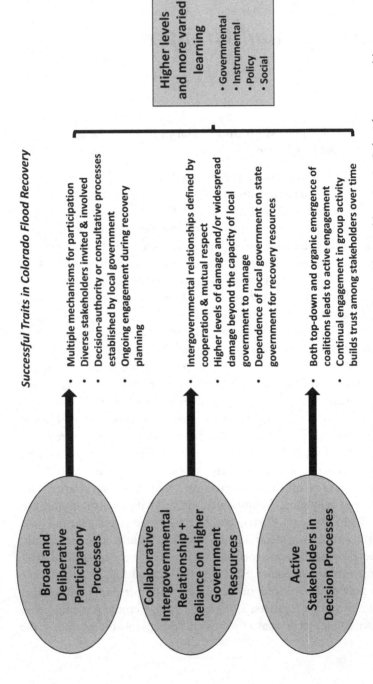

Figure IV.1 Participation, stakeholder activity, intergovernmental relationships, and learning in Colorado communities

nature of local government collaboration, engagement, and social capital with the various internal and external stakeholders during the recovery process proved to be vital to learning and eventual disaster recovery outcomes.

This part discusses the importance of stakeholder engagement dynamics and relationships – with other governments and within a community – that can encourage or limit learning and resilience during disaster recovery. To begin, Chapter 7 discusses the variety of participation mechanisms that local governments used to inform and encourage active engagement by their residents and other local stakeholders. The chapter then focuses on groups of individuals within communities called coalitions that coordinate to try to influence local government decisions. Finally, Chapter 8 examines the relationships and dependence that local governments have with state agencies. These dynamics are examined as they relate to learning outcomes for disaster-affected communities. Figure IV.1 illustrates the dynamics observed in the study communities and how they combine to influence learning within local governments.

This part focuses on group-level dynamics and governmental processes instituted that involve collaboration, participation, and engagement in decision-making. These chapters draw most heavily from interview and document data (see Appendix A for a detailed description of the research methods). This part of the book sheds light on the processes for post-disaster recovery that can be helpful in building the community resilience Chapter 1 discusses as important to reducing vulnerability to future risks.

7 | Stakeholder Engagement and Community-Level Disaster Recovery toward Resilience

For a variety of reasons – including soliciting disaster experiences to inform potential policy changes, increasing buy-in from local residents, and disseminating safety information – local governments may convene public meetings to discuss disaster recovery, along with potential policy changes (Albright & Crow, 2015b; Wachinger et al., 2013). In their review of the flood risk literature, Wachinger et al. (2013) concluded that public participation is a critical, and often the most effective, way to increase public awareness of flood disasters and to increase trust in government officials. Recovery processes vary across communities in breadth and depth of public participation. In some communities, experts may dominate recovery processes, but those processes then may be less open to community members and other nonexpert stakeholders (Albright & Crow, 2015b; Crow, 2010a; Schneider & Teske, 1992). Alternatively, some communities may engage the public in deep discussions about their perceived risks and policy preferences toward how the community recovers and rebuilds after the disaster. Building on Part III, this chapter focuses attention on the public engagement, information dissemination or collection, and deliberation processes that are sometimes instituted by local governments during disaster recovery to provide input, reimagine, and plan for a community's future. This chapter primarily focuses on processes and group-level dynamics involved when stakeholders participate during disaster recovery.

Through these public engagement processes, local government officials communicate about risk among themselves, as well as with external experts and the general public. Those individuals who participate in recovery processes and trust local government in flood management may report greater levels of support for flood mitigation policies. Alternatively, it also may be that those who support mitigation policies are more likely to view government as a legitimate actor and therefore engage in participatory processes, as Chapter 6 discusses.

Strengthening civic capacity around issues of disasters, risk, and hazard mitigation is time consuming, often resource intense, and frequently ephemeral (Page, 2016). Engaging community members on topics of hazard mitigation may present many challenges, both outside and inside the response and recovery periods. Outside of the immediate disaster response window, discussions centered on hazard mitigation may fall on disinterested ears because the ideas discussed are not salient (Godschalk, Brody, & Burby, 2003). Within the disaster response period, people who have suffered damages to their homes, are displaced, have limited transportation, or have limited individual capacity may not be able to engage in discussions about flood recovery. Disaster recovery processes may therefore further disenfranchise groups and community members who were previously marginalized from community decision-making processes. For example, residents who lack citizenship are less likely to seek support or interface with government officials, for fear of legal consequences. An official in Estes Park described training their staff to work with flood survivors and connect with them to better serve them:

We did some other things I thought were really useful; we brought in I think it was a psychologist that did training for all our staff on secondary trauma—not primary ... as training for my staff for how to react to people dealing with trauma. To say you're dealing with people who have lost their homes, they're displaced, they're frustrated. What to look for, what to look for when they need help, how to suggest they get help. The psychological impact of this. And that kind of training, those kinds of things, it was really easy, it was only like an hour and a half but to have all my staff sit down and go through that and say hey, if you see these symptoms in somebody, these are things to look out for, these are things to be careful about, this is where you might want to get somebody help. (EP-01)

How communities engage with stakeholders and community members after a disaster may influence the extent to which issues stemming from the event are discussed and failures in previous policies and practices are identified. In turn, these discussions may lead to or potentially inhibit revision or adoption of local-level policies during the recovery process. Through examining participatory processes across the seven Colorado communities, lessons can be learned about effective approaches of stakeholder and public engagement in the aftermath of a disaster. Local officials described how they involved the public in their recovery processes in interviews. In Longmont, outreach to residents focused attention on planning for recovery along the main river corridor:

We want to make sure that people have door hangers, that they have videos depicting what's happening, that they're able to see things on the web site, that they can subscribe to e-notifications around the St. Vrain River. There's tons of different ways that people can engage about getting the information. Obviously, we have signs, and we put things in the newspaper, and we put things in our newsletters and things like that. There's probably 20 different media outlets that we used. (LG-02)

The task force planning process in Lyons focused on sector-by-sector issues such as housing:

And so it's made up of volunteers from the community; it represents a lot of different interests—some folks that live in the confluence [heavily flooded] area, some folks that live in the outlying area where we may do a replacement housing project, and then some business people. So it's a combination of folks. (LY-02)

In Estes Park, the local government solicited input from residents, but despite efforts felt that many were still uninformed:

Because we would stream the meetings live and allow them to email in questions. And we did that during the fires too. So it was not unusual for us to answer people's questions in Southern California. We talked to people in Florida, Houston, that have homes here. They could get online, they could see what everybody is talking about and they could ask their own questions and get them answers and we got a lot of good feedback from that. We have as many as 1300 people watching the streaming live. So that went really well. We've done a lot of, we do a lot with social media so we had a couple twitter accounts, we have a Facebook page that was good just sharing information, getting information out really quickly. We had people sign up on, we do push notifications to people to find out what's going on. Some cases like the no flush zone we worked door to door. We made door hangers to let people know that they can't flush. English on one side, Spanish on the other side. And boy scouts went door to door and handed them out. So amazingly enough this was four days—probably a week after the flood started, they actually ran into people that didn't know there was a flood. (EP-01)

The City of Boulder solicited information from residents through surveys and meetings focused on neighborhood-level issues:

So the neighborhood meetings have been critical in that right now ... it's almost like a debrief. We're asking the residents to come tell us what their experience was and also what they think, and it's been fascinating to watch them come to the flood maps and say, "No, that's not how it happened; this is how it happened." ... It's kind of letting the community vent, but also debrief, because that will help us gather data. (BO-01)

Community documents over a three-year period after the floods indicate that each community adopted a variety of approaches to engage with the public and stakeholders in recovery-related decisions (Table 7.1). Boulder, Longmont, Lyons, and Estes Park adopted the most engaged and extensive outreach to their communities. Each of the study communities adopted unique approaches to engage community members after the floods. Engagement with community members differed across three dimensions: frequency of engagement, breadth in topics covered during interactions, and the role that community members played in the recovery process. Lyons implemented strategies to engage its residents throughout the recovery process, displayed more in-depth learning, and adopted a greater diversity of policies, as well as a community-wide recovery plan that integrated many community sectors and issues. Lyons developed multiple sector-focused flood task forces that were composed of residents, local officials, and federal officials to tackle such issues as public infrastructure, housing, and parks. Evans formed one centralized task force with representatives selected from various groups, whose charge was to discuss the redevelopment of the downtown core. While both Evans and Lyons experienced devastating damages, the damage in Lyons was more widespread, whereas in Evans damage was centralized in neighborhoods near the river. Pre-flood individual-level capacities in the two communities differed as well, with lower median household income in Evans, as well as higher rates of undocumented community members.

Also important to note in this discussion of local participatory processes is whether they were purposely cross-sector in nature, drawing from residents, businesses, and other organizations. The literature presented here suggests that diverse participatory mechanisms can provide better results in terms of eventual decision outcomes, stakeholder support for decisions, and stakeholder understanding of underlying problems and constraints that governments face. In several study communities, local officials reported engaged members of the business community during recovery planning. In Estes Park, the business community comprised mostly small, local businesses that worked together to assist the business community during recovery.

Table 7.1. *Participatory process characteristics across study communities*

	New institutions	Task force/ stakeholder process	Public meeting participation	Survey of residents	Participants	Depth of involvement	Sector of process focus	Scale of participatory processes
Boulder	No	No	Yes	Yes	Staff, commission, public	Consultation: community-wide and neighborhood specific	Open space and floodplains	Moderate
Longmont	Yes	Yes	Yes	Yes	Staff, commission, public	Delegate power: stakeholder processes	Parks	Moderate
Lyons	Yes	Yes	Yes	Yes	Staff, Public, local businesses	Public control: multi-sector planning process	Multi-sector	Broad
Loveland	No	No	No	No	Staff, council, commission	Zero to limited input from public for infrastructure, consultation for parks	Infrastructure and parks	Moderate
Estes Park	Yes	Yes	Yes	No	Staff, Public, commission, local businesses	Consultation/ delegate power: public forum	River corridor	Moderate

Table 7.1. (*cont.*)

	New institutions	Task force/ stakeholder process	Public meeting participation	Survey of residents	Participants	Depth of involvement	Sector of process focus	Scale of participatory processes
Evans	Yes	Yes	No	No	Staff, council, task force (residents, businesses)	Public Control/ delegate power: stakeholder process	Infrastructure and river corridor	Broad
Greeley	No	No	Yes	No	Staff	None	None	None

But some creative things going on; there's a group of business people who are putting together a virtual Estes Park. They've got a website out there and encouraging people to get out there and say hey, you can't get up here and shop for Christmas but look, here are all of the businesses you love in Estes Park online, you can shop with us anyway. So that's worked really well. (EP-01)

Beyond assisting their own business community, businesses in Estes Park, Lyons, and Evans also participated in the planning processes instituted by their local governments. This pattern was observed more often in smaller communities with tight networks. Owners of small businesses were more often viewed as part of the community and engaged in participatory processes like other residents of the community than large businesses owned or operated from outside the community.

In a small community, you meet many of the business owners, so you already have that working relationship, which has been helpful. It's not—when someone says, "My property on…" you know, "was damaged, and this is"—you can picture exactly where it is. You don't have that learning curve, the—if you had an organization that's just constantly turning over. (EP-02)

And so it's made up of volunteers from the community; it represents a lot of different interests—some folks that live in the confluence area, some folks that live in the outlying area where we may do a replacement housing project, and then some business people. So it's a combination of folks. (LY-02)

In Loveland, local officials found that preexisting relationships and networks with local small businesses proved important during the extensive recovery process throughout the community, despite not using participatory processes similar to other communities.

It takes a village. You hear that all the time, but it really does, and it has to do with different groups, relationships, having that community capacity, if you will, in order to deal with these kinds of things ahead of time. Because if you need to create them when you're in the middle of the disaster, that's not the time to do it. So it's planning. (LV-02)

The cross-sector nature and openness of some public engagement processes – notably those in Lyons, Estes Park, and Evans – stand out compared with those in other communities where local governments were less inclusive of nongovernmental and public stakeholders during

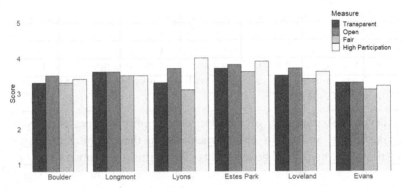

Figure 7.1 Civic engagement: measures of transparency, openness, fairness, and community participation in flood recovery processes[1]

their participatory planning processes. Interestingly, compared with the discussion in Chapter 2 focused on nongovernmental sector involvement during disaster response, the faith-based community and other civil society organizations were not involved in the participatory processes presented in Table 7.1. When the processes were cross-sector, it was primarily local government, residents, and sometimes the business community who engaged. This is notable given the extensive literature on the importance of civil society in disaster recovery introduced in Chapter 1. It is also notable that the business community occasionally engaged in these processes, but only those small businesses that were integral components of community civic life. In other words, the local franchises of national and multinational businesses were not identified as participating in the disaster recovery processes in the study communities.

Levels of public engagement in disaster recovery varied across communities. Survey respondents from Lyons and Estes Park on average perceived that their recovery process involved high levels of public engagement (Figure 7.1). Evans, a lower resourced community with a more conservative belief system on average, reported the lowest level of engagement in participatory processes and formed one centrally led task force. Communities that showed more in-depth participatory processes were those communities with the highest levels of per capita wealth and formal education, both of which are typically associated

---

[1] Agreement with the statements were measured on a five-point scale: Strongly disagree (1) to Strongly agree (5).

with higher likelihood of political participation among individuals in the United States (e.g., Brady, Verba, & Schlozman, 1995). The variety of participatory processes established by local governments in these communities was also associated with group-level activity observed during disaster recovery, which is explored next.

7.1 Coalitions and Participation during Disaster Recovery

Policy literature often focuses attention on groups (Koontz & Johnson, 2004; Leach, 2002; Wolfe & Pulter, 2002) and individuals – like those who engage in the participatory processes described earlier (Crow, 2010b; Mintrom, 1997; Mintrom & Normal, 2009; Roberts & King, 1991; Schneider & Teske, 1992; Teske & Schneider, 1994) – who work to influence decisions and policy outcomes. These actors can raise the salience of issues, advocate for specific outcomes, and shape broader understanding of issues, which can shape the policy process (Baumgartner & Jones, 2009; Baumgartner, Jones, & MacLeod, 2000; B. D. Jones & Baumgartner, 2005; Rivera, 2010). Issue attention and salience can shift quickly after disaster response is complete and allow technical experts to dominate decision-making during later phases of disasters, such as the recovery period (Birkland, 1998). However, groups of stakeholders have the ability to keep government attention focused on problems related to disasters and keep those problems on the public agenda, thus influencing the potential for policy change (Albright, 2011; Chui, Feng, & Jordan, 2014; Johnson, Tunstall, & Penning-Rowswell, 2005; Pierce, 2016; Rivera, 2010; Sabatier & Weible, 2007b). Because theoretical understanding of groups or coalitions within disaster policy subsystems is newly emerging (Crow et al., 2021), understanding processes through which disaster policy is formed is incomplete. The development of a clear definition of a disaster policy subsystem and the coalitions or groups that work within those systems to influence policy decisions was a major contribution of the study this book presents.

Policy process theory lends some insight into the roles that groups of stakeholders can play in policy decision-making. Coalitions, according to the Advocacy Coalition Framework, are groups of stakeholders that share common beliefs on a given policy issue (e.g., anthropogenic climate change requires drastic reductions of carbon emissions) and who coordinate their policy-focused activity in an effort to advance their goals (e.g., a carbon tax is an effective way to address carbon emissions) (Sabatier & Jenkins-Smith, 1999). These coalitions can influence policy outcomes depending on the resources they bring to bear on the policy process, the dynamics between competing coalitions who vie for policy success, and the strategies they use.

Other bodies of literature also examine groups of actors and their influence over decisions within the policy process, offering overlapping and complementary descriptions of group activity. Among the other group-focused explorations of policy activity are studies of networks (Henry, Lubell, & McCoy, 2010; Kapucu & Garayev, 2012; Lee & van de Meene, 2012; Robinson, Eller, Gall, & Gerber, 2013; Weible, 2005; Weible & Sabatier, 2005), collaborative groups (Margerum, 2008), and watershed partnerships (Moore & Koontz, 2003). While some of these – such as advocacy coalitions and ally networks – form based on shared beliefs and coordinate group activity (Sabatier et al., 2005; Sabatier & Jenkins-Smith, 1993a, 1999; Sabatier & Weible, 2007b), others do not. Coordination networks (Provan & Milward, 1995; Weible & Sabatier, 2005), for example, are not bound as clearly by shared beliefs and require something like occasional coordination rather than the sustained coordination of advocacy coalitions (Weible & Sabatier, 2005).

Becoming more common over the past two decades, a higher governmental authority typically establishes collaborative governance processes and convenes diverse groups of stakeholders to inform governmental decisions (Ansell & Gash, 2008; Busenberg, 1999; Lubell, 2004; Weible, Sabatier, & Lubell, 2004). Unlike the groups formed around shared beliefs, groups engaged in collaborative processes can build trust and social capital despite sharing a history of policy-related conflict. The goal of these processes is to find mutually acceptable policy solutions and change the ongoing conflict within a policy process (Koebele, 2015; Leach & Sabatier, 2005a, 2005b). These collaborative groups are different than the other groups discussed earlier due to the divergence of beliefs among actors as well as the top-down instituted nature of the collaborative processes involved. Shared beliefs may not, therefore, be the foundation for coordination between actors in these governance processes (Koebele, 2019). Rather, coordination may be more likely when actors in a collaborative governance process share an opponent (Henry et al., 2010), or view others as trustworthy or useful to achieving their goals (Calanni, Siddiki, Weible, & Leach, 2015). Despite a significant body of literature focused on various versions of policy actor groups, disaster policy subsystems at the community level are a blind spot in our knowledge of policy actor groups, specifically with regard to the emergence, shared goals or beliefs, and composition of actors in the groups.

The term *coalition* is used in this study to describe actors who work together within a disaster policy subsystem to advocate for and achieve their shared policy goals, which is different than the earlier definition employed in the Advocacy Coalition Framework, wherein shared beliefs form the foundation of coalitions (Crow et al., 2021). A higher authority – such as in collaborative governance processes – may institute these coalitions or they may emerge organically like advocacy coalitions. The actors involved may include numerous stakeholders as would be observed in any type of public policy process, but may also involve distinctions due to the nature of disasters wherein experts often wield more significant influence and consideration of victims dominates much policy-focused discussion after a disaster. These actors involved in community-level policy and governance processes can include local officials and other experts, residents, businesses, civil society groups, and media (Rivera, 2010). The goals of groups that form in disaster policy subsystems may range from advocating for extensive policy changes based on ideological (or other) beliefs or they may be narrower goals about disaster recovery policy outputs such as rebuilding or risk mitigation.

Based on the assumption that coalitions may be potentially important to policy process dynamics and that coalitions may form to achieve a variety of goals, the analyses from flood-affected communities in Colorado focused on three dimensions of coalitions that may be key to understanding policy actor group engagement in disaster recovery processes: (1) how a coalition is formed (emergence), (2) who participates in the coalition (composition), and (3) the goals coalitions seek (purpose) (Crow et al., 2021). Each of these characteristics is summarized next with examples from interview data to illustrate how these community-level disaster policy coalition characteristics were identified in the study communities.

7.1.1 Coalition Emergence: Coalition Formation in a Disaster Policy Subsystem

Across flood-affected communities in Colorado, two primary mechanisms for coalition formation were observed: *organic emergence and top-down initiation*. Community members with shared goals who focus on influencing disaster recovery policy decisions within their communities came together organically in some instances. These coalitions formed in Boulder neighborhoods in 2016, three years after the floods and focused their attention on project-based goals rather than community-wide long-term planning or risk reduction policies as described by a Boulder official:

People tend to organize when there's a specific decision. So there was a group of residents along Gregory Creek who are pretty active right after the flood ... they got less active or dispersed once there wasn't sort of a focal point. (BO-02)

The initial meetings were in focused areas around neighborhoods, which generally correlated to a specific drainage area and specific impacts, and that's the way that they've organized. (BO-06)

Coalitions of individuals that were convened by some higher authority (e.g., a local government or state agency) also emerged in some communities. The State of Colorado helped establish some collaborative groups in watersheds to help with regional-scale flood mitigation planning, such as the ones described by officials in Evans and Loveland:

It's a coalition of all the land owners along the river. And it will ultimately culminate in a river plan. And so that would include everything from opportunities for trails and public access, to flood mitigation. (EV-01)

And we got the [specific river] River Coalition ... So [now] there's communication and understanding ... rather than just thinking about my little stretch of the river, have people think more holistically. (LV-02)

These coalitions sometimes morphed over time after creation by higher authorities, often as a result of the trust and social capital built among group members wherein they identified their own personal beliefs and coalesced naturally at later stages. This pattern of coalition evolution was observed in both Lyons and Estes Park. In Lyons, groups held planning meetings focused on community recovery planning for more than two years. Those same groups later emerged as powerful advocates for their shared interests and goals as described by a Lyons official:

That neighborhood was the hardest hit. They literally—we met every Wednesday with them for the first full two years. Just to help communicate

need, but also just helping people navigate insurance, and regulations, and be a support to each other at the same time. They're down to meeting once a month now as a formal group...
They meet on their own in their neighborhood every week still. (LY-01)

In Lyons, this group-based recovery planning process changed over time, from a top-down instituted collaborative process focused on sector-specific discussions to include coalitions of community members who coordinated with one another to advocate for shared goals, more like the advocacy coalitions that work within policy processes.

Table 7.2 shows the various coalitions that emerged at two time points during disaster recovery in the Colorado communities studied. The findings from Lyons and Estes Park where the local government initially formed coalitions of community members including residents and local businesspeople that evolved into more organic coalitions with shared beliefs suggest overlap in the coalitions and collaborative governance literatures and provide insight into a potentially fruitful role for local governments to play in helping nurture social capital within their communities.

7.1.2 Coalition Composition: Policy Actor Group Involvement

As discussed in Chapter 1, disaster policy subsystems change over time. They can merge with other subsystems after a disaster when damage necessitates. They can then also go back to their pre-disaster composition once recovery is complete. Fung (2006) describes a continuum along which a variety of actors – *from technocrats and experts to the broader public and community organizations* – may engage in political activity. In the Colorado study communities, government agencies were critical participants by convening coalitions in several examples, as described in the previous section, but the public, neighborhood groups, and nongovernmental organizations also engaged in the disaster coalitions observed in many communities, such as described by officials in Boulder and Longmont. While these civil society groups were not deliberately engaged during the local government planning processes, they did advocate in some instances highlighted here.

There's Friends of Boulder Open Space, Plan Boulder County, the Audubon Society ... the Boulder Mountain Bike Alliance, and the trail runners' group, and the climbing group [that all worked together to advocate for open space and trails projects]. (BO-05)

Table 7.2. *Coalition emergence across study communities*

Community	Early disaster recovery: 2013 coalitions	Mature disaster recovery: 2016 coalitions	Coalition summary
Boulder	Loose coalitions focused on open space	Neighborhood coalitions of residents	Organic emergence of coalitions during both phases
Longmont	None	Neighborhood groups advocated through established formal channels and liaisons	Later coalition emergence due to prior engagement with formal municipal boards and commissions
Lyons	Planning groups composed of residents and government officials established by local government	Neighborhood coalitions of individual residents that emerged from top-down coalitions	Initial emergence due to municipal creation of multi-sector process. Later evolution into organic coalitions due to trust building.
Estes Park	Neighborhood groups facilitated and established by local government	Neighborhood groups of residents that emerged from top-down coalitions Externally established collaborative groups of local stakeholders	Initial emergence due to municipal creation of multi-sector process. Later evolution into organic coalitions due to trust building.

Table 7.2. (*cont.*)

Community	Early disaster recovery: 2013 coalitions	Mature disaster recovery: 2016 coalitions	Coalition summary
Loveland	None	Externally established collaborative groups of local stakeholders	Later coalition emergence due to formally established groups.
Evans	Task force including public and organized interests and experts established by local government	Externally established collaborative groups of local stakeholders	Both phases saw formal establishment of groups by government authorities.
Greeley	None	None	None

We had a neighborhood group leaders' association that was in place before the flood. They represent their neighborhoods, and so what's great is that they're able to use those pathways that are already established to advocate for things for the neighborhoods. (LG-02)

Existing inequities in access and political power can influence who participates in coalitions after a disaster. For example, Evans saw limited involvement by residents in a recovery task force instituted by the local government. A local elected official argued that this was, at least in part, due to the disproportionate disaster burden borne by undocumented residents and their low likelihood of engaging in government processes. Instead, the formal task force established by the local government recruited participants from targeted sectors of the community such as businesses and engaged residents.

We indicated that we did in fact want specific types of individuals on the task force: we wanted business owners, we wanted residents, we wanted potentially our Chamber, so our economic development experts, those type of people on the task force . . . What we did was we just opened it up for anyone [to apply], and tonight the Council I think will be appointing ten people to that task force, and then as we break that task force down into specific areas. (EV-03)

Along Fung's (2006) participation continuum, this type of group falls somewhere in the middle of the participation axis. While a number of different types of individuals were asked to participate, they were recruited and appointed rather than invitations being open to anyone who wanted to participate. This was a more closed process than the one observed in Lyons, for example.

Due to Lyons' government's limited capacity, the town asked all residents and businesses to commit to helping with the recovery planning across various sectors of the community.

Last night after we talked about the timeframe and the different areas that people can get involved in, we had them break in to [sic] those eight groups . . . and commit to being part of this process the next eight weeks. And then the state is providing a facilitator for every meeting . . . We had probably 78, 80 people in each group last night. (LY-01)

Although the process was initially anticipated to last eight weeks, some of the recovery groups in Lyons were still meeting two years after the flood. Based on these findings, a spectrum of coalition membership in disaster policy subsystems ranges from coalitions with broad involvement (Lyons) to those where previously engaged individuals or experts (i.e., business experts as identified in Evans) comprised the groups (Evans and Longmont).

7.1.3 Coalition Purpose: Policy, Projects, or Other Shared Goals

Two distinct purposes for group activity typified the coalitions observed across the Colorado communities – *project-focused coalitions and broader policy-focused coalitions*. It is important to note that some coalitions can work toward multiple goals or shift their focus over time, so these characterizations can be fluid.

The belief-based coalitions described in much of the policy literature – those focused on broad policy revisions or changes – were not commonly observed in the Colorado communities. Instead, shorter-term project-focused coalitions were observed most often. For example, in Estes Park, residents who did not share a history together formed a coalition focused on the restoration of specific open space land and ponds that had been damaged:

It was a committee that helped steer the vision that was made up of residents on the corridors ... There were some residents in the immediate area surrounding the ponds that did not like the plan at all ... They were concerned that it wouldn't provide fish habitat; there were some boardwalks shown [on the original rebuilding plan], and they were concerned about that type of intense, or perceived intense use of the open space. (EP-02)

While they were less common, in two instances the longer-term belief-based coalitions that focus on policy goals did emerge. In Lyons, the town-wide recovery planning process examined Town goals and actions around building community resilience over time. In Boulder, some project-focused neighborhood coalitions evolved into longer-term, policy-focused groups:

There's kind of a neighborhood group that started after the flood and lobbied considerably to move the mitigation study forward ... And they've worked really hard to constructively influence decision-makers. I mean, they have the hours they put into to go to the advisory board meetings and council meetings and planning board meetings to keep this on the radar. It's been fairly impressive effort on their part. (BO-02)

The most common pattern observed in Colorado flood-affected communities involved groups of neighbors coalescing around shared project goals rather than shared beliefs. Their goals focused on specific flood mitigation or rebuilding projects. When groups focused on broader policy change (e.g., policies designed to prevent building in floodplains to reduce risk from floods), coalitions organized around shared beliefs and focused on longer-term goals, while groups that focused on projects had shared interests but often diverged on beliefs.

7.1.4 A Typology of Disaster Policy Coalitions

The three characteristics identified in the literature – emergence, composition, and purpose – form the structure of this description of disaster policy coalitions. As articulated in more depth elsewhere (Crow et al., 2021), the cube presented in Figure 7.2 illustrates the dimensions of disaster policy coalitions observed in Colorado. Each axis of the

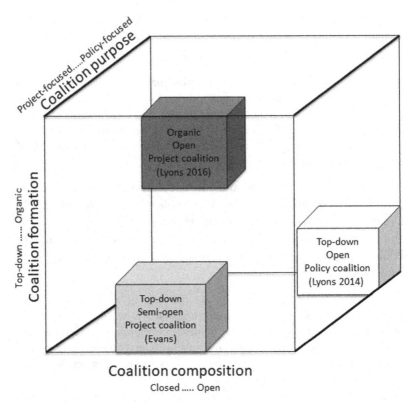

Figure 7.2 Typology of coalitions in a disaster policy subsystem from observations in Colorado communities (Crow et al., 2021)

cube shows the spectrum of observed traits for the coalition emergence, composition, or purpose. For coalition emergence, the spectrum is defined by the end points "top-down" and "organic." Along the composition spectrum are the end-points "technocratic" and "broad public involvement," which are drawn from established literature (Birkland, 2006; Fung, 2006; Gormley Jr., 1986). Finally, coalition purpose articulates the empirical observations of "project-focused" and "policy-focused" goals of coalitions.

Beyond advocating for policy change, Birkland (2006) argues that the presence of stakeholder activity can keep disaster-related policy issues on the policy agenda and can influence the likelihood of government learning after a disaster. In the Colorado communities, observations suggest that there are numerous ways that those groups can form and numerous ways they can advocate for their goals. These findings suggest that the ability of coalitions to maintain policy issue salience and energize policy debates in local governments may be more nuanced than previously thought. These coalitions are not uniform in how they emerge, what they look like, or what they advocate. As such, their role in government learning after disaster is also likely more nuanced than previously thought. These coalitions within communities can play important roles on the path to recovery, advocating for a variety of policy goals and engaging diverse stakeholders. As the literature observes, such groups can influence eventual policy decisions.

As Figure IV.1 illustrates, variation in learning is associated with different factors discussed in this chapter. Lyons used the most sustained, deep, and diverse stakeholder engagement process during disaster recovery. The sector-specific task forces used in Lyons to assist in recovery decision-making and planning were the exception, however. Most communities used task forces or stakeholder processes that relied on previously known parties from specifically selected groups to inform the decision-making conducted by local governments. A similar variation was observed when analyzing the coalitions of actors that emerged during the recovery period. In some communities, such as Boulder, coalitions emerged to focus on specific projects and needs in hard-hit sections of the community. In other communities, coalitions emerged after the local government established a sanctioned group of stakeholders to help inform the recovery decisions made by local officials. Chapter 8 expands upon the questions of learning to argue that more in-depth learning is associated with diverse, sustained, and deep engagement from community members. The extent to which these characteristics were observed through participatory processes or coalition activity varied substantially between communities.

Beyond the intra-community collaborative dynamics discussed here, there are also critical intergovernmental dynamics that can influence disaster recovery outcomes. These relationships and collaborations discussed in Chapter 8 extend beyond the community but can be just as important as the internal dynamics of a community in achieving recovery success. The discussion of collaboration and group dynamics that can influence eventual learning and policy change toward resilience continues with an examination of intergovernmental dynamics between local and state governments in Colorado after the 2013 floods.

8 | *Intergovernmental Relationships and Successful Disaster Recovery and Learning*

This book focuses on learning after disasters within communities, with particular attention on the processes, decisions, and resilience-related policy outcomes of local governments. As discussed in Chapter 1 and throughout the book, federal and state governments can also support or constrain local government efforts. This chapter, therefore, examines the dynamics between state and local governments as they relate to community-level learning after disasters.

Local governments are the core of all community disaster recovery decision-making. That said, the U.S. states develop their own disaster recovery processes and policies (Gerber, 2007; G. P. Smith, 2012). Depending on the national context, these processes and policies supersede local government policies and are also embedded within the context of national policies, funding, and mandates (Bea, 2010; G. P. Smith, 2012). More frequent engagement between governments across levels and jurisdictions can increase the availability of resources and knowledge available to both governmental parties, which can encourage learning among individuals within governments. This, then, may result in more successful disaster recovery outcomes if learning is, in fact, enhanced (Krause, 2011; C. B. Rubin & Barbee, 1985). The role of states, therefore, may be critical for understanding whether local governments learn, change, and adapt in the wake of a disaster.

Community disaster response and recovery in the United States places federalism in the spotlight. During emergency response, local governments may depend on mutual aid agreements with nearby communities as well as the state government. States may provide support from the National Guard, resources for response, and recovery aid. Many disasters, however, require resources beyond the capacity of state governments to support the needs of local governments. The initial response to a disaster can be constrained by higher authorities beyond the local government. This dynamic is amplified during disaster recovery, which is longer term, more nebulous, and becomes less salient over time.

As Part I describes, when a disaster strikes in the United States and is declared a Federal Disaster, the Stafford Act requires that federal government agencies coordinate with and support states in disaster recovery (Bea, 2010; Moss et al., 2009; "The Stafford Act, as amended, and Emergency Management-related Provisions of the Homeland Security Act, as amended," 2016). State governments fill a fiduciary role in federal disaster recovery and are conduits for federal assistance and resources such as training and grants for local governments (Bea, 2010; C. B. Rubin & Barbee, 1985). In their role as administrators of federal disaster aid, states place requirements that local governments must follow, beyond what federal law dictates, including capping funding levels or instituting supportive or restrictive policies. These roles that states play can constrain or support local governments as they navigate the disaster recovery process. The dynamics wherein local governments are reliant on states and states are governed by federal rules increases the complexity of disaster recovery. These intergovernmental dynamics can lead to successful, often collaborative relationships between government entities. They can also lead to competition, conflict, and negative relationships that can hamper successful disaster recovery for local governments.

The literature depicts a dichotomy between collaborative and opportunistic/coercive intergovernmental relationships (Conlan, 2006; May & Burby, 1996; McGuire, 2006). While intergovernmental relationships appear quite important to disaster recovery, it is unclear whether they lead to greater learning between the governments involved or whether the collaborative nature of the relationships matters to learning (Kincaid & Stenberg, 2011). If intergovernmental relationship dynamics influence learning, lower level authorities' (local government, for example) dependence on higher authorities (state or federal government) during recovery and the degree to which that dependence plays out positively or negatively may matter to outcomes. Dependence may be shaped by pre-disaster capacity or disaster damages as described in Chapters 3 and 4 (i.e., even a high pre-disaster capacity government may be dependent on higher authorities during a catastrophic event).

Building on Chapters 3 and 4, it is clear that disaster damage and resource characteristics within communities are important for understanding post-disaster learning that takes place. As the discussion in this chapter illustrates, intergovernmental relationships may also influence post-disaster learning. Relationships between governments in this chapter are identified along a spectrum of collaborative to coercive (Conlan, Posner, & Rivlin, 2009; May & Burby, 1996; McGuire, 2006; McGuire & Silvia, 2010). *Coercive* relationships involve a state government exerting power over a local government through punitive means such as sanctions in an effort to get the local government to act in certain ways. *Collaboration*, on the other hand, involves more shared decision-making and peer-to-peer type of inter-actions between the government entities. While these ends of the spectrum represent the poles, *cooperative* relationships exist wherein positive dynamics are present, but shared decision-making is missing. The degree to which an intergovernmental relationship is collaborative or coercive may be a function – at least in part – of the dependence that a lower authority has on the higher authority, as discussed earlier.

8.1 Intergovernmental Relationships and Local Government Autonomy

The following sections focus on the intergovernmental influences over post-disaster learning that were observed in local governments in the Colorado study communities. These relationships are connected to the resources and damage that the study communities sustained, based on the discussion presented in Chapters 3 and 4. All local governments in the study communities that experienced major damage and also required assistance from the State of Colorado engaged in learning, based on the summary of resources, damage, and learning. Instrumental learning was the most common form of learning observed in local governments, often related to the complex federal grant-making process and the logistics of navigating the federal rules to maximize local government reimbursements.

Nearly all local governments studied in Colorado described positive relationships with the State of Colorado during disaster recovery. This does not mean, however, that the interactions were only positive. Several local governments described more nuanced and sometimes fraught relationships with specific state agencies or personnel. Because the State serves an oversight role in its fiduciary capacity for federal   funds,   challenging   and   sometimes   conflictual intergovernmental relationships emerged in two Colorado communities – Lyons and Evans. Conflict appears to have been a function of the degree to which local governments were dependent on the State for resources (as connected to capacity and damage) as well as whether those resources were supplemental or necessary for basic recovery to commence.

The most positive state–local intergovernmental relationships involved local governments with relatively high internal pre-disaster resources, while other relationships involved conflict or distrust by one or both parties at times. Some instances of conflict and distrust were fleeting although significant (e.g., Lyons), but others were more sustained (e.g., Evans). These conflicts arose due to the paternalistic nature of state–local government relationships and control of financial resources for disaster recovery. In the following, interview data illustrate the areas where intergovernmental relationships between the State of Colorado and local governments in disaster-affected communities were positive and areas where conflict emerged.

The fiduciary duty of the state to distribute and manage federal funds caused some conflict between government entities, as described by state officials:

But then as for the planning program itself, I've been working on my technical assistance log for a couple of days. And so we do an extraordinary amount of handholding and technical assistance in all of the communities. (STATE-01)

Across the board we're working with folks who are new to CDBG [community development block grants] and certainly CDBG-DR [CDBG disaster recovery], both new to those requirements and new to the projects and across the board understaffed. Blanket, everywhere, essentially everywhere understaffed. (STATE-01)

Now, there have been a lot of challenges because the federal rules are a lot more stringent than what they're used to. Particularly with things like labor requirements and environment review requirements, they're [local governments] not used to doing that. They want to be proactive and just go and get projects done. But when they don't do procurement right or do the environmental reviews, then all of a sudden, they make their spending ineligible for our money. That's a hard thing to hear, especially if you've got a $150,000 annual budget, and all of sudden somebody's telling you, "We can't reimburse you for that $50,000 procurement you did." That's going to cause tension. (STATE-02)

State–local relationships were commonly viewed as successful with regard to the state's role in convening collaborative groups to share information among local governments, according to officials in Boulder, Estes Park, and Lyons:

And the State, in response to some concerns I think, that the local communities were having they developed an advisory group, public assistance program advisory group which meets usually monthly, either in person or by phone just to talk about some of the higher-level policy issues and challenges that people are having and then have all the communities talking about the same thing. (BO-07)

That's been really great because we had at the table our senators, and congressional member staffers there. And that was really helpful with our lessons learned, trying to figure out where can we make an impact. Because we didn't know if it was state or federal. If it was legislative or it was a department. And so that was really helpful because they actually—we gave them the list and they actually did all the research. (EP-05)

That collaboration between all of the groups and even the different committees that have been set up for the Public Assistance Advisory Committee, which met with the HSEM [Department of Homeland Security Emergency Management] and you had mayors and finance people and trying to make some high-level decisions or bringing awareness of the issues. It's the weekly calls, the bi-weekly calls. And there's still a lot of collaboration between a lot of different people to try to improve everything. And then it will continue. (LY-04)

The State was viewed as helpful in its role of providing external resources, including technical expertise and information for local governments, as an Estes Park official described:

We really figured our role in community development was to help with—and this was encouraged by CWCB [Colorado Water Conservation Board under the Department of Natural Resources] during this, the stream team meetings. They basically told people, you know, really for—to restore and have an ecologically healthy river and a river that's resilient, you need to have private property owners working together, and you need to be doing some master planning. So yeah, you can do your short-term stuff before the spring runoff; your longer-term stuff will take probably 18 months, if not longer. And that you need a coalition of people along the drainage to be working together to determine what they want the river to be like. (EP-02)

Local government openness to state involvement in their recovery processes was a critical factor in whether relationships were viewed as successful as well, but was sometimes difficult to achieve according to state and local officials:

But in that, I think one of the roadblocks has also been the fact that the State is developing their systems, and handing us guidance as they're coming up with it, which means a lot of it is untested. So, we're kind of working on a fast, lean process; we're trying to actually anticipate and develop processes that don't necessarily exist with the state, closeout being one of them. We've been expected to start closing out projects for over a year now, and the State really only recently released their guidance for it. (LG-07)

[describing a specific concern related to the reimbursement process, while the overall relationship was deemed positive by officials]

But yeah, there's a couple that have been working together, and there's others that we've offered to connect them with other communities saying, you know, these guys are willing to help you. They're a little bigger than you. They've got similar projects to you. And it was, "Nope, we've got it. We don't want any help." (STATE-04)

I would say it's the politics, in my opinion, at the local level. It's where there is kind of the shortsighted, you know, not looking at the long-term but rather what is this going to do to us in the short-term. We've seen just so much of that. And I think some of it we've been able to overcome through just kind of pounding away at it or providing helpful resources. I think there are some areas where it, frankly, still exists and we're still battling it. (STATE-05)

To understand learning experienced by local governments as it relates to intergovernmental relationships with the State of Colorado and federal government, documents were first analyzed for changes in policies. Those policy changes were then categorized according to the type and degree of changes that they involved (see Appendix for discussion on policy change and learning analysis). Table 8.1 presents policy changes identified in local government documents between 2013 and 2015 only focused on financial issues to narrow the scope of possible sectors of learning. This table brings together many of the same policy changes presented in Table 4.3 in the discussion of capacity-building strategies used by local governments. This time the analysis focuses on policy changes that are centered on relationships or external actors to the study communities.

This example of a single domain of policy changes during disaster recovery illustrates the relative significance of external intergovernmental factors, which are highlighted in the table. This demonstrates

Table 8.1. *External resources: financial policy change and lessons*

Community	Total documents coded	Flood recovery policy changes	Policy changes related to finance (% of total)	Types of financial changes related to flood recovery
Boulder	526	185	57 (30.8%)	• **Lessons about FEMA rules, personnel turnover, and navigating the reimbursement process** • Increase fund for open space • Issue bonds for future capital projects • Increase sales and use tax • Increase personnel for flood recovery • Budget reserve increase
Longmont	292	108	60 (55.6%)	• **Lessons about FEMA rules, personnel turnover, and navigating the reimbursement process** • Wastewater fee change • Approval of bond ballot initiative • Park fee for flood recovery • Extended transportation sales tax for ten years • **Acceptance of grants and approval of grant proposals for recovery funding**

Table 8.1. (*cont.*)

Community	Total documents coded	Flood recovery policy changes	Policy changes related to finance (% of total)	Types of financial changes related to flood recovery
Lyons	408	278	78 (21.8%)	• **Lessons about FEMA rules, personnel turnover, and navigating the reimbursement process** • **Approve grant applications and acceptance of grant funding** • Hired personnel for recovery finance • Budget reserve increase
Estes Park	159	53	22 (41.5%)	• **Lessons about FEMA rules, personnel turnover, and navigating the reimbursement process** • Suspend normal procurement/ contracting rules to expedite recovery projects • Fee increase for floodplain permits • **Accepting of grants and MOU adoption for grants and collaborations** • Budget reserve decrease

Table 8.1. (*cont.*)

Community	Total documents coded	Flood recovery policy changes	Policy changes related to finance (% of total)	Types of financial changes related to flood recovery
Loveland	268	94	38 (40%)	• **Lessons about FEMA rules, personnel turnover, and navigating the reimbursement process** • Rate increase for power customers • Funding for flood recovery finance position
Evans	134	95	48 (50.5%)	• **Lessons about FEMA rules, personnel turnover, and navigating the reimbursement process** • Wastewater fee change • Hired personnel for recovery finance Consolidated staff working on recovery under the Deputy City Manager
Greeley	38	14	8 (57.1%)	• Funding for rain gauge monitoring system
Totals	**1,825**	**827**	**311 (42.5%)**	

Bold = Policy changes or lessons related to external resources or relationships.
Note: The right-hand column begins with a statement of the most common lessons in each community, as derived from the interview data. All other data in the table draw from coded documents and finance documents.

the salience of intergovernmental issues in post-disaster discussions in the Colorado communities. Policy changes highlighted in the table are associated with local government relationships with federal and state agencies; procedural and staffing changes to help local governments work more within complex state and federal agency processes to attain maximum reimbursement for disaster recovery expenses; and modifications focused on compliance with federal and state procedures for disaster recovery reimbursement.

The State of Colorado went through its own learning process, as did the local governments. The State had dealt with significant wildfire disaster recovery in the years prior to the 2013 floods, but the floods spanned numerous local governments and caused more widespread damage than even the record-setting fires of 2012 and 2013 (Crow, Lawhon, et al., 2017). As such, the State was learning lessons from its own interactions with the federal government and with the local governments it was meant to support. Interviews with officials in Evans described the complexities of these intergovernmental dynamics:

These incidents are not technical incidents, they're people incidents. And there's a lot of relationship issues between government agencies, between people that are impacted, between businesses. You know, it's all people related, relationships, information processing, all those kinds of things that are tremendously resource intensive. (EV-02)

Regardless, somebody at the state we never heard of, we'd get a copy of an email a week later that said, "Oh, yeah, the state needs to meet about this landfill in Evans," because somebody had heard about it. The one guy from the state agency didn't know this other guy from another state agency was already working with the city. So the state itself didn't talk to themselves about the issue. (EV-03)

The major lesson the State learned from the flood recovery period was that having an office dedicated to supporting communities' efforts to build resilience, identify hazards, and prepare for disasters was vital in moving Colorado beyond a reactionary posture to a more long-term view of risks and planning for future events. This permanent entity was also essential to establishing knowledge of community needs and improving the intergovernmental dynamics experienced during flood recovery. In 2018, the Colorado General Assembly established the Colorado Resiliency Office (CRO), which had been previously created as a temporary office within the Governor's Office after the floods

(Colorado Department of Local Affairs, 2017; CRO, 2019). The new office was to be forward-looking with the mission of supporting local governments in risk identification and reduction goals to achieve resilience. This state-learned lesson can be characterized as organizational learning in that the State of Colorado focused on appropriate structure and reporting arrangements to promote disaster recovery across Colorado. It may represent social learning related to the CRO's focus on identifying underlying hazards faced by communities and working proactively to break the lingering disaster response cycle where communities rebuild, replace, and maintain the status quo.

8.2 Internal or External Stakeholders and Learning in Disaster Recovery

As this section describes, participatory processes and the engagement that local stakeholders have with decision processes undergone by their local government during disaster recovery varied significantly in Colorado's flood-affected communities. These various types of engagement were also observed when assessing the presence, composition, and purpose of coalitions of actors that formed during disaster recovery. Finally, positive intergovernmental engagement was associated with support such as resources and knowledge. Dependence of local governments on state government, along with the collaborative or coercive nature of the relationships varied across communities as well.

Learning in the study communities varied substantially, as described throughout the book and summarized in Chapter 9. Most communities experienced instrumental learning and often learned how to better navigate the complexities of the recovery process, particularly involving reimbursement and federal funding requirements. Some communities also experienced government learning wherein they examined and changed organizational structures, personnel, or similar aspects of their organization to better cope with disaster recovery in future crises. Less common were instances of higher levels of learning such as social learning through which the local government examined broad goals and underlying assumptions of community planning and development to create more resilience going forward.

With regard to intergovernmental relationships, both Estes Park and Evans depended heavily on resources from the State, but lower levels of learning were observed in these communities than in Longmont,

Boulder, or Lyons. Similarly, Lyons, Longmont, and Boulder all enjoyed constructive relationships with the State overall. Loveland and Estes Park did as well, but experienced lower levels of learning as well as lower resource needs from the State. The combined importance of resources from the higher governmental authority – most important to communities with low pre-disaster capacity or high flood damage – and the character of the intergovernmental relationship with the State of Colorado was associated with the type of learning observed in these local governments. More collaborative or cooperative state–local intergovernmental relationships appear important to successful disaster recovery, but these relationships only encourage higher levels of learning in local governments that are also reliant on state-level disaster recovery resources. If either of these characteristics (positive relationships or dependence on state resources) is absent, less learning by the local government was observed. Furthermore, learning that did happen when these characteristics were absent was less likely to fall along the more deliberative end of the spectrum. For example, in Loveland where intergovernmental relationships with the State were strong, but resource needs were moderate, learning was less common. In Evans, where resource needs from the state were high, but the state-local intergovernmental relationship was stressed, learning was also less common.

As discussed throughout this section, relationships and collaboration between individuals within a community as well as between governments may be critical to understanding the local government learning that takes place after a disaster. The picture that emerges from these findings is one of nuanced and varied coalitions of individuals who come together in disaster-affected communities to advocate for project or policy goals. Those groups can help maintain focus on disaster policy issues even as a community wants to return to normalcy and move beyond the disaster. These activities can maintain the focus needed to make policy changes more likely and learning possible. Beyond the individual level, this chapter also presents a picture of intergovernmental dynamics that can greatly influence learning outcomes in both the lower- and higher-authority government organizations. This is just part of the puzzle of understanding what factors make local governments more likely to learn after experiencing a disaster and undergoing the complex and often frustrating process of recovery. In Part II, the damage incurred and the pre-disaster capacity and post-disaster capacity-building that local governments conduct is examined as they relate to learning that took place after disaster. In Part III, the characteristics internal to a community – from trust in government to the beliefs held by community members – are discussed as they relate to this puzzle. In the final part of this book, these community processes and characteristics are tied together to present a framework for understanding community-level disaster recovery and learning that can increase resilience to various risks that communities around the world face.

Review

Box IV.1 Key lessons from Part IV

1. Participation by residents and other stakeholders leads to higher levels of learning by local governments, but it appears that this happens when the following procedural characteristics are present:
   a. Inclusion of diverse stakeholders from a broad spectrum of the community rather than only residents and business owners
   b. Deliberative engagement rather than pro forma information sharing with the stakeholders
   c. Sustained engagement by stakeholders over time
2. Coalitions of individuals within disaster-affected communities can actively seek to influence their local government's decisions, but these do not always emerge, and can take varying forms along the following traits:
   a. Establishment of the coalition by higher authorities or through organic means
   b. Composition of groups according to narrow or broad inclusion approaches, with broader inclusion connected to greater advocacy activity by the coalition
   c. Purpose of the coalitions, with some more focused on narrow projects and others interested in longer-term planning and community-wide issues
3. Intergovernmental relationship dynamics matter because they can provide resources for disaster-affected communities. When relationships are characterized by both dependence on the resources and collaborative or cooperative relationships between the entities, learning is more likely within disaster-affected local governments.

Connections, Conclusions, and Recommendations

Disasters can serve as focusing events that increase agenda attention related to disaster response, recovery, and preparedness. Increased agenda attention can lead to policy changes and also to learning. The degree and type of learning that occurs after a disaster within a government organization or the broader community can matter to policy outcomes related to individual, household, and community-level risks and resilience. Compared to federal-level disaster policy-making, we know less about learning within communities where a local government oversees disaster planning and recovery, which motivated the study of Colorado's 2013 floods. Local governments are the first line of disaster response, but also bear the bulk of the burden of performing long-term disaster recovery and planning for future events. And yet, scholars do not have a clearly articulated framework for understanding if, how, and with what effect local governments learn after a disaster strikes their community.

Drawing from the lessons presented in this book, this part presents a framework of community-level learning after disaster. This framework builds upon the established knowledge of learning after disaster in other jurisdictional scales of analysis, but tailors existing frameworks to address the nuances of local-level disaster policy processes. This concluding part then applies the major lessons from the Colorado study communities and the framework presented in Chapter 9 to other cases of disasters in the United States and Europe. Finally, this part concludes with a discussion of recommendations for practitioners and future directions for scholars who seek to expand upon and strengthen the work presented in this book.

Disasters as Catalysts for Change and Learning

Throughout this book disasters are described as events that impact communities, causing disruption to various social processes and local livelihoods (Perry, 2007). They can act as focusing events, which draw the attention of policymakers and the public to a problem simultaneously that may not have previously been recognized as a problem, or acknowledged as a problem in need of governmental attention through policy reform (Birkland, 1997, 1998). This attention to a disaster may highlight failures of existing policies or gaps in policy attention, potentially catalyzing policy actions aimed at reducing communities' vulnerability to future hazards (Schwartz & Sulitzeanu-Kenan, 2004).

The decisions made by local governments in the wake of disaster will determine the extent to which a community recovers in the weeks, months, and years afterward (Aldrich & Ono, 2016; Becker, 2009; Crow et al., 2018; Donahue, Eckel, & Wilson, 2014). Yet, while they are key to disaster recovery, local governments are nested within a larger intergovernmental context of state (or province), national, and sometimes supranational (e.g., European Union) resources and requirements (Bea, 2010; G. P. Smith, 2012). U.S. states institute their own disaster recovery processes and policies that layer on top of – and sometimes in competition with – local governments (Gerber, 2007; G. P. Smith, 2012).

Disaster recovery is considered to be more ambiguous than emergency response, which is dominated by questions about saving lives and property in the immediate aftermath of a disaster. There has been less emphasis by scholars and practitioners on planning for recovery, perhaps due to this uncertain and less defined area of governmental action (G. P. Smith & D. Wenger, 2007). Despite sufficient knowledge about the components of successful disaster recovery, "the [United States] has yet to fully develop an actionable pre-event disaster recovery policy or provide appropriate funding to carry out what remain vague, often uncoordinated federal goals" (G. P. Smith, Martin, & Wenger, 2018, p. 595).

In addition to policy hurdles for successful disaster recovery, it should come as no surprise that "the principal impulse" for communities is often "to return to what is familiar – that which defined the community prior to the event – even if pre-event conditions may have been fraught with social injustice, high hazard vulnerability, inadequate housing and public infrastructure, economic fragility, and poor leadership" (G. P. Smith, 2012). Not only can this impulse prevent communities from conducting deliberative processes to rebuild better and reduce vulnerability to future disasters, but it can also result in recovery policies that actually increase future hazard risk (Ingram, Franco, Rumbaitis-del Rio, & Khazai, 2006). Residents and local officials may also ignore or deny the continual risks they face to future disasters (McCaffrey, Toman, Stidham, & Shindler, 2013), which reduces their likelihood of conducting and participating in deliberative planning processes. Compounding all of these factors is the limited "window of opportunity" that local governments have to substantively change their policies and plan in a manner that may increase the resilience – and therefore reduce their risk – to ongoing hazards (de Vries, 2017; Koebele et al., 2015; Peek, 2012), with many survivors pointing to the one-year anniversary of a disaster as the closing of many windows of opportunity for change (Koebele et al., 2015). This timeline will necessarily be longer for a disaster that requires multiple years of active rebuilding and readjustment by the community where event-related salience remains high for a longer period of time.

Increasing the likelihood of positive change that may help create more resilient communities is a goal many administrators at all levels of government share. It requires awareness of disaster risks, political will, community support, and a variety of resources to accomplish. What makes this change possible in some instances – and what policy-makers and administrators can do to encourage it – are not just intellectual questions aimed at understanding disaster processes, but are also key to encouraging communities to do better after a disaster. These links will be further explored in the concluding chapters, beginning with Chapter 9 and a presentation of a framework for community-level learning after disasters.

9 | *Building Community Resilience*

The other thing that we have been doing a lot of in the county is around individual and neighborhood and community resilience. So BoCo [Boulder County] Strong was formed county-wide and Longmont has been doing— we already do a lot of work in our neighborhoods and so it was not a big stretch to start talking about resilience within our neighborhood work and particularly in the neighborhoods that were hit; we started with those. So we did a lot of outreach just around what resources were available to them to recover but then into resiliency, so what do you need?

(LG-07)

Community resilience centers on the capacity to anticipate, learn from, and adapt to past shocks. It calls for the integration of new knowledge to identify, reduce, and address vulnerabilities to decrease the likelihood and impact of future disasters. Communities that are more resilient tend to view and address risks and vulnerabilities broadly and comprehensively, often system wide (Johansen et al., 2017). Through building resources and strengthening capacities – financial, administrative, technical, and civic – communities may be able to rebound from disaster and reduce a variety of future risks to a greater extent than otherwise. Furthermore, communities that can rely on their own resources instead of those external to their community are often more resilient (FEMA, 2011).

The goal of this book is to understand how disaster-affected communities move forward after a disaster to recover, learn, institute policy changes, and move toward resilience. In so doing, they can become better able to withstand future crises and stressors. The study communities that showed the greatest shift toward resilience were those that also engaged in greater depth of community member engagement. How local government officials think about and operationalize resilience in their community's recovery process varied across communities. All told, communities that showed deeper learning and policy changes that address a broad range of risks moved closer to resilience. Four resilience-related themes emerged from interviews with local officials: fiscal resilience, resilience of physical infrastructure systems, ecological resilience, and social resilience (Albright & Crow, 2019b). By achieving resilience across many of these dimensions, communities can move toward greater overall community-level resilience.

Boulder is a community with relatively strong fiscal, technical, and human capacity. Local officials in Boulder discussed resilience across all four themes, while Greeley officials did not mention resilience in their interviews. Nearly all study communities talked about resilience according to physical infrastructure. In particular, the focus was on strengthening and creating redundancies in existing water, storm water, and wastewater systems. Loveland (low civic capacity) officials discussed resilience within physical systems such as replacing hydro-electricity with more flood-resilient solar facilities and increasing redundancies in water infrastructure:

Like, let's say a couple of lessons may be that, for example, at the water treatment plant, where we lost two out of three water lines, the placement of those water lines and the original thought behind them was to establish redundancy so that if one of the lines failed, you still had two left. What we've learned is, if you're going to have redundant systems, they need to be spaced and planned so that they can be truly redundant and not wiped out by the same event. (LV-01)

Officials in Estes Park also emphasized ecological resilience of local river corridors to a greater extent than physical or social resilience:

So then, for long-term, we really figured our role in community development was to help with—and this was encouraged by CWCB during this, the stream team meetings. They basically told people—to restore and have an ecologically healthy river and a river that's resilient, you need to have private property owners working together, and you need to be doing some master planning. So yeah, you can do your short-term stuff before the spring runoff; your longer-term stuff will take probably 18 months, if not longer. And that you need a coalition of people along the drainage to be working together to determine what they want the river to be like. (EP-02)

The presence of in-depth deliberative processes, learning, and policy changes suggest a more resilient community. Lyons, and to a lesser degree Boulder, Longmont, and Estes Park, exhibited greater patterns of resilience, based on these measures. Lyons sought to increase all four types of capacity (fiscal, technical, administrative, and civic), and demonstrated the greatest extent of community resilience-building across the study communities. In this small town, members of the community substantively engaged in deliberative processes of recovery, and as a result, the community adopted a breadth of policy changes across a number of sectors, and formalized these changes in a community-wide recovery plan.

This discussion suggests an important link between the capacity-building strategies that local communities adopt and how communities frame resilience after disaster in the long term. The decisions that local governments make in the immediate aftermath of disaster, such as how to engage community members and how best to capture and leverage external funding and technical support may influence how a community envisions its path forward, as well as the breadth and types of risks and community needs that are addressed. This link between capacity, learning, and resilience is key to our understanding of community-level resilience. As communities face growing and more numerous risks in the future, they also need to consider the mechanisms by which they can build more resilience into their existing systems so that in the face of any shock – whether a climate-related disaster, economic shock, or pandemic – they can withstand and rebound afterward. Table 9.1 brings together findings presented in previous chapters focused on capacity-building, policy changes, type of learning observed, and the type or extent of resilience-building communities engaged in during their disaster recovery efforts between 2013 and 2016. To achieve community resilience, resilience-building work must span multiple sectors listed in the table.

9.1 A Framework for Understanding Community-Level Learning in the Aftermath of Disaster

As this book presents in detail, after a disaster strikes a community, local governments and stakeholders will grapple with decisions about how to recover and what, if any, changes they want to make as they plan for rebuilding, future disaster response and recovery, and associated issues. These decisions may involve promulgating new policies, changing former policies, or revising implementation approaches to current policies. These decisions are made in the context of learning

Table 9.1. *Linking capacity-building strategies, policy change, learning,*
and resilience (Albright & Crow, 2019b)

Community	Capacity-building and resources	Policy change[a]	learning	Types of resilience indicated[b]
Boulder	High (F, H, T, C)	Broad and numerous	Governmental Instrumental Policy Moderate social	Financial Physical Ecological Social
Longmont	Medium (F, H, C)	Broad and numerous	Governmental Instrumental Policy Moderate social	Ecological Social
Lyons	High (F, H, T, C)	Broad and numerous	Governmental Instrumental Policy Social	Physical Ecological Social
Estes Park	Medium (F, T, C)	Moderate, broad changes within a specific corridor of town	Instrumental Policy Moderate social	Ecological
Loveland	Medium (F, T)	Narrow, focused on infrastructure	Instrumental Policy	Financial Physical Ecological
Evans	Limited (F, limited C)	Narrow, focused on downtown	Instrumental Policy	Financial Social
Greeley	Minimal	Minimal	Minimal	Minimal

[a] In column 2, F = fiscal capacity, H = human capacity, T = technical capacity, C = community capacity

[b] Findings in column 5 (resilience) are from the analysis of transcripts from interviews with flood personnel.

that takes place due to the disaster and the ensuing learning that happens at individual, organizational, and community scales. Whether and how learning takes place can be influenced by the complexity, severity, and breadth of the problem (i.e., the disaster), as well as current and incoming resources that a local government has at its disposal (Sabatier, 1999). The chapters in this book also highlight the importance of internal community characteristics such as beliefs and trust, relationships and engagement among various community stakeholders, and intergovernmental dynamics. This complex puzzle is dissected in this chapter to develop a framework for understanding what factors make community-level learning after disaster more likely.

Learning is a complex subject that is difficult to measure in organizations or communities because while attention may be on collective learning, learning must take place at an individual level. Within policy processes, learning can be defined as "a process in which individuals apply new information and ideas or information and ideas elevated on the agenda by a recent event, to policy decisions" (Birkland, 2006, p. 22). At times, learning can lead governments to various changes to reduce local vulnerability to risks and future disasters (Albright & Crow, 2015b; Birkland, 2004; O'Donovan, 2017). Because disasters typically open brief windows of opportunity to enact policy changes before the salience of the issue fades and political will and inertia fade with it, there is a similarly brief window within which learning may take place (Birkland, 1997; Birkland & Warnement, 2014; Koebele et al., 2015).

Learning takes place along a continuum ranging from simple lessons from an experience that help improve processes or programs (single-loop learning) to in-depth evaluations of an organization's underlying learning processes or goals of an organization (double-loop learning) (Argyris, 1976, 2000), as discussed in Chapter 1. For example, as discussed in Chapter 4, a government may learn how to better financially prepare for disasters by adopting new fees or taxes to pay for improvements to its infrastructure, likely representing instrumental learning. Government learning may be observed in instances where a government restructures its hierarchy to be more efficient during disaster response or recovery, indicating learning about organizational processes and failures (Bennett & Howlett, 1992; Etheredge, 1981), as observed with the State of Colorado's establishment of a resiliency office after the floods. Policy-oriented learning is observed in instances where goals of policies and organizations are reconsidered and possibly revised (Sabatier & Jenkins-Smith, 1999). Social learning (Hall, 1993), which is the highest level of learning in the continuum, entails deliberation about existing policies and policy failures related to the disaster, as well as an examination of necessary changes in goals and priorities.

9.1.1 Learning at the Local Level

As disasters are experienced most directly at the local level, learning processes after a disaster may look different than at higher levels of government. Compared to the national level where disaster policy-making is often viewed as a technical exercise, in communities, non-experts such as community members and civic organizations may be more likely to engage in post-disaster governmental decision-making. However, because communities may be directly affected by a disaster, learning by local governments may be constrained by inadequate resources that often exist in the aftermath of a disaster, potentially limiting the capacity for learning. Community members may press local officials for a quick return to pre-disaster normalcy, or alternatively, support changes in disaster-related policies. External flows of resources from other levels of government and nongovernmental organizations may also incentivize or limit learning. This tension between increased agenda attention and resource availability and constraints may add complexity to the dynamics of local-level learning that are not as pronounced at other levels of governance.

Disaster and policy scholarship suggest that local-level policy changes and learning may occur after disaster (Brody et al., 2009; Johnson et al., 2005), but the mechanisms that connect a disaster to change are less clear, as are the types of learning that may drive these changes. Longitudinal studies of learning stemming from disaster at the local level have been limited to date (Brody et al., 2009; Johnson et al., 2005; Nohrstedt & Nyberg, 2015). Whether learning happens within a community after a disaster can determine if policies are changed, terminated, or newly developed. Birkland's event-related learning model provides a framework for understanding post-disaster variables that may lead to learning and policy change (2006, figure 1.2). The model, however, was developed to focus on national-level learning after disaster and therefore may not address some of the unique characteristics and challenges faced by local governments after disaster. These characteristics can be described as constraints or influences both internal and external to the disaster-affected community.

In the previous chapters, post-disaster observations were presented related to learning at the community-level, with a specific focus on local governments engaged in disaster recovery. In the seven communities studied in Colorado, learning was identified across the continuum of types of learning – from instrumental learning to more robust social learning. While instrumental or political learning are most common outcomes in local governments – primarily with regard to reimbursement requirements, logistics, and financial processes – deeper learning can occur and is linked to various factors. More open and transparent post-flood decision processes are observed in cases with greater deliberation, learning, and more substantive and frequent policy change. Additionally, the importance of resources that come into a community after disaster (essential to smaller or severely damaged communities) combined with the nature of the intergovernmental relationships (particularly with state agencies and personnel) is associated with learning observed in local governments. This deeper learning leads governmental organizations to reexamine their goals, long-term planning and management, and overall risk to hazards that may create future disasters.

Local governments are the first line of disaster response, but also bear the burden of performing long-term disaster recovery and planning for future events. And yet, we have not previously had a clearly articulated framework for understanding if and how local governments learn after a disaster strikes their community. In the previous chapters, a set of factors were identified – both internal and external to individual communities – that may encourage or impede local-level learning. The internal and external factors that may create different processes and outcomes for local governments are addressed in turn here so that a framework can be articulated that brings together the confluence of factors that increase the likelihood of learning after a disaster that can move a community toward resilience.

9.2 Factors Associated with Learning in Local Governments after Disaster

Before disasters, local governments differ across demographics, economic sectors, resource availability, extent of public engagement, and public beliefs and support of policies, among other factors. After disaster, communities face different internal and external constraints and incentives to learn and change. Some of these differences stem from external factors, such as higher-level policies that constrain their activity or external resources that support local government action. Other factors relate to the internal characteristics of the disaster-affected community or its government. Each of these factors was associated with the extent or type of learning that takes place within a local government after disaster. Resources that aid in disaster recovery, which are also related to the extent of damage incurred in a disaster, can be internal to a community or come from external sources, and are therefore presented separately.

9.2.1 Resources and Damage as Catalysts for Learning

Prior to a disaster, local governments may have varying levels of capacity to govern, a measure of financial, administrative, technical, and civic resources that a government can bring to bear to perform governing duties. After a disaster, resources may also increase significantly and rapidly for a community as support comes from external governments, NGOs, and insurance or other private sector sources (Albright, 2011; Albright & Crow, 2015b; Sabatier & Weible, 2007b). The nature and extent of resource inflows matter for community-level recovery and associated policy processes, with previously limited-capacity governments potentially being affected to a greater extent than higher-capacity governments that may be able to fund greater portions of their own recovery projects, and therefore are less subject to influences and constraints from external higher authorities (Crow et al., 2018). Questions about capacity are especially crucial when discussing disaster recovery in low-capacity or severely damaged communities, which may depend on external resources to restore even basic functions.

Four categories of resources are important to delineate when describing their influence on learning and policy changes that may take place after a disaster. First, fiscal resources are critical to virtually everything a local government does after a disaster, including emergency response, disaster recovery, and rebuilding. Governments may work to build fiscal resources from disaster reimbursement programs from state or federal agencies, grants available from government and nongovernmental organizations, internal resources such as municipal taxes or fees, and external loans (Crow et al., 2015; Crow et al., 2018; Garrett & Sobel, 2003; McDonnell, Ghorbani, Desai, Wolf, & Burgy, 2018; A. Rose et al., 2007). Second, technical resources (e.g., GIS mapping of disaster zones, etc.) can be helpful for local governments as they try to understand the disaster causes and effects, as well as future risks that they face. These types of data and information can inform internal decision processes during disaster recovery and planning. Technical resources can exist internally to a local government or they may be provided by external individuals or organizations (Heikkila & Gerlak, 2013; Huber, 1991). Third, government personnel and administrative resources can encourage learning within a government. Their leadership, expertise, personal experiences, relationships, or knowledge gained during disaster response and recovery can all influence the learning that takes place within a government organization (Beck & Plowman, 2009; Becker, 2009). Within local governments, personnel may also be limited in disaster experience, which may necessitate hiring of additional outside staff, which can disrupt an organization in either positive or negative ways. Finally, the civic capacity of a community, catalyzed in part by local government processes established after a disaster, is critical to recovery outcomes.

In the preceding chapters, evidence showed that both resources and relationships with other government agencies were associated with learning, and most importantly that resources alone did not matter but rather how much a community depended on those resources based on internal capacity and the extent of disaster damage incurred (Crow & Albright, 2019). Extensively damaged communities also mobilized diverse categories of resources, compared to communities with less damage (Albright & Crow, 2019b), both from internal and external sources (Crow et al., 2018). However, the findings suggest that damages experienced do not fully explain the variation in type and extent of resource mobilization across communities. Capacity-building strategies and resource availability can be tied to the varied learning that happened across the communities. Local governments with low internal capacity were less able to take financial risks and more likely to rebuild in nonresilient ways that conform to existing federal guidelines (Albright & Crow, 2019b). Policy changes also varied across communities, with in-depth and broader changes observed in communities with more civic-capacity building.

9.2.2 External Constraints

Local governments operate within the context of a nested system of governance and are therefore bound by the constraints that state and national governments place on them and the degree of autonomy they have over their own affairs. In the context of disasters, local governments are resource dependent on federal and state governments, which for low-capacity governments or severe disasters can dictate much of disaster recovery.

9.2.2.1 Intergovernmental Interactions and Federalist Dynamics

When a disaster event strikes a community in the United States, the federalist structure of the U.S. system of governance influences eventual local-level disaster recovery outcomes to a significant extent. A local government first faces emergency response focused on saving lives and property, where they often depend on assistance from the National Guard, which is under state jurisdiction. Once disaster response concludes, a longer-term and more uncertain process of disaster recovery begins. The intergovernmental nature of disaster management is made more complicated when government entities at multiple levels hold differing perceptions of the disaster (including its causes and outcomes) and divergent preferences about disaster recovery policies (Crow & Albright, 2019; Paudel, Botzen, & Aerts, 2015; Surminski et al., 2015). In the United States, response to a disaster and recovery from it are funded in large part from higher authorities rather than local governments as discussed in Chapters 1 through 4, whereas decisions regarding local-level planning, zoning, and building codes are under local authority, but may be constrained by federal requirements (e.g., FEMA reimbursement, National Flood Insurance Program (NFIP)).

During disaster recovery – when a disaster in the Unites States is declared a Federal Disaster – the Stafford Act dictates that federal government agencies work with states to assist in disaster recovery (Bea, 2010; Moss et al., 2009; "The Stafford Act, as amended, and Emergency Management-related Provisions of the Homeland Security Act, as amended," 2016). State governments serve an oversight role in federal disaster recovery and are conduits for funding, training, and other resources for local governments (Bea, 2010; C. B. Rubin & Barbee, 1985). States can therefore enact requirements that local governments must follow, including limiting funding or instituting requirements and processes to access federal disaster aid. States can inhibit successful disaster recovery or encourage it, which can result in direct local effects and recovery outcomes. Dynamics of dependence on higher governmental authorities for necessary resources and the rules and processes instituted by those higher authorities make disaster recovery a difficult process to navigate for local governments. In the analysis of intergovernmental relationships and learning presented in Chapter 8, collaborative or cooperative intergovernmental relationships were linked to successful disaster recovery. And yet, they only encouraged more extensive or deep learning when a local government is also dependent on the state government for disaster recovery resources (Crow & Albright, 2019).

9.2.2.2 Local Government Autonomy

In the United States, local governments have varying levels of authority over their ability to raise revenue through taxes and fees. States can allow local governments to be Home Rule, giving them more authority over their affairs, or they can abide by Dillon's Rule, which makes them dependent on the state legislature for revenue, taxes, and associated resources (Vanlandingham, 1968; Weeks & Hardy, 1984). Colorado, where this study was situated, has a unique and difficult fiscal environment. As a Home Rule state, Colorado grants budget authority to local governments for many issues. However, it also has the Taxpayer Bill of Rights amendment, or TABOR, which requires all tax increases to be put forth to voters for approval. Local governments can put a vote before their residents to be TABOR exempt, but few have done this. The level of autonomy that a local government enjoys may therefore dictate the extent to which they are legally capable of engaging in deliberation over areas of policy that affect or interact with taxation.

Chapter 4 indicated that local governments used a number of tools to increase resources for flood recovery, including levying taxes and fees, seeking external grants, and accessing reimbursements for damages from federal programs (Crow et al., 2018). Those local governments that had greater levels of internal resources, and therefore more independence from other levels of government, had greater flexibility in their recovery processes. This independence also shortens the timeframe of disaster recovery for communities since all federal disaster recovery processes are reimbursement based, meaning that low-capacity local governments may have to conduct disaster recovery by iteratively focusing on single projects rather than multiple simultaneous projects.

9.2.3 Internal Dynamics and Constraints

Many of the differences between federal and local processes during disaster recovery relate to scale in various ways, including the physical proximity community members have to a disaster, which may affect learning and governmental policy changes that take place. Additionally, factors such as the likelihood that officials know their constituents or hear from them directly and frequently, the information received about a disaster by residents of a community and their associated trust in their local government, and the capacity of a local government are all important in disaster recovery and related to community size. The various factors related to the internal dynamics of local governments and their communities were discussed in detail in Chapters 5 through 8.

9.2.3.1 Flood Experience, Problem Severity, and Worldviews as They Relate to Floods

Disasters do not affect communities equally, and within communities, residents are not equally affected. Some residents will be inconvenienced or have friends and family who were impacted, while others will be seriously and personally affected by a disaster. Directly or indirectly experiencing a disaster may influence an individual's awareness of, concern for, and willingness or capacity to engage with disaster-related issues on the government's agenda. Disaster experiences may also alter how the public understands causes of disasters and the associated damage and whether or not they support policy actions to address future risks of similar disasters (Brilly & Polic, 2005; Wachinger et al., 2013). Disaster effects on individual-level beliefs about problem severity and the causes of disaster may bring groups of individuals together to advocate for new policies that address ongoing problems (Albright, 2011; Nohrstedt & Weible, 2010; Sabatier & Weible, 2007b), or a widening gap between the public and experts (officials and government personnel in particular), or conflict within the community can emerge, potentially impeding changes in policies. Additionally, individual policy preferences and support for government actions may be influenced by how individuals understand the underlying causes of and place blame for a disaster (Stone, 2011).

9.2.3.2 Information, Participation, and Trust in Government

Individuals form their beliefs about risks, problem severity, and policy preferences through information acquisition and other social processes (Ho et al., 2008; Lin et al., 2008; Rogers & Prentice-Dunn, 1997). Disaster-related information may influence beliefs about the causes and effects of a disaster as well as the importance of actions to reduce future risk (Wachinger et al., 2013). Whether residents of a community perceive greater risks is typically linked to the information they consume as well as the degree of trust in the sources of information (Heitz et al., 2009; Wachinger et al., 2013). Individuals are most likely to seek information from sources they already trust and are also likely to consume information that supports their prior beliefs (Nickerson, 1998).

Local governments may convene public meetings to disseminate information, discuss disaster recovery, and deliberate over potential policy changes (Albright & Crow, 2015b; Wachinger et al., 2013). Participatory mechanisms used during disaster recovery vary widely in terms of openness and deliberative characteristics. Open and collaborative processes are those that engage nonexpert stakeholders to a greater extent, and these processes may encourage higher levels of learning (Albright, 2011). These stakeholders can include a variety of actors, from community residents, local officials, businesses, civil society, faith-based groups, and media, to name several. The openness of post-disaster processes, however, has not been viewed as a central element of disaster planning or response to a disaster. Experts may dominate some post-disaster stakeholder processes, which may marginalize nonexpert stakeholders (Albright & Crow, 2015b; Crow, 2010a; Schneider & Teske, 1992). Alternatively, the public may be invited and encouraged to engage in deep discussions about their perceived risks and policy preferences in an effort to conduct long-term planning in partnership with local governments (Albright & Crow, 2015b). Wachinger et al. (2013) argue that public participation is critically important to increasing public awareness of disasters and increasing trust in government officials.

The support individuals have for government actions in a post-disaster situation is influenced by these participatory processes as well as the trust they have in the government. Those who participate in post-disaster recovery dialogues may have higher support for policy actions, for example. The disaster event itself can erode trust in government (Cooper & Block, 2007; Han et al., 2011; Menzel, 2006) at multiple levels of governance, including federal, state, and local governments (Haddow et al., 2010). Higher levels of trust in government may also encourage people to participate in the post-disaster processes their government holds, and more in-depth participation in recovery processes may affect the level of trust residents have for their government. This connection between trust in government and support for the actions that government takes after a disaster is important to understanding the internal dynamics of a community.

In the aftermath of the Colorado 2013 floods, communities adopted distinct flood recovery processes in which levels of public engagement varied significantly, from minimal participation to in-depth and broad participation. The depth and breadth of public engagement was not simply a function of extent of disaster damage experienced nor solely resource availability, but was also related to pre-disaster levels of government resources, education, and participatory capacity (Albright & Crow, 2015a, 2015b). In the post-disaster context, communities that engaged more deeply and across a wider range of sectors (e.g., housing, transportation) – and that notably invited a variety of stakeholders from within the community to participate such as residents, businesses, and other groups – demonstrated more in-depth learning compared to communities with more limited engagement (Albright & Crow, 2019b).

Community members' direct experience of disaster, as measured by extent of damage to personal property, was related to increased information acquisition about the disaster and disaster recovery (Albright & Crow, 2019a). Individuals who reported greater levels of damages in their neighborhood and community reported higher levels of support for some flood mitigation policies (e.g., floodplain development policies). Community members who reported more damage in their neighborhood also reported lower levels of trust in their local mayor and government staff in dealing with flood issues. The findings also suggest participation in flood recovery processes was associated with beliefs about problem severity of the local floods. These findings suggest that perceptions about problem severity may be driven, at least in part, through the social process of formal flood recovery discussions, where public engagement processes led by local governments may be an effective tool to increase risk awareness (Wachinger et al., 2013). Community members' support for local government actions after a disaster is a function of a variety of factors, including community and neighborhood-level damage, participation in flood recovery processes, previously held beliefs, and perceptions about causes and severity of the disaster. These complex processes also involve the central role of information – obtained from various sources such as governments, media, and interpersonal relationships – in influencing the formation of beliefs and perceptions, but also in engaging the public in more deliberative recovery processes.

9.2.3.3 Coalitions in Disaster-Affected Communities

Participation may be important for building trust in government and informing residents and other community members about policy decisions, but because attention often shifts quickly away from disaster-related topics as communities rebuild, experts can dominate disaster recovery deliberations (Birkland, 1998). During disaster recovery, stakeholders inside and outside of government – including the public – have the opportunity to influence policy decisions made (Albright, 2011; Chui et al., 2014; Johnson et al., 2005; Pierce, 2016; Sabatier & Weible, 2007b). Coalitions of stakeholders may emerge through multiple mechanisms – including top-down instituted groups or organically emerging groups – and can include a wide variety stakeholders (Ansell & Gash, 2008; Koebele, 2019; Koontz & Thomas, 2006; Sabatier, 1988; Sabatier & Jenkins-Smith, 1999; Weible, Sabatier, & McQueen, 2009). The goals of these coalitions can focus on long-term community-scale policy change around a shared belief set, or they can be shorter term and focused on specific narrow projects or programs. Actors from the professional policy community – such as transportation or parks and recreation – may mobilize to influence policy change within the areas they work (Birkland, 1998). This can happen either when there are no other stakeholders active in the issue area or because the technical nature of the issues or processes can shut other actors out.

Chapter 7 suggested that stakeholders may participate more in smaller communities due to the scale, trust, or closer community connections that may be present. This may be one reason that the same stakeholder participation patterns of technocratic decision-making found in federal-level processes were not present in the study communities. Coalitions of stakeholders emerged in numerous study communities and were more diverse than what may be observed in federal policy processes (Crow et al., 2021). Local disaster coalitions in Colorado ranged from organic to top-down created, focused primarily on project-specific issues but occasionally also resembled belief-based advocacy coalitions described in the policy literature, and also varied in their composition between open to local residents and dominated by previously engaged stakeholders (Crow et al., 2021).

9.2.4 Adapting Our Understanding of Learning after Disaster to Local-Level Learning

Learning is difficult to accomplish and tendencies among disaster-affected communities are to rebuild and find normalcy after a crisis that strains the community. Most of what scholars know about learning after disaster focuses on federal-level policy regimes. Learning within communities that are directly affected by a disaster and in which local government oversees disaster planning and recovery have not been investigated to the same degree. In this chapter, a variety of factors are outlined that are potentially important in local government disaster policy processes, particularly with regard to inhibiting or encouraging learning that influences policy change after disaster.

First, resources available to a community's local government after a disaster are critical to processes and outcomes of disaster recovery. These resources can be internal to a community or external, and may result in significant inflows of new resources. Resources are connected closely with a second factor: type and extent of damage incurred. Low capacity governments or those that face significant disaster damage may be more reliant on the external resources for successful disaster recovery and their processes may even be dictated by a higher governmental authority. Beyond resources and damage, *external to a community*, the intergovernmental dynamics and relationships with higher governmental authorities are important to consider when applying this understanding of learning after a disaster to local governments. Additionally, the level of autonomy a local government enjoys is vital to consider with regard to the degree to which a local government can actually enact changes. *Internal to a community*, the scale of the disaster and also the size and demographic composition of a community may relate to factors such as proximity of disaster experiences, beliefs about the cause of the disaster and risk perceptions of future disasters, deeply held beliefs of community members, the capacity of the community and the local government, and trust community members place in their local government. Also internal to a community, the participatory processes established during disaster recovery and planning are important – particularly with regard to who participates and the depth of participation, as is dissemination of risk and disaster-related information to the public. These various internal community factors may also influence the degree to which individuals are concerned about the disaster, and this in turn may influence community member support of policy decisions made by their local government during disaster recovery.

Birkland's model of event-related learning (Figure 9.1, adapted from Birkland, 2006) informs the model presented here. While Birkland's model was developed based on national-level disaster policy processes, it helps distill the essential components for disaster policy processes. First, differences that may be observed in local government disaster policy processes along the various categories Birkland presents (agenda attention, group mobilization, etc.) are discussed. Then several characteristics of local government disaster policy are described that require adaption of Birkland's model in order to represent local government learning after a disaster accurately.

Through the lens of this model of event-related learning, the likelihood and extent of learning associated with increased agenda attention after a disaster as well as whether groups mobilize to engage in discussion and deliberation related to policy changes are critical to examine. These factors increase the likelihood of policy change taking place, but learning may or may not happen despite changes to policies, according to Birkland. These factors are important in local-level disaster policy processes as well. However, how they are understood may be different in local-level disaster policy. Agenda attention to any individual disaster may be greater at the local level because people have more proximate experiences with the disaster. Local governments that directly engage with community members may have to grapple with issues related to public support, beliefs, and risk perceptions that impede or promote policy change. In communities, individuals or small groups of vocal individuals may have a relatively strong voice in the decision-making process, as compared to federal policymaking processes where singular voices of the populace may be diluted across a larger population and by more powerful actors. As a result, local-level disaster

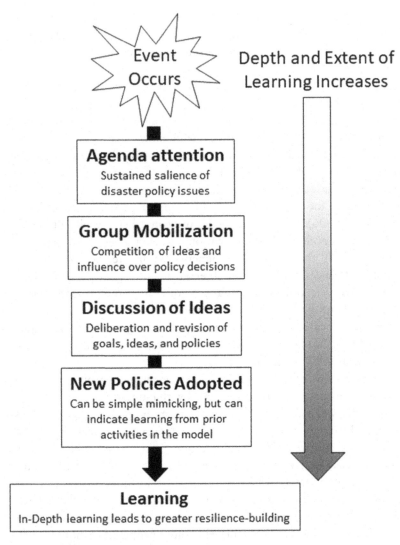

Figure 9.1 Disaster events and depth or extent of learning

policy processes and outcomes may see more community-to-community differences, in part based on the deep core beliefs held by community members prior to disaster occurrence.

Group mobilization takes place at the local level as Birkland suggests, but most mobilization may be focused on discrete recovery projects rather than broader policy goals and deliberation over community-wide planning. As a result, the extent to which coalitions are engaged in the discussion of broad policy goals and planning may vary across communities. It also may be the case that local governments can develop venues where they can bring together members to form top-down groups to engage in discussions rather than relying on them to emerge organically. Discussion of ideas is critical for local disaster policy processes, as it is in national-level processes, but may look different than national-level deliberation. The analysis of participatory mechanisms in Chapter 7 points to the importance of openness of these participation processes to encouraging learning and policy change. This suggests that it is not only important for discussion to happen, but also for it to happen in certain ways that are more open to a variety of stakeholders across a community. Based on the analyses in Chapters 3–8 and summarized in Table 9.1, a spectrum of learning can take place after a disaster. While instrumental and political learning – the easiest and "thinnest" types of learning where tools, processes, or tactics to accomplish discrete goals are learned – are most common, communities can and do engage in more deliberative and in-depth types of learning processes aimed at changing future goals, plans, and vulnerabilities in the face of ongoing hazards.

9.3 A Framework for Understanding Local-Level Learning after Disaster

In addition to understanding several aspects of Birkland's model in the context of local government, there are several areas where it is necessary to expand on the model in order to accurately reflect the policy process and potential learning and policy change among local governments.

Directly related to the disaster event, *proximity*, *scale*, and *severity* of the disaster are important at the local level because in local contexts attention is focused on events that occur nearby and therefore have real impacts on individuals and communities. The extent to which a community is damaged, what areas and sectors of a community were damaged, the relative portion of a community that was affected, and whether the severity of the damage is widespread or focused are all related to whether or not community members widely know about the disaster, understand its severity or impact, and support the actions their government is taking to address the damage.

The level and changes in resources after a disaster are important to consider, particularly for local governments engaged in disaster recovery and long-term planning. Not only do existing resources matter to how much a government may have planned prior to a disaster event,

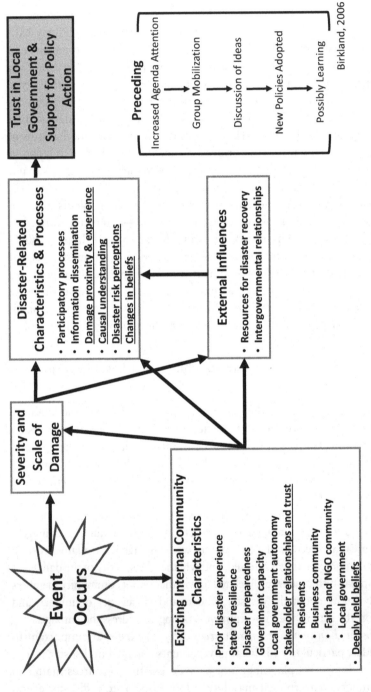

Figure 9.2 Community-level event-related learning

but these resources also matter when it comes to post-disaster rebuilding, planning, and community engagement. More open processes are associated with higher levels of learning in Chapter 7, but these open processes are also more resource intensive.

Associated with "Increased Agenda Attention" are changes in *beliefs about risk or causes of a disaster* after a disaster event takes place. These beliefs about increasing risk and causes of the risk are associated with higher support for policy changes by governments that seek to reduce risks from ongoing hazards and reduce the likelihood of future disasters to a community.

During disaster recovery, the *intergovernmental relationships* that a local government develops are important to local government learning after disaster. As was observed, collaborative or cooperative (rather than coercive) intergovernmental relationships were associated with higher levels of learning among local governments in Colorado. These relationships are often characterized by dependence of the local government on higher authorities and that dependence can impede local-level recovery planning because local governments will be restricted in their decision-making authority or flexibility if they do not also have the ability to raise revenues and control their internal decisions. *Local government autonomy* is also therefore vital to consider in the local disaster policy process context.

These factors that are important to community-level learning after a disaster are illustrated in Figure 9.2, situated as a precursor or foundation upon which Birkland's model can further explain learning after a disaster as a function of increased agenda attention and group mobilization, among other factors. The factors illustrated in Figure 9.2 are internal to a community and external, and are portrayed in the figure according to those categories. Underlined factors relate to individuals, while other factors describe community or government characteristics and processes.

Next, the framework presented in this chapter is applied to cases of disasters beyond the 2013 floods in Colorado that is the focus of the book to this point. Chapter 10 tackles the major factors discussed in this book – from resources and damage to individual beliefs to participation and engagement – with the goal of highlighting that these factors are not unique to Colorado or to flood disasters. Rather, this framework was developed with the goal of applicability to disaster-related learning in communities with varying characteristics and disaster experiences.

10 | Examining Community-Scale Disaster Recovery and Resilience beyond Colorado

Chapter 9 presented a framework for understanding the factors that make community-level learning after disasters more likely, thereby increasing the likelihood of resilience-building within communities to reduce vulnerability to future risks, building on the analyses presented throughout the book. In this chapter, those lessons are applied to cases beyond Colorado and the United States and in other disaster events beyond flooding.

Prior to disasters, communities have varying capacities and resources that they can leverage during the immediate response to and long-term recovery from disasters. When disasters strike, the impacts and extent of damages vary within and across communities. Variation in disaster damage (extent and type) and internal capacities to fund and administer disaster recovery influence the ability of a community to learn from, change policies, and build resilience to future events. Internal community characteristics also influence disaster recovery processes and decisions made by local governments. Direct and indirect disaster experience can influence the degree to which residents view disasters as an increasing and urgent problem for their local governments to address. Additionally, the role of stakeholders in forming coalitions to advocate for disaster recovery policy solutions can play important roles in the decision process after a disaster. Finally, the nexus of local government information dissemination and participatory processes established during disaster recovery can serve two important roles: (1) garnering support for local government action and trust in government decisions, along with (2) incorporating a range of views beyond only technocratic experts to build innovative policy solutions. The level of autonomy that local governments enjoy over their fiscal and decision-making processes as well as their relationships with state and federal agencies are also important to the discussion on disaster recovery and resilience-building.

The previous chapters established that these factors were important during flood recovery in Colorado communities. This chapter expands the discussion of these dynamics by examining climate-driven disasters in four contexts: (1) Hurricane Katrina, which struck the Gulf Coast of the United States in 2005, causing catastrophic damage; (2) extreme flooding in Columbia, South Carolina, United States, caused by Hurricane Joaquin; (3) extreme floods in Hungary, the European Union; and (4) wildfires in California, United States.

10.1 Hurricane Katrina

The Gulf Coast of the United States, including regions of Texas, Louisiana, Mississippi, Alabama, and Florida, is no stranger to the devastation wrought by hurricanes. The coastline spans over 1,600 miles and supports diverse communities and economic sectors, including tourism, ports, fisheries, agriculture, and oil extraction and production. Communities range in size from Houston, Texas, a city of more than 3 million, to small, unincorporated towns in the bayous of southern Louisiana. This region has a long history of hurricanes and tropical storms, from the deadly Galveston Hurricane of 1900 that caused approximately 8,000 deaths (National Oceanic and Atmospheric Administration (NOAA), 2000) to Hurricane Harvey in 2017 that flooded much of Houston and beyond, becoming one of the costliest cyclones in history ($125 billion).

10.1.1 Damages Wrought by Hurricane Katrina

Prior to Hurricane Katrina in the late summer of 2005, many of the communities in the Gulf Coast region of Louisiana and Mississippi were under-resourced, as measured by higher levels of poverty compared to the nation as a whole. African American residents, who comprise a large percentage of the population in this region, have been marginalized and disenfranchised from engagement in education, political, and economic systems in the Southern United States and face a disproportionate burden from environmental hazards (J. R. Elliott & Pais, 2006). The devastating impacts of the hurricane rendered many individuals, families, and communities even more resource-constrained than prior to the storm. In the aftermath of the large-scale disaster, an estimated 700,000 people were directly impacted, with over 645,000 residents of Louisiana and 66,000 residents in Mississippi displaced (Gabe, Falk, Mason, & McCarty, 2005). As often occurs with disasters, Hurricane Katrina disproportionally affected communities of color and low-income households. The Congressional Research Service estimated that approximately a third of individuals displaced by Hurricane Katrina had incomes less than 1.5 times the poverty rate, while more than 40 percent of those displaced were African American (Gabe et al., 2005). Prior to Hurricane Katrina, vulnerability to the risk of flooding from hurricanes was borne unequally across community members of the region as a whole and more specifically in the City of New Orleans (Fussell, 2015).

10.1.2 Federalism, Intergovernmental Relationships, and Resources

In late August of 2005, Hurricane Katrina wrought death and destruction in New Orleans and other areas of southern Louisiana. Numerous scholars of the policy process and federalism have pointed to the multilevel government response as a massive policy failure (Birkland & Waterman, 2008) – a failure of FEMA, the State of Louisiana, and the Mayor of New Orleans. Birkland and Waterman (2008) suggest that the system of federalism in disaster management as established by the Stafford Act, along with a weakening federal capacity to manage disasters after the 9/11 attacks, lessened the focus on preparation for hurricanes and other weather-related disasters. In the aftermath of 9/11, FEMA was restructured and placed in the newly formed Department of Homeland Security (DHS), which led to further institutionalizing the prioritization of national security threats from terrorism above other potential hazards. Key federal administrators departed the agency, and those who stayed had their access to decision-makers reduced, decreasing the agency's administrative capacity to manage large-scale disasters such as Hurricane Katrina (Birkland & Waterman, 2008; Derthick, 2007).

As discussed in Chapter 4, in the aftermath of a disaster, the inflow of resources from external sources may increase dramatically and rapidly (e.g., external funds or increases in personnel), along with a redistribution of resources internally and externally, including financial and technical resources, personnel, networks, and other external support (Albright & Crow, 2019b; Crow et al., 2018;

Muñoz & Tate, 2016). In addition to the influx of external resources, intergovernmental relationships, as discussed in Chapter 8, influence the ability of communities to successfully recover, learn, and build resilience after a disaster.

In the aftermath of Katrina, the federal government and philanthropic organizations dispersed funds to state and local governments, local organizations, and households to help fund recovery in New Orleans and the surrounding region. Federal funding came from a variety of programs, departments, and agencies, including FEMA Public and Individual Assistance grants, Hazards Mitigation grants, and the Flood Mitigation Assistance Program. Department of Housing and Urban Development (HUD) funding came in the form of Community Development Block Grants (CDBG). The U.S. Congress appropriated more than $100 billion for Hurricanes Katrina and Rita recovery. CDBG-DR grant money dispersed by HUD totaled to more than $19 billion for recovery after Hurricane Katrina, the largest in U.S. history (Gotham, 2015, 2017). Congress legislated a new program through the GO Zone Act of 2005 that offered tax incentives in the hurricane-affected Gulf Region for redevelopment (Gotham, 2015). Despite the inflow of these federal funds, the recovery of the region, and specifically New Orleans, was slow and often contentious, uneven across racial and socioeconomic demographics, and largely inadequate in reaching the goals of an equitable recovery (Comfort, Birkland, Cigler, & Nance, 2010; Fussell, 2015; Gotham, 2015). More than fifteen years later, the slow pace of recovery is still apparent in the region.

10.1.3 Long-Term Recovery and Planning Processes

After the deadly hurricane hit, killing more than 1,800 residents and displacing hundreds of thousands of others, several long-term recovery processes were initiated at the federal, state, and local levels. One process, led by the Urban Land Institute, a national think tank, drew upon national organizations and experts to develop a recovery framework for the city (Comfort et al., 2010). The Unified New Orleans Plan (UNOP), another recovery process, was a local effort funded in part by the Rockefeller Foundation. The Bring New Orleans Back Commission, along with neighborhood groups and local organizations also spearheaded several recovery processes, such as Neighborhood

Rebuilding Plans and the Association for Community Organizations for Reform Now (ACORN). The City's Office of Recovery Management developed the Recovery Implementation Plan, building on the work of UNOP. Individual planning efforts involving a wide array of governmental and nongovernmental organizations numbered more than fifteen (Comfort et al., 2010). Some processes and plans were initiated at the federal level (such as FEMA's ESF-14 Plan) whereas others were centered in individual neighborhoods. The U.S. Army Corps of Engineers led local and regional recovery projects, including the Mississippi Coastal Improvements Program. This complex of processes that engaged an array of diverse stakeholders did not lead to significant measurable outcomes in the immediate years following the hurricane. Five years after the disaster, only a handful of recovery projects were completed (Comfort et al., 2010).

10.1.4 Inequities in Recovery

Scholars have pointed to a variety of causes that may explain the delayed response to and incomplete recovery from Hurricane Katrina, including lack of leadership at all levels of government, inadequate resources, and preexisting resource constraints across the region. Explanations of failures in response and recovery to Katrina often center on the flow of resources from the federal government to local communities where funds were deployed. Much of the federal assistance to Louisiana came through block grants, funneled from the federal government through the State of Louisiana Recovery Authority (LRA) to be dispersed to communities and residents in need of money for rebuilding. Five years after the storm, only 55 percent of the applicants had received aid, and evidence suggests that the monies were not allocated evenly across neighborhoods, with neighborhoods with lower home values receiving less funding (Gotham, 2015). Scholars point to the role of privatization of the housing recovery program, through the contracting of ICF International to manage the Road Home Program, leading to these inequities (Gotham, 2015).

Within the City of New Orleans, neighborhoods faced different levels of risks and vulnerabilities prior to Hurricane Katrina. The devastating disaster and recovery processes led to even greater inequities across neighborhoods (Fussell, 2015). Gotham (2015) argues that by including regions that were less impacted by the disaster, the structure of the Go Zone tax relief and incentive program favored communities that had capacity to apply for funding, further disadvantaging communities that experienced greater devastation or had more limited capacity.

At the end of the first year after the hurricane, the City of New Orleans was markedly whiter, wealthier, had higher levels of formal education, and was older compared to the city before the storm. Depopulation after the disaster was greatest in neighborhoods with highest level of exposure and vulnerability to flooding (Finch, Emrich, & Cutter, 2010; Fussell, 2015). Fussell (2015) suggests that the inflow of resources from housing assistance programs did not adequately compensate for the differences in vulnerabilities across neighborhoods in New Orleans during post-hurricane recovery. The Urban Land Institute (2015) reflected on the unevenness of recovery and shifts in demographics a decade after the disaster:

Although African Americans make up nearly 60 percent of its population, nearly 100,000 moderate- and low-income African Americans fled the city after Katrina, never to return. The disparity in median income between white and black households was 54 percent in 2013, higher than the 40 percent disparity that exists nationally between the two groups, according to the New Orleans Index at Ten. And a recent NPR/Kaiser Family Foundation survey revealed a stark divide in how blacks and whites perceive post-Katrina New Orleans: 70 percent of white residents believe the city has recovered, while only 44 percent of blacks do.

10.1.5 Resources, Capacity, and Recovery

In the Colorado communities, as discussed in Chapter 4, and communities affected by Hurricane Katrina, pre-disaster capacities influence how communities can recover, adjust, and learn after disaster. Disasters impact communities heterogeneously – and these communities also have varying access to resources before, during, and after disaster. Similar struggles seen in Hurricane Katrina occurred in Evans, Colorado, a community with a relatively low administrative capacity and resources and relatively larger communities of color. After disasters, external resources are mobilized from a complex landscape of governmental and nongovernmental organizations. This was true in the communities affected by the 2013 Colorado floods and communities along the Gulf Coast after Hurricane Katrina. In the case of

Hurricane Katrina, the capacity of state officials to allocate funds to households was limited, which lead to privatization of the recovery program. Scholars suggest that local officials on the Gulf Coast focused too little on addressing the vulnerabilities of their community members to hurricane-related disasters (Burby, 2006), while others argue that the lack of state-level capacity led, at least in part, to slower and more inequitable recovery in Louisiana (Fussell, 2015), underscoring the role of capacity, resources, and multiple levels of government to support recovery.

10.1.6 Flooding in South Carolina

Communities, households, and individuals are evermore vulnerable to floods as the climate changes and development, land use policies, and historical settlement patterns come into conflict. Low-wealth communities and households often bear a disproportionate burden of disaster, frequently worsening preexisting inequities, as illustrated in the discussion of Hurricane Katrina. During the first week of October 2015, in part due to the presence of Hurricane Joaquin, a Category 3 Atlantic hurricane off the coast, incessant rain drenched much of South Carolina. This pattern of precipitation led to a 1,000-year flood event across the state, including low-wealth communities and communities of color. Reports indicated that flooding led to seventeen deaths and left significant damage in its wake (Columbia, 2016; FEMA, 2015). The floods damaged public infrastructure, including 10 miles of Interstate 95 leading to its closure, and drinking water supply systems, causing more than 40,000 residents to lose access to potable water. Several dams across the state were breached, and hundreds of residents were displaced from their homes. Governor Haley declared an emergency for forty-six counties across South Carolina (Columbia, 2016; FEMA, 2015). A resident of Columbia described her experience with the flood:

I remember it had rained and rained and rained. And then my husband works rotating shifts, so he was on the 7 p.m.–7 a.m. shift. So he went at seven that night, and got off at seven that morning. So when I woke up that morning, I saw the water outside ... So then they started showing, you know, like on the news, everything that was closed because of all the flooding. So it normally takes him an hour to get home. It took him five hours that day because he was driving into the flood. So I went berserk because he said that everywhere he went, there was just water flowing everywhere.

10.1.7 Resources and Risk Perceptions

As discussed in Part III, direct and indirect experience with disasters, trust in local officials, and causal understanding of disasters are important to understanding how residents perceive future risks of similar events. This section looks at the same factors presented in Part III by examining how resources and flood experiences influence risk perceptions after an extreme flood in Columbia, South Carolina.[1] The flood damaged many neighborhoods across Columbia but most severely affected low-wealth and majority African American areas of the city and nearby communities. Many apartment complexes were significantly damaged or even destroyed by the flood, a disaster that occurred in part due to a series of dam failures that caused a wall of water to rush downstream into lower-wealth neighborhoods.

Communities with less financial wealth and individuals who live within them are often exposed to greater risks of climatic events. Perceptions of risk may correspondingly differ spatially across communities, in part depending on the proximity to hazardous locations, which may, at least in part, be a function of community financial resources (Laws et al., 2015). Neighborhoods and communities with less wealth are frequently located on marginal, low-lying lands that may be more at risk to flooding, hurricanes, and other natural hazards (Caniglia, Vallée, & Frank, 2016). As such, individuals in lower-wealth communities may perceive greater future risks of flooding than those in wealthier communities because of their increased exposure. Communities with less wealth may not be able to provide needed assistance to residents to prevent and mitigate flood risks, potentially increasing residents' risk perceptions and decreasing perceptions of their ability to recover from a flood. A lack of home ownership may

---

[1] See Appendix B for a description of the methodology of collecting and analyzing interviews and survey data collected from Columbia, South Carolina, residents in the months following Hurricane Joaquin.

Columbia is a mid-size city (population of 385,000) in the U.S. South. Residents in Columbia were interviewed and surveyed about their experiences with the flood and the recovery three months after the devastating flood.

directly or indirectly influence an individual's vulnerability to flood events, independent of income level or other measures of wealth. This increase in vulnerability may affect how flood risks are perceived. Home ownership may capture a number of dimensions, including a greater sense of individual agency in recovery process, economic security, stability (R. Palm, Palm, & Hodgson, 1992; R. I. Palm, 2019; L. A. Russell et al., 1995), or generational wealth, whereas self-reported income likely represents current financial status only.

Approximately half of the survey respondents in Columbia had low- to lower-middle income, with 31 percent of respondents reporting pre-tax income of less than $25,000 a year, and 26 percent of respondents reporting between $25K and $50K annually, which is comparable to the general population of the city. Fixed effects regression models of risk perception demonstrate a consistently positive relationship between income and risk perception, yet a negative relationship with home ownership (home ownership reduces risk perception) (see Appendix B for more details). Based on this analysis, home ownership was a significant factor in residents' risk perceptions in South Carolina, with renters significantly perceiving greater flood risks than home-owners. The home ownership theme was prevalent in the interviews with residents as well. One apartment resident described his experience with the flood and recovery:

My apartment complex has shoddy maintenance policies, so it took forever for somebody to come out there and fix the road, which means that for days, for weeks, we weren't—the garbage man wouldn't be able to come over that little bridge to pick up the trash, so it was there for a long time. People were getting disgusted by the smell. There are people who are moving out of other apartments.

Another apartment resident discussed the months following the flood:

My apartment complex, like I said, they didn't want to let anybody out their lease, so everybody over there—I want to say it's like maybe 115 families over there that were struggling. Me and my three kids had to go to different hotels. I didn't receive that much assistance from FEMA. FEMA did not assist me till the end, and I only got $1,500, which it helped but it wasn't enough, you know. So my hotel bill came up to like $5,000. I had to stay at this one hotel for ten days, and another hotel for two weeks, and then I just stayed at one hotel until I got – the last hotel – until I got another apartment. I missed days [of work] because my kids were constantly sick. Their immune system has been compromised due to us living in the mold environment. And because of this, I lost my job.

A third flood-affected resident recalled her experience:

The flood experience was very, what's the word, traumatic. And it kind of separated us for a little bit because we had repairs that need to be done [sic] our apartment. And we had some things we had to throw away that we wouldn't— we didn't get back; we went and replaced. We got sick. My kids got sick. And I got sick also. So we were separated for a couple weeks because I didn't want them to stay in the apartment. And I went and stayed with friends and relatives. And they stayed with their dad. So now, I had repairs done to the apartment. And we're still doing work. So we're together but we're still going through the flood issues. We see it daily because it's our neighborhood, it's in our apartment complex. We have basically condemned apartments that, you know, a lot of our neighbors are not staying in those apartments anymore. So it's like it's kind of empty now. Where we used to see kids running and playing, we don't see that too much anymore. We still see a lot of water. And every time it rains it's an issue.

Very few studies examine the role of home ownership as an influence of risk perception, especially after the occurrence of an extreme event. Renters are often more difficult to capture in randomly sampled household surveys, as demonstrated in the Colorado study. In communities with a significant renting population, studies of risk perceptions may underestimate the perceived risks to the community if renters are systematically underrepresented in the survey. As discussed in Chapters 4 and 7, resources and public participation are critical in encouraging community-level learning and change. Due to lack of resources and less control over their own properties, residents who live in apartments, like those studied in South Carolina, may be less likely to be able to participate in recovery processes as well as fully recover themselves after a disaster. Chapter 4 emphasized the importance of resources to recovery, including resources and capacity before and after a disaster. This discussion of flooding in South Carolina expands on the findings in Chapter 4 to suggest that the role of individual- and household capacity after a disaster also influences capacity to recover.

10.2 Floods in Hungary

Disastrous floods struck a number of European countries in the first part of the twenty-first century, causing extensive damage across the continent. In 2002, nations in Central Europe, including Germany, Austria, and the Czech Republic, experienced catastrophic floods, causing loss of life and damages exceeding $15 billion (Helmer & Hilhorst, 2006). Extreme flooding returned to Central Europe in 2009, again leaving catastrophic damages and loss of life in its wake. To manage these floods and disasters, communities, states, and nations have developed approaches and policies to prepare for, mitigate risks of, and recover from disasters.

10.2.1 The Importance of Intergovernmental Relations

Similar to the U.S. context where the dynamics of federalism are key to disaster management, disaster policymaking in the European Union occurs at multiple levels of government, including at the supranational level (the E.U.), in each individual nation, and within states and communities (Hooghe, Marks, & Marks, 2001; Liesbet & Gary, 2003; Marks & Hooghe, 2004; Marks, Hooghe, & Blank, 1996). As discussed in Chapter 8, and in the Hurricane Katrina example in this chapter, intergovernmental dynamics can play an important role in disaster recovery processes. Higher levels of government may provide external funding for disaster recovery and may also mandate, incentivize, or constrain the actions of local governments in how they prepare for, mitigate risks of, and recover from disasters.

Since its formation, the European Union has built capacity for managing risks and disasters, including adopting laws that mandate member states to assess risks and submit their assessments to the European Commission (Boin & Rhinard, 2008). After the catastrophic flood of 2002, the European Union formed a Solidarity Fund (EUSF) to provide financial assistance for disaster recovery efforts in member states (Aakre et al., 2010; Surminski et al., 2015). Since its inception, EUSF has allocated more than 5 billion Euros to twenty-four member nations for disaster recovery. In addition to the EUSF, the European Union has adopted hazard-specific legislation, such as the European Union Floods Directive (Directive 2000/60/EC). This directive requires member states to conduct flood risk mapping and develop flood management plans. In doing so, much discretion has been left to member states to implement the directive (Hartmann & Spit, 2016a, 2016b). It is up to individual nations to decide how to allocate risk and disaster management among levels of government. Nations must decide how centralized or decentralized their system of disaster management should be. As a comparison, the Netherlands, which has actively managed floods through structural approaches (e.g., dikes, levees), has adopted a centralized approach to flood management, while sub-national states in Germany take the lead in flood risk management.

10.2.2 Floods in Hungary during a Time of Change

Hungary, which is located in Central Europe, experienced a series of extreme floods during the period of democratic and economic transitions of the 1990s and 2000s, providing both challenges and opportunities to flood recovery. The 1980s and 1990s brought sweeping political, economic, and social change to many nations in Central and Eastern Europe (CEE). The fall of the Berlin Wall in 1989 and the opening of the fence between Hungary and Austria marked an end of Communist rule in many nations across the region, including Hungary, a country of approximately 10 million people. During this period of democratic transition, including accession into the European Union in 2005, Hungary experienced a series of 1,000-year flood events in the Danube and Tisza river basins. These events, in combination with a shift toward a more open society, allowed for a greater number and diversity of voices to participate in discussions surrounding flood management. These shifts, in part, led to a change in approach to managing floods during this time period (Albright, 2011). The story of Hungary's extreme floods and policy response in the late twentieth and early twenty-first centuries underscores the importance of intergovernmental dynamics, civic capacity, coalitions, and participatory processes as potential drivers of learning after a disaster.

10.2.2.1 The History of Flooding in Hungary

The Tisza River, one of the major tributaries of the Danube River, flows through the predominantly rural and agricultural eastern portion of Hungary. The river basin of the Tisza includes land of four neighboring nations – Slovakia, Romania, Ukraine, and Serbia – encompassing more than 60,000 square miles. The river basin is surrounded by the Carpathian mountain range from which several tributaries feed into the Tisza. The river runs through the flat lowlands, much of which are agricultural fields that were drained during the nineteenth century to increase agricultural production (Borsos & Sendzimir, 2018; Matczak, Flachner, & Werners, 2008). Floods have been common during the history of Hungary, including many floods in the nineteenth and early twentieth centuries. During the nineteenth century, Hungary adopted an engineering approach to manage the floods, an approach centered on the development of an engineered system of wetland drainage, levees, and pumps (Szlávik, 2003), not too dissimilar to the historic management of the Mississippi River described in Chapter 1. This engineering approach remained largely intact until the late twentieth century, as the communist era emphasized agricultural production and engineering solutions, despite large flood events in the early twentieth century (1913 and 1932) (Szlávik, 2003).

As the late twentieth century brought political and economic transitions across CEE, including Hungary, the nation shifted from one political party to a multiparty system, and legal and institutional frameworks were reinvented, including the adoption of the Environmental Framework Law in 1995. During the economic transition, environmental issues were not prioritized on the government's agenda (Buzogány, 2009; O'Toole Jr & Hanf, 1998), although the public became more involved in protests that included environmental issues, such as protests against a major dam project on the Danube in 1988, when more than 100,000 people petitioned and protested (Deets, 2009).

10.2.2.2 Local-Level Mobilization Pushing for Policy Change
After extreme flood events between 1998 and 2000 in the Bodrogköz area in the Tisza River basin, a few mayors in the region reached out to a local environmental organization to discuss flood management issues (Albright, 2009). The Bokartisz partnership, founded on July 5, 2001, included mayors of twelve communities, two local environmental organizations (The Palocsa Organization and E-Mission Association), and the Hungarian Environmental Economics Centre. From these beginnings, the Bokartisz partnership of local environmental organizations and twelve towns evolved. The members of the Bokartisz partnership met in face-to-face meetings, including annual meetings with all of the partners, as well as individual meetings between the partnership director and local town officials (Albright, 2009). The Bokartisz partnership was successful in applying for and receiving various grants from external sources. The regional environmental directorate, in

partnership with Bokartisz, was awarded a series of European Union Interregional Program grants from 2004 through 2008 to further develop their sustainable flood management program within the Bodrogköz region. A mayor described the vision of the alliance:

We have been a member of Bokartisz partnership, and I naturally agree with the targets of Bokartisz. So Bokartisz was founded mainly for the renewal of traditional water management, and is devoted to nature-friendly technical solutions. So according to their ideas we do not have to struggle with internal flood waters, but have to develop a productive technology, an agricultural system which tolerates the floods, and moreover, utilizes them. (Mayor from Bodrogköz region, 2006)

The convergence of the following four dynamics set the stage for a shift in approach in the management of the Tisza River: (1) a history of an engineering approach to river management, which failed to protect Hungary from the devastating floods of the 1990s and 2000s; (2) newly E.U.-mandated processes for governance and environmental management; (3) newly restructured national environmental management institutions with weakened financial and human capacity; and (4) increased role of local mayors in governance (Albright, 2011). The national water directorate employed more than 25,000 staff prior to 1990, but by 2003, these numbers were reduced to around 4,000 (Vari, Linnerooth-Bayer, & Ferencz, 2003). Frustrated with a lack of national action addressing flooding and local-level concerns, in 2006 a coalition of mayors from forty-two local governments, twenty-eight environmental organizations, and many farmers in the region formed a broader alliance to push for policy change at the national level. This coalition wanted to see a more comprehensive approach to flood management, stepping away from the historical focus on engineering solutions to include environmental protection and regional development (Albright, 2011). A mayor of a small community in the Tisza region described the actions of a coalition of mayors concerned about flooding and economic development:

We went to demonstrate, one of the mayors went on a hunger strike, and we saw that all was in vain, so we had to draw the conclusion and we decided to find a new tactic: to increase our strength, to increase our capacity to represent the interests of our cities. So we decided to try to gain the support of more city leaders, whose interests are similar to ours, and my idea was that I suggested that we should create an association which stands on four major pillars. One would be the city councils, the other the farmers, who are directly interested in this question, the third would be the civic organizations, local or not local but those who are dealing with the Tisza, and the fourth would be science, those scientists who are researching the Tisza and to whom they listen to. My idea was that if we would have all these four supports, we would be covered from every angle. So this is what the city councils want, but what are the farmers saying? Yes, they want the same. The civil organizations ... Well, they also want the same thing. And finally even the scientists say the same. I was hoping that this way we would be able to close the circle. (Tisza Mayor, 2007)

This alliance of local governments and environmental organizations pushed for change at the national level. A leader of an environmental organization described an increased openness to input from national officials during this time period:

I think the main role was played by [Mr. A] who was state secretary at that time who was responsible for water management and his deputy [Mr. B]. And he was the one that told us if you know what you want, then come and tell us. So it was really uncommon for the Hungarian system, because you very rarely get heard. (Technical expert, 2007)

An environmental leader discussed mediation between local-level government and national-level officials:

In March 2003, we had a debate with the water management side, and the Ministry people, and my role was mediation between the parties. That was the meeting that the Ministry people understood that [the Director of the partnership] is not insane and that what he is explaining makes sense and that the two sides became much closer, the two opinions, and that there is a way to merge the floodplain management idea into the Vásárhelyi planning concept ... You know when there are two sides and they have different views and they very often just don't understand each other, because they don't have the ability to listen, and that meeting was a bit different because they tried to focus not on the differences but on the common things and it worked very well. (Environmental organization, 2007)

A national plan for the Tisza region was adopted in 2003, called the revised Vásárhelyi Terv Továbbfejlesztési (VTT) and was made possible by these discussions between local and national officials, scientists, and environmental organizations. The VTT incorporated a broader approach to flood management in the rural Tisza region, including issues of rural development and a more ecological focus through increased retention of waters on the floodplains and in emergency reservoirs and shifts in agricultural practices (Borsos & Sendzimir, 2018). The process of democratization in the late 1980s, accession to the European Union, along with a series of extreme floods set the context in which this dialogue occurred. Changes that occurred external to the flood policy subsystem (i.e., the end of the state-socialist era, the accession into the E.U.) alone were not enough to motivate changes to the core of the government's flood program. For changes to occur, including changes in beliefs about flood policy solutions, changes in the political system were required, which allowed for more diverse voices within the policy process. These political changes and a series of extreme events were necessary for major changes in the national government's flood management program to occur.

Although the VTT plan was adopted in 2003, suggesting policy change and a shift in beliefs about solutions to flooding, implementation of the plan stalled, as well as participatory processes in the Tisza region.

From the middle of 2004, the preparation and planning of the VTT slowed down, the social discourses became less frequent, as did the frequency of the VTT Inter-Ministerial Committee sessions. Consequently, the transparency of the planning process declined considerably, and in some particular areas, like the Cigand-Tiszakarad emergency reservoir and land management pilot area (in the Bodrogköz), the information flow to stakeholders and the consultations with them were practically terminated. (Cselószki, 2006)

To date, a few of the proposed emergency reservoirs have been built. The European Union has designated more than 50 billion Euros from 2014 to 2020 for the completion of the projects. As implemented, Borsos and Sendzimir (2018) argue that the VTT plan "does not offer sufficient capacity to cope with or adapt to the impacts of increasing climatic variability."

The case of flood management in the Tisza River basin in Hungary underscores the importance of several disaster-related dynamics discussed in previous chapters, including the role of resources, beliefs about flooding, coalitions of actors, and intergovernmental relationships, all with the potential to influence the path of disaster recovery, including policy changes and learning. As discussed in Chapter 4, flows of resources from external sources and internal capacities may be critical to disaster recovery. In the case of Hungary, the flow of external resources from the European Union, new European Union mandates, and limited national-level administrative capacity have been important in the management approach in the Tisza River. The analysis of the trajectory of flood management in this region of Hungary over centuries suggests that long-held beliefs and policy preferences toward flood management can play a critical role in policy change after extreme flooding. Chapter 5 demonstrated that local officials and the public may become more concerned about flood risks after a disaster and that risk perceptions are formed through the lens of values, beliefs, and experiences. The example of flood management in the Tisza demonstrates the importance of post-disaster beliefs and participatory processes. The series of disasters brought local-level leaders, environmental organizations, and farmers together who shared similar beliefs about policy failures and solutions. This coalition of local-level actors then engaged in discussions with national leaders who held different beliefs about flood management and disaster recovery. A compromised flood management plan was developed that incorporated policy preferences from both local and national officials. Chapter 8 described the importance of intergovernmental dynamics in local-level post-disaster recovery. In the Hungarian case, policy change at the regional level (The Tisza River basin) was influenced by intergovernmental dynamics between local-level officials who demanded a change in approach to flood management and officials at the national level whose organizations were embedded in a history of engineering-centric flood management. Accession into the European Union, and along with it adoption of E.U.-level policies and practices, encouraged a more democratic approach to flood management in the early 2000s that allowed for increased dialogue between officials who held competing beliefs about flood management.

10.3 Wildfires in California

Extreme floods are only one type of climate-influenced disaster. Wildfires have increased in intensity and frequency in certain regions such as the western United States and Australia and are predicted to become more widespread and intense due to climate change, in part because of increased drought conditions (Departments of Interior & Agriculture, 2001; McCaffrey, 2015). Extreme, extensive, and relentless wildfires burned areas across the State of California, much of

Australia, and in the Amazon of Brazil the first two decades of the twenty-first century. The National Institute of Standards and Technology estimates that the annual economic costs of wildfires in the United States total between $7 and $62 billion, with annualized losses ranging from $63.5 to $285.0 billion (Thomas, Butry, Gilbert, Webb, & Fung, 2017). The increasing risk from wildfires is not unique to the western United States. Extensive and catastrophic wildfires in Australia during 2019–2020 spread across 18 million hectares, devastating multiple economic sectors including agriculture, homes, and natural habitat for many species (United Nations Environment Programme, 2020). Ash from wildfires in Australia choked rivers in the southeastern region of the nation, leading to fish kills, as one example (Welz, 2020).

Wildfire risk mitigation, preparation, management, and recovery are becoming even more critical as the earth warms, drying forestlands and making them more susceptible to wildfires. Changes in climate have led to increased heat and dryer conditions in forests in these regions, often making them even more vulnerable to wildfires and lengthening wildfire seasons. Millions of residents across these regions have been displaced, homes have been destroyed, and habitats rendered inhospitable to wildlife. Beyond climate change, as human development encroaches on and intermingles with forests [known as the wildland–urban interface (WUI) (Departments of Interior & Agriculture, 2001)], more human lives, homes, and communities are at risk of disaster. How residents perceive risks from wildfires and act to mitigate these risks is critical for the protection of lives and property. In a wildfire-prone area of Colorado, when residents perceived greater risks of fire, they were more likely to adopt risk-mitigating behaviors (Brenkert-Smith, Champ, & Flores, 2012). Risk-reducing actions, such as hardening of structures, thinning of wildfire fuels, and providing defensible spaces – areas surrounding homes that are cleared of wood and other material that may fuel fires – may be crucial to help protect both lives and property.

10.3.1 Risks, Trust, Causal Understanding, and Community Recovery

Risk perceptions, as discussed in Chapter 5, are affected by numerous factors, including information sources, deeply held beliefs, and level of trust in government agencies charged with risk management. Personally experiencing a disaster may increase the public's information-seeking behaviors and may influence the level of trust they hold in government officials. Community members in Colorado who directly experienced flood damage to their personal property reported being more informed about flooding and had participated more fully in local-level flood recovery processes. And those whose neighborhoods were most severely impacted by the disaster reported lower levels of trust in local governments managing the disaster. Just as these factors affect risk perceptions about flooding, studies suggest they also influence how individuals perceive future risks of wildfires (Velez et al., 2017).

Trust between wildfire managers and the public is paramount to the health and safety of residents who live in areas prone to wildfires. Prior to a wildfire, trust in officials and information may affect the extent to which residents adopt risk-mitigating behaviors (Koebele et al., 2015). As a wildfire approaches, government officials may convey information about immediate risks and means of reducing exposure to these risks, such as information about the severity of an expected disaster and mandated or voluntary evacuations. Residents who trust the information they receive about recommended actions and act upon it will likely fare better than those who do not. Lack of trust in wildfire managers and the information they share may lead to slower evacuations or residents deciding to stay in place, placing them at greater risk (Velez et al., 2017).

Trust is just as essential during long-term recovery from a disaster, as it is in the days or hours preceding a disaster. Social scientists who study the management of wildfires have examined the role of trust in information dissemination, information seeking, risk perceptions, and risk-reducing behaviors (McCaffrey et al., 2013). After a disaster occurs, government officials disseminate information to support emergency response in the immediate aftermath of a disaster, such as where and how community members and organizations can seek or provide aid. Post-disaster messaging from officials and others may also focus on long-term recovery issues, such as policies, programs, and behaviors that could mitigate future risks of disasters. The media, using both conventional and social platforms, often mediate these messages from government officials to community members and organizations (Crow, Lawhon, et al., 2017; Steelman et al., 2015). Just as information dissemination from local governments was important in Colorado's flood recovery, this information is key to numerous factors that can lead to higher levels of government trust which in turn is vital for local government learning and change after a disaster.

10.3.2 Risk Perceptions and Risk-Mitigating Behaviors in California

In California, living with wildfire has always been a fact of life, but in the early twenty-first century, wildfires have grown and caused catastrophic damage, and are often attributed to changing climate (drought) and development in the WUI (CDP, October 10, 2019; Diffenbaugh, Swain, & Touma, 2015; Hagerty, 2019; C. S. Kennedy, Weise, & Maschke, 2017). California is so familiar with wildfire risk and response that the CalFire model is often referenced as the impetus for the National Incident Management System that FEMA uses and trains nationwide emergency management professionals to use (Buck, Trainor, & Aguirre, 2006; J. Jensen, 2011). In the 2019 Verisk Wildfire Risk Analysis, it was determined that more than two million properties in California were at high or extreme risk from wildfires (Verisk, 2019). Multiple scholars have investigated the extent to which homeowners perceive risks from wildfires in California. In their 1987 study, Gardner, Cortner, and Widaman (1987) found that residents in Southern California demonstrated low awareness of fire risks and an unwillingness to adopt risk-mitigating behaviors. The awareness of wildfire risk has changed in the decades since early social science work was conducted in California. Wildfire risk is now central to many residents' concerns. Prior experience with wildfires, knowledge about wildfires, and past preparedness actions all influence how much a person knows about wildfire risk and what types of information sources they seek to learn more (Velez, Diaz, & Wall, 2017), so higher risk perceptions and knowledge should be expected in California. Wildfires are so numerous in California that studies have examined risk perceptions as they relate to specific experiences during a wildfire disaster – staying at home, evacuating, experiencing damage to homes, and other nuances of individual-level experiences that can all affect risk perceptions about future wildfire events (McGee, McFarlane, & Varghese, 2009). Risk reduction behavior in the form of evacuating from a wildfire is more likely among individuals with higher education and children, while older, lower-income individuals with pets are less likely to evacuate, even including those who have evacuated in past wildfires (Wong, Broader, Walker, & Shaheen, 2020). This brief review of literature indicates that our understanding of past disaster experience as it influences risk perceptions is still developing, in part because risks are increasing and the field of study is evolving rapidly.

10.3.3 The Camp Fire-Engulfed Paradise, California

Wildfires are not new to Northern California. A 1923 fire ignited in the grasslands outside of Berkeley, California, and moved quickly into town, destroying more than 500 homes (G. E. Russell et al., 1923). The Marble Cone fire, sparked by lightning, in 1976 enflamed more than 170,000 acres of land in Monterey County (CalFire, 2019). Fifteen of the twenty largest wildfires in California's history have occurred since the year 2000. The State of California experienced unprecedented drought during the first two decades of the twenty-first century, increasing the risk of wildfires.

California is currently in the midst of a record-setting drought. The drought began in 2012 and now includes the lowest calendar-year and 12-mo pre-cipitation, the highest annual temperature, and the most extreme drought indicators on record. The extremely warm and dry conditions have led to acute water shortages, ground-water overdraft, critically low streamflow, and enhanced wildfire risk. (Diffenbaugh et al., 2015)

Drought, driven in part by anthropogenic climate change, coupled with increased development in the WUI and faulty infrastructure, set the stage for the deadliest wildfires in California's history. In 2018, the Camp Fire engulfed the region of Butte County (population more than 200,000), including the community of Paradise, California, with a pre-fire population of 27,000.

It started around 6:30 am on November 8, 2018, a so-called red flag warning day with the ideal conditions for a wildfire: whipping Diablo winds paired with heat and low humidity. The cause, the state's fire-protection agency, Cal Fire, concluded after a six-month investigation, was a few sparks that had flown off electrical transmission lines near Pulga, California. Fueled by vegetation that was tinder-dry after years of drought, it quickly outgrew Pulga, tearing into the neighboring Butte County towns of Concow, Magalia, and Paradise. (Hagerty, 2019)

On the day the fire started, Governor Gavin Newsome declared a State of Emergency, followed by a major disaster declaration by President Trump four days later. Two weeks after the fire started it was declared contained. More than 18,000 structures were destroyed across 240 square miles, and damages exceeded $16.5 billion, of which $4 billion were uninsured (Butte County District Attorney, 2020; Ruiz-Grossman, 2019).

By seventeen months after the disaster, 3,000 residents had returned to Paradise, leaving roughly 24,000 living elsewhere (Kuz & D'Orio, 2020). The wildfire sparked lawsuits, with about 7,000 homeowner claims against Pacific Gas and Electric (PG&E), due to equipment and transmission lines that sparked the flames (Penn, 2020). In May of 2020, PG&E reached a settlement with Paradise homeowners for $13.5 billion. PG&E plead guilty to eighty-four counts of involuntary manslaughter.

10.3.4 Community Member-Driven Disaster Recovery Process

A gift from the Butte Strong Fund supported the development of a resident-driven long-term planning process that began in January 2019. This process led to the development of the Paradise Long-term Community Recovery Plan (Urban Design Associates, 2019). The plan included a fourteen-week engagement process in which residents of Paradise engaged in conversations about the strengths and weaknesses of Paradise, both before and after the disaster. Seven listening meetings were held, in which community members provided input that filtered into a Community Vision with several goals and approximately forty recovery projects (Urban Design Associates, 2019). The focus on goals and objectives in these meetings, followed by the development of projects echoed a similar process that occurred in Lyons, as described in Chapters 4 and 7. Table 10.1 lists selected goals included in the Recovery Plan.

In a survey and community listening meetings, Paradise residents identified perceived weaknesses of their community, both before and after the fire. Policy failures were identified – such as a lack of fire breaks, inadequate evacuation routes and road networks, and lack of tree and brush maintenance. Several residents noted a lack of walk-ability, poor planning and haphazard development, and lack of a

Table 10.1. *Goals of community members developed through a series of community member engagement process*

- Create a safer street network.
- Improve evacuation, fire safety, and emergency notification system.
- Remain accessible to families, individuals, and seniors.
- Provide a full spectrum of housing choices.
- Create more parks, green spaces, and outdoor event spaces.
- Create a walkable downtown.
- Rebuild in a more resilient way – as an example to the world and other rural communities.

Source: Urban Design Associates, 2019

sewer system (Urban Design Associates, 2019). Similar to Lyons, Colorado, a set of tangible recovery projects that stemmed from these discussions was identified.

10.3.5 Paradise: A Slow Recovery and Compounding Risks

A year and a half after the fire, progress toward these goals and development of these projects was impeded by a compounding disaster, the COVID-19 pandemic, although some concrete progress was achieved during recovery. A Building Resiliency Center opened in January 2020 to assist residents in rebuilding by providing information sources and a one-stop shop to complete permit applications (Mackey, 2020). Funded by a grant from the U.S. Department of Agriculture Rural Development program, the Butte Strong Fund, and corporate donors, the Center aimed to ease and streamline the process of recovery for homeowners, businesses, and organizations (Kaenel, 2020).

A year and a half after the wildfire, the Town of Paradise had received approximately 1,000 building permit applications and has issued 832 permits. A total of 166 homes have been rebuilt by the end of May 2020, out of the approximate 16,000 homes that were destroyed (Goyer, 2020). It is too soon to tell what recovery will look like in Paradise in the coming years, including how many homes and businesses will be rebuilt or what lessons will be gleaned from the fire. Recovery from the disaster has presented many challenges, as recovery from all disasters do. Funding and reimbursements have been slow and bureaucratic, and housing is insecure. Community members are spread across the region and country, requiring online public engagement processes to supplement in-person meetings. These challenges echo those experienced by some communities in Colorado in 2013 and beyond. But now, community members face another crisis that is complicating and slowing the already slow recovery process.

In late 2019 and early 2020, the COVID-19 pandemic spread across much of the world, including California and Butte County. As a result of this public health crisis, states and local governments adopted stay-at-home orders and mandated social distancing practices. The town spokesperson describes how COVID-19 has affected recovery in Paradise:

It's been hard because our whole focus was a face-to-face interaction … Rebuilding is an emotional thing. People are overwhelmed. We wanted to be able to sit down and literally and figuratively hold their hand during the process. Now, this makes that impossible. (Branson-Potts, 2020)

Recovery from the devastating fires will continue, even if slowed by the COVID-19 pandemic. Homes and businesses will be rebuilt, but it is unclear how many and where. Community members may return to their community, but many will stay relocated as a part of the Camp Fire diaspora, similar to evacuees that never returned to New Orleans after Hurricane Katrina. The California State Assembly passed legislation in 2019 to help fund risk-mitigating actions and provide defensible space guidelines (McCann, 2019), underscoring the role of external resources in disaster recovery and mitigation. Time will tell if communities in California will learn from the experience of Camp Fire.

10.4 Common Threads across Disasters and Communities

Through an examination of a set of disasters in a diversity of settings, including hurricanes on the coast of the Gulf of Mexico and in South Carolina, extreme floods in the Central European nation of Hungary, and devastating wildfires in Northern California, several broad themes emerged that underscore the dynamics that played out in post-disaster recovery in the aftermath of the Colorado 2013 floods. As highlighted in Chapter 4, resources and capacity were critical in disaster recovery in the flood-affected communities in Colorado. Resources also proved important in the examination of Hurricanes Katrina and Joaquin. Chapter 8 presented the importance of intergovernmental dynamics in post-disaster recovery, with higher-level governmental authorities influencing action at the local level. These dynamics were important in New Orleans and in Hungary, both in terms of resource flows and in support (or in opposition) of policy preferences and processes at the local level. The examples of development of the VTT plan in Hungary and the recovery planning process after the wildfire in Paradise, California, underscore the importance of engagement in post-disaster recovery dynamics, discussed in Chapter 7. Perceptions of future flood risks and beliefs about problem severity, causes of flooding, and policy preferences are highlighted in Chapter 5. Dynamics of beliefs and risks were illuminated in the discussions of wildfires in California and flooding in South Carolina. The argument herein does not suggest that the dynamics discussed in this chapter are the only dynamics at play in long-term recovery of disasters. Each story of recovery is complex, often with many potential drivers or impediments to learning and change. It does become clearer though that the dynamics discussed in this book are not solely relevant to recovery from the 2013 floods, but, rather, may play out in a diversity of disasters and geographic locations.

11 | Conclusions, Recommendations, and Future Directions

This book articulates a specific problem that all communities across the globe may grapple with in the coming decades – if they have not already had to. In a scenario of a changing climate where human development, technological advances, and conflicts among nation-states may increase, communities are likely to see increasing risks. Those risks may come from their environment, a legacy of outdated infrastructure, and modern cyber infrastructure or energy grids, or may come from other humans through conflict or sabotage. To become more resilient in the face of those growing risks and increase their likelihood of rebounding successfully after a crisis or disaster, communities and their local governments must learn from their own experiences, their neighbors' experiences, and those of other disaster-affected communities.

The degree and type of learning that they experience is connected to whether and how local governments change policies that can improve their community's resilience. Common lessons from a disaster are relatively simple to incorporate into existing policy regimes, but may not do much to change a community's overall risk profile and move the community closer to resilience. Less common learning that is deep and sustained can lead to more substantive changes but is difficult to achieve. In this book, the factors that can make such learning more common are presented. The framework and recommendations presented in this concluding chapter are designed with the intention of contributing to community-level governance and learning that can help achieve resilience. While risks will not decrease for communities – regardless of whether they sit along coastlines, in drought-stricken regions, in the wildland-urban interface, or in floodplains – the capacity of humans to adapt and change in the face of risks is potentially profound. While the Colorado communities described in this book demonstrated varying levels of learning, some communities successfully built back more resilient than prior to the 2013 floods. Such changes are not easy to accomplish or even expected. But, this possibility of change makes otherwise dire future scenarios more optimistic. With the types of learning and change discussed in these pages, communities can and must become places where their residents can live and thrive even in the face of increasing risks.

11.1 Community-Level Learning after Disaster: A Summary

The book presents a study of disaster recovery in communities across Colorado, United States, after extreme flooding in 2013. These floods caused vast and varied damage across the seven study communities, which had different levels of pre-disaster capacity. The resources – including financial, human, technical, and civic – that communities built after disaster were important to their recovery. At the individual level within communities, the beliefs and risk perceptions held by community members, along with the trust that they have in their local governments, are critical to understanding the support that local governments enjoy in their post-disaster recovery planning processes. The book also examines the relationships between state and local governments, along with the groups and coalitions of actors that engage in policy activity after disasters. The participatory processes established by governments after disaster prove to be an important factor in the learning that local governments see. All of these factors combine to influence the extent of learning that communities experience after disaster. That learning can lead to policy changes, which in turn can help build resilience to future and ongoing risks that a community faces. Chapter 9 presented a framework that combines these factors to understand how learning after a disaster can increase.

11.2 Recommendations

Despite their potentially devastating effects, disasters can afford learning opportunities for communities. The recommendations given here can assist public servants – emergency managers, town administrators, state agency personnel, and myriad others – in establishing processes and helping create the factors that can aid in catalyzing learning within communities and governments. These recommendations are offered with the goal of furthering community-level resilience and the changes necessary to accomplish resilience-building. The following recommendations are based on the findings presented throughout this book and the framework presented in Chapter 9. These recommendations are tailored toward local officials, but through viewing them as scalable to other jurisdictions, state government officials can also adapt them for their use.

While the hazards a community faces and the severity of a disaster are only partially within the power of a community to mitigate, the other characteristics discussed in this concluding chapter provide local governments and decision-makers with opportunities to build resilience by increasing their likelihood of learning and making policy changes prior to a disaster rather than waiting for one to strike. If practitioners hope to increase the likelihood of successful community recovery from disaster as well as increase resilience to ongoing and future risks, these recommendations can help build the community characteristics that increase success as well as the organizational capacity needed to support such processes. Resilience-building through learning and policy change need not wait for a disaster but can be a continual effort within a community. Reflecting on the disaster cycle discussed in Chapter 1, if communities are continually in some disaster-related phase – including preparedness, response, recovery, and mitigation – then there are ongoing opportunities for communities to work to enhance or create the characteristics identified in this book as important to the learning necessary for resilience-building.

11.2.1 Existing Internal Community Characteristics

11.2.1.1 Improve Community Resilience and Relationships

1. Identify existing relationships in the community – with residents, businesses, civil society organizations, faith-based groups, and others – who will be important points-of-contact after a disaster to access, engage, and communicate with various segments of the population.
2. Work with trusted leaders within neighborhoods and segments of the community rather than relying only on government-run or established leadership to promote resilience-building. Expand beyond already-established commissions and task forces to include diverse demographic segments of the community, business owners from various types of businesses (large, small, various sectors, etc.), and other nongovernmental organizations and groups.

3. Conduct a hazard identification and risk assessment to clearly identify the variety of risks that the community faces, including potential compounding risks (e.g., wildfire + public health risks). Grant funding is often available to assist with this process and some states provide technical assistance for such work.

4. Train local government personnel in resilience concepts, particularly those related to community resilience that encompass aspects such as the natural environment, infrastructure, social capital and government relationships with the community, housing, public health, education and welfare, and economic health of the community. By understanding resilience holistically, government departments and personnel not traditionally viewed within the resilience framework can begin to see themselves as part of this important work.

11.2.1.2 Disaster Preparedness

1. Have both an emergency plan and a recovery plan in place prior to a disaster to work with constituents and identify community segments that may be most affected by a disaster.

2. Conduct a disaster recovery planning process *prior to a disaster event*, similar to existing disaster preparedness processes but including the processes and personnel that will guide recovery.

3. Work to develop a strategic and specific plan to identify, build, and strengthen relationships to work with diverse segments of the community during disaster planning and recovery. In this planning process, be sure to include various sectors, types of organizations and groups, and residents from various neighborhoods, backgrounds, and demographics.

4. Seek assistance from faith-based organizations, businesses, and community nonprofits that are already working with residents who face barriers to accessing government aid programs and decision-making processes.

5. Where appropriate, work across governmental departments, such as human services, health, animal control, and code enforcement, to find points of positive engagement with residents regarding risk and resilience.

6. Invest in digital infrastructure and equipment that synchronizes with federal procurement processes to save time and resources during disaster response and recovery.

11.2.1.3 Government Capacity

1. Incorporate disaster finance planning in all government departments rather than sequestering the skills only within a single department. Consider requiring an existing training module (or developing a more robust shared module for communities within a single state) for emergency managers and financial and procurement staff and train them in the requirements for response and recovery documentation.
2. Determine an appropriate level of budget reserves and clearly document the justification for this level so future government staff and elected officials have insight into past budgetary decisions.
3. Include disaster-related skills in personnel decisions – even in non-disaster hiring – such as experience with CDBG applications and management, project management skills, etc.

11.2.2 Disaster-Related Characteristics and Processes

11.2.2.1 Participatory Processes

1. Develop a forum to bring together leaders of existing neighborhood, business, and community groups to facilitate conversations about including diverse residents in planning and advocacy, identifying important mitigation/recovery resources, and partnering within local government and other organizations on recovery goals.
2. Coordinate with groups of diverse stakeholders, such as existing NGOs and businesses, to identify and engage additional community members from risk-prone areas that may be interested in participating in broader planning processes.
3. Think creatively about who, how, and where to engage community members. From little league baseball to churches to homeowner associations, local governments often forget the existing capacity and social ties within their communities that can assist in long-term planning processes.

11.2.2.2 Information Dissemination

1. Develop an outreach plan that uses multiple forms of communication (i.e., digital, traditional, face-to-face, etc.) to create government-to-resident and resident-to-resident networks so that even the most isolated individuals can be reached during disasters.

2. Create a dialogue using multiple methods of communication and education, including methods targeted at specific segments of the community (e.g., children, older adults, immigrants) as well as coordinated efforts throughout the year and during seasonal times when risk increases.
3. Provide opportunities for community members to participate so that local government can listen and learn from their experiences. Information dissemination should be viewed as a two-way process between local governments and their communities.

11.2.2.3 Risk Perception and Causal Connections

1. Maintain an ongoing dialogue between local officials and community members to facilitate in-depth understanding of local hazard risks and risk reduction strategies.
2. Capitalize on residents' direct experiences with hazards to learn more about potential high-risk areas; incorporate these residents into the process of developing risk reduction tools such as hazard maps.
3. Make risk maps available to the public, using simple color-coding or other systems, so that individuals can clearly see their own risk as well as their neighborhood and community risks.

11.2.3 External Influences

11.2.3.1 Resources for Disaster Recovery

1. Connect with businesses, nonprofits, and other nongovernmental groups with access to funding beyond that which is available internally to investigate opportunities for collaboration on planning and recovery projects, especially those that span jurisdictions or fall outside local government priority areas.
2. Establish relationships with business organizations that can support disaster planning and recovery through funding and collaboration on rebuilding projects, planning processes, and other areas where resources such as technical, fiscal, and personnel are vital and can be supplemented by organizations outside of government.

11.2.3.2 Intergovernmental Relationships

1. Develop pre-disaster relationships and formal partnerships (e.g., MOUs) between larger- and smaller-capacity governments to aid

smaller communities, including with fiscal management, during disasters.

2. Work with state government contacts to make sure local government personnel understand the processes, requirements, and other details that the state government will use during and after a disaster.

11.3 Study Limitations and Future Directions

The study of seven Colorado communities after a disaster presented in this book helps move disaster research forward. In two primary ways the study expands upon our current state of knowledge. First, many disaster studies focus on single cases of disaster events within individual communities or nations (Klinenberg, 2003; Muñoz & Tate, 2016; Rivera & Nickels, 2014; C. B. Rubin et al., 1985; Wilson, 2009). This study reaches beyond the single-case analysis approach that is common and necessary in much of the discipline to offer a cross-case analysis of a single disaster event across a region. This helped provide comparative analyses of the factors that make community-level learning more common after a disaster. Second, this study moves the literature forward by focusing on local-level learning rather than national-level government learning after disasters. The literature on national-level learning after disaster forms the foundation of much of what we know in the field – and of this book – which provides an opportunity to fill the important gap of knowledge wherein local governments who are most affected by disasters have not been studied as extensively as other governmental scales. Analyses of national-level policies that emerge or change after disaster frequently do not explicitly address the roles of public and public perceptions, or resources in policy learning. The prior disaster literature also does not focus attention on intergovernmental relationships or collaborations within a disaster policy subsystem as broad as a community to the extent done here. Rather, it focuses on more narrow communities of policy actors and decision-makers. The framework in Chapter 9 moves the field forward by focusing on local-level government learning after disasters.

Despite these important contributions, this study – like any – has limitations that pose opportunities for future research. Because this study focuses on community-level factors and questions, it does not examine each factor in as much depth as it might if it were the sole focus of the study. For example, in a study that focuses exclusively on risk perceptions, or singularly on participatory processes after disasters, the findings may be far more nuanced. This provides an opportunity for scholars to dissect, clarify, and expand the framework presented in Chapter 9 to understand each mechanism of community-level learning to a greater extent. Additionally, this study focuses on flood disasters in one U.S. state. As such, there are ample opportunities to explore, test, and expand upon the findings presented in this book in different geographical locations, in different disaster contexts, to other hazards, and beyond the United States. Whereas the bulk of the book focuses on learning within individual communities, research is needed to more clearly elucidate and understand when and how learning occurs among communities after disaster. Finally, while the book attempts to examine the role of a variety of stakeholders in community-level disaster recovery processes, studies could examine each sector in more fine-grained detail by focusing exclusively on one, from businesses and faith-based groups to civil society groups. This would move the literature forward in important ways since much of the work done on these various groups and organizations has been conducted focused on disaster response rather than longer-term recovery efforts.

Our hope is that students, scholars, and practitioners can take lessons from this study to understand and improve community-level pre-disaster planning and post-disaster processes. By making improvements – and investigating the links and causal connections between the factors discussed in this book – we hope that understanding and practice of disaster governance at the community level can improve so that communities across the globe can reduce their vulnerability to risks that they face. This is critically important as risks increase due to climate change, population growth, and other natural and human-caused factors.

Appendix A
Research Design and Methods

A.1 Colorado's 2013 Floods: A Multi-method Comparative Case Study

The framework for community-level learning after disasters presented in this book – and the specific findings that inform the framework – was developed based on a study funded by the National Science Foundation's Infrastructure, Management, and Extreme Events Program (award #1461923 and #1461565). Chapter 2 describes the disaster case study, the 2013 Colorado floods, in depth. From that case, a comparative multi-method case study research design to study learning after disaster in local governments was developed (Yin, 2003, 2013). Communities were selected for inclusion in the study from Colorado's three hardest-hit counties (Federal Emergency Management Agency, 2013). The comparative case analysis of seven communities allowed examination of the internal community and government characteristics, external influences, and disaster-related dynamics associated with learning after a disaster event.

This research design allows for case variation based on size of community and associated local government capacity, extent of disaster damage incurred, and community demographics. Table A.1 presents basic characteristics of each community, including the damage experienced from the floods. Damage estimates based on interviews with disaster recovery personnel as well as FEMA and local government documents were gathered between September 2013 and September 2016. The number of people interviewed during each of three rounds of in-depth interviews for each community is also listed in the table.

Table A.1. *Community characteristics, damage, and interview subjects*

County (2014 pop.)	Community	Approx. size (2010 census)	Approx. size (2014 census)	Extent and type of flood damage	Interviews conducted Round 1: 24 Round 2: 24 Round 3: 23
State of Colorado		5,029,196	5,264,890[b]	Extensive damage along major urban corridor to residential, commercial, and infrastructure	0 R1 2 R2 3 R3(3 new)
Boulder (313,333)	Boulder	101,800	105,112	Moderate infrastructure and residential damage in specific zones	4 R1 5 R2 (4) 6 R3 (1 new)
	Longmont	88,600	90,237	Significant damage to infrastructure and moderate damage to residential in specific zones	6 R1 4 R2 (0 new) 3 R3 (1 new)
	Lyons[a]	2,000	2,102	Significant damage to infrastructure and residential, extensive throughout town	2 R1 2 R2 (1 new) 3 R3 (2 new)
Larimer (324,122)	Estes Park	6,000	6,165	Minor to moderate damage to residential, infrastructure, and commercial in specific zones	3 R1 4 R2 (1 new) 3 R3 (1 new)

Loveland	67,039	72,651	Moderate damage to infrastructure and commercial in specific zones	5 R1 2 R2 (1 new) 3 R3 (1 new)
Weld (277,670) Evans	19,500	20,473	Significant damage to infrastructure and residential in specific zones	3 R1 5 R2 (2 new) 3 R3 (2 new)
Greeley	95,300	98,596	No lasting damage	1 R1 2 R2 (1 new) 2 R3 (1 new)

[a] Data for Lyons, CO, was obtained from www.City-Data.com.
[b] 2014 data from Colorado State Demographer: https://demography.dola.colorado.gov/demography.

A.2 Concepts, Variables, and Data Used for Measurement

Throughout this book, concepts were presented to study whether and how local governments learned after Colorado's 2013 floods and what types of learning occurred. To understand this learning, changes in policies were examined along with the depth and subject of learning. For example, more in-depth learning about the causes and long-term risk of floods may lead a local government to change policies that relate to building and planning in order to become more resilient to future extreme events like the 2013 floods. Chapters 3–8 then examine specific characteristics of the community disaster recovery process to understand the factors that help influence learning within local governments. Table A.2 presents these concepts – or the variables embedded in the research questions that guide this study – along with an explanation of the concept and the data source(s) that this analysis drew from to examine each variable. The following section explains each data collection and analysis method used in the study identified in Table A.2. Finally, this appendix includes the descriptive tables from the two surveys described here.

A.3 Data Collection and Analysis Methods

The comparative case study research design was constructed to draw upon multiple sources of data to allow comparison of multiple communities (and their local governments) but also understand the nuance within each community. Four sources of data were collected for this study: (1) in-depth interviews with key disaster recovery personnel in both state and local governments; (2) all documents from local government city councils, boards, and commissions related to disaster recovery and planning; (3) resident surveys in six of the study communities; and (4) local official surveys in all seven communities. Each data source and the analytic methods used is described in the sections to follow.

A.3.1 Metadata for Study

While the data collection and analysis methods are described here, to replicate any aspects of this study, researchers will also need the instruments used for data collection and document coding. Those metadata, along with published findings, and a practitioner-oriented report are available on the National Science Foundation-funded

Table A.2. *Concepts, definition, and data sources*

Concept	Definition	Data source(s)
Guiding concepts (outcome variables)		
Learning	Uptake of new information that leads to revisions in goals, policies, or other governmental procedures	Documents Interviews Surveys
Policy change	Changes to existing policies or adoptions of new policies	Documents
Part II (Chapters 3 and 4)		
Damage	Type (sector) and extent of damage incurred from the flood disaster	Documents Interviews Surveys
Resources	Capacity in the areas of financial, human, technical, and civic held by a community before or after a disaster	Documents Interviews Surveys
Part III (Chapters 5 and 6)		
Risk perceptions	Individual belief about future risk from extreme floods	Surveys
Causal beliefs	Individual belief about the causes of the 2013 floods	Surveys
Trust	Individual opinion about the trustworthiness of their local government or other actors	Surveys
Policy support	Individual opinion about the benefit of new policies or processes local governments established after the floods	Surveys
Problem severity	Individual belief about the severity of the 2013 floods	Surveys
Part IV (Chapters 7 and 8)		
Intergovernmental relationships	Interactions between government entities along a continuum of cooperative to conflictual, also examined according to the dependence of one government on the other for resources	Documents Interviews
Coalitions		Interviews

Table A.2. (*cont.*)

Concept	Definition	Data source(s)
	Groups of actors working together to achieve a goal during disaster recovery	
Participatory processes	Processes instituted by local governments to solicit information, deliberate about planning, or engage external stakeholders in decision-making during disaster recovery	Documents Interviews Surveys

project website Learning from Disasters: www.learningfromdisasters .org/researchers/flood_metadata.html.

A.3.2 In-Depth interviews

In each study community, three rounds of in-depth semi-structured interviews (H. J. Rubin & Rubin, 2005) were conducted. The first round of interviews took place as each community completed emergency response and began disaster recovery in late 2013. The second and third rounds of interviews were conducted in early 2016 and 2017. Due to personnel changes, changes in organizational structures, and hiring of dedicated flood personnel in some communities, interview subjects in Rounds 1, 2, and 3 overlap but are not identical.

Additionally, state personnel working on flood recovery were conducted in 2016 ($n = 2$) and 2017 ($n = 3$). These interview participants include the personnel most involved with disaster recovery decision-making and local government outreach for the State of Colorado who worked for the agencies charged with disaster finance, emergency management, and local government support. The State of Colorado focused its flood recovery efforts among personnel in the Governor's Office (then called the Office of Resiliency and Recovery), the Department of Local Affairs, and the Division of Homeland Security and Emergency Management.

All interviews were conducted in person or via video conference (interview subject pools are listed in Table A.1), digitally recorded, and transcribed verbatim. Interview questions asked about flood damages, flood recovery processes and decisions, and in-depth information on specific policy actors and actions within each community and statewide.

A.3.2.1 Interview Coding and Analysis

Interview transcripts were coded manually using NVivo 11 software. Codes for the variables analyzed in the study were developed from the literature. Coding of interview data involved a process by which coders developed and discussed a codebook based on literature and theoretical concepts, conducted pilot coding, discussed the coding choices among several researchers until agreement among coders was reached, and then individually coded transcripts by hand to categorize interview data into bins or codes (Auerbach & Silverstein, 2003; M. B. Miles, Huberman, & Saldaña, 2013; Weston et al., 2001).

Using NVivo, coding involved categorizing content found in interview transcripts into corresponding digital "bins" where all related content is stored. After transcripts were coded, researchers revisited the bins of interview data that corresponded to each code. Coders then employed a constant comparative approach to analyze coded data, where in-depth narratives of individual cases (e.g., communities) were developed to explore the nature of each case study fully. These narratives were used to compare communities and discover cross-case patterns according to the topical codes. Using these analytical procedures of coding, developing case narratives, and searching for cross-case patterns, researchers developed the findings presented in this book (M. B. Miles et al., 2013). When quotations from interviews are used in the book, alphanumeric identifiers are used to attach the quotation to an interview subject within a specific community. The alpha portion of the ID is the community (LY = Lyons, for example), while the numeric portion is the interview subject number. The ID is always attached to the same individual through multiple years of interviews. For subject confidentiality and to conform to Institutional Review Board requirements to protect human subjects, individuals are not identified in the research reports published from this study.

A.3.3 Documents

All documents related to flood management planning, emergency response, evaluation of policies, and community responses to the floods were collected from the date of flood occurrence (September

11, 2013) through September 15, 2016. The document dataset includes local government outreach, city/town council minutes and memos, planning session documents, and other documents as appropriate to each community (n = 1,825). Documents were accessed from local government websites for all boards, commissions, task forces, or city/town councils in each community.

In addition to the general governmental documents, financial reporting documents for each community were collected. Local governments produce two primary forms of financial reporting documents annually. First is the annual budget, which communicates a community's priorities and is approved by elected officials. The budget is a prospective planning document. Local governments also issue a Comprehensive Annual Financial Report (CAFR) to report actual spending each fiscal year (FY). The CAFR includes a narrative summary of the previous year's spending and important events or decisions, along with actual spending levels.

A.3.3.1 Document Coding and Analysis

Documents were used to understand multiple aspects of disaster recovery and learning in this study. The primary difference with the document coding approach (compared with interview coding explained earlier) is that it was categorical, where coders used drop-down lists in spreadsheet columns to assign a code to documents for each question prompt.

Policy Change and Learning Coding. Policy changes identified in documents were categorized according to the presence or absence of the following: (1) goals and goal revision, (2) policy failures (inadequacies of past policies), and (3) specific lessons drawn related to needed policy improvements (e.g., processes or procedures) as indicated by the explanations found in meeting minutes, agendas, and similar documents. Policy change was coded when final decisions to enact (or not) new or revised policies were observed in documents. Discussions of policy changes were coded and referenced when coding for final policy decisions, which is relevant to sustained attention on various discussions of policy change.

Two researchers coded policy changes after pilot coding sessions to create a common understanding of categories of codes, subjectivity, and other potential problems, as recommended in similar studies (Lyles & Stevens, 2014; Stevens, Lyles, & Berke, 2014). The coded data about policy change were then linked to learning by classifying the types of policy changes observed according to the types of learning outlined in Chapter 1. Specifically, researchers considered whether policy changes represented an attempt to address a discrete or limited problem through a new strategy, an administrative change (both indicating instrumental learning or organizational learning), learning about relationships or strategies to use with other actors and organization, or whether it indicated a more systemic type of change (which could indicate social learning). The "Measurements of Learning" presented in Chapter 1 were used to develop the document codebook researchers used to measure policy change, while the types of disaster learning presented by Birkland were used to connect the coded policy changes to categories of learning experienced by local governments.

Analysis of Financial Data and Policies. Financial documents from the flood-affected communities were used to determine the relative magnitude of the disaster across the communities and how the key financial policies changed in the years during and following the flood event. Specifically, financial data, policies, and flood response information were collected from 2011 to 2015 to allow researchers to understand pre-disaster financial conditions as well as post-disaster changes. CAFRs were the primary source of data used since they detail actual spending levels and categories, but for fiscal years (FY) 2016 and 2017, annual budgets were used since CAFR data were not available at the time of the study. Colorado local governments use the calendar year as their FY. For the analysis, the pre-flood comparison period generally includes the 2011 and 2012 FYs, while the flood/post-flood period represents 2013 and 2014.

A financial flood impact measure was created by comparing the response and recovery spending reported to FEMA for public assistance reimbursement to the average annual governmental expenditures of the two years prior to the flood event. Estimated state and federal reimbursement rates supplement this information to build a complete picture of financial impact. Local governments depend, in part, on financial reserves (or fund balance) to provide additional resources during a current budget cycle for disaster response and recovery. The level of reserves a local government has is guided by a local government's existing financial policies. The most appropriate measure of reserves available for emergencies is the unrestricted general fund balance from the Governmental Funds Balance Sheet (Marlowe, 2012).

A.3.4 *Surveys*

A.3.4.1 Resident Survey

A random survey of residents was conducted in six flood-affected communities in Colorado in 2016 and 2017 according to standard survey design methods (Dillman, Smyth, & Christian, 2014). The sampling frame for the resident survey was developed using geographic information systems (GIS)-based data of residential parcel ownership and 2013 county-based flood inundation maps. Residents who rent were included in the sampling frame by mailing the survey notification and survey instrument to the physical address of the land parcel listed in the GIS database. Because of a relatively high rate of nonresident property ownership in Estes Park, surveys were mailed to nonresident property owners. When flood inundation maps were not available from counties, inundation was estimated from municipal floodplain maps and aerial photos. Flood inundation data served as one measure of physical flood exposure in the analysis. The inundation data only captured flooding from the 2013 event and not any previous or later flooding.

From the GIS data, 500 residences in each of six communities (Boulder, Longmont, Lyons, Estes Park, Loveland, and Evans) were randomly selected across two stratifications: inundated residences and noninundated residences. In each community, 150 residences were sampled from flood-inundated areas and 350 from noninundated zones for each round of the survey to ensure an overall sample of flooded households would be adequately large to detect differences between flood-affected and unaffected residents. Residents received at least three mail contacts inviting them to participate in an online or paper survey. A total of 903 responses were collected across the six communities for an overall response rate of approximately 17 percent.

The resident survey included questions about: (1) perceived damages resulting from the floods, (2) perceived future flood risks, (3) policy preferences for managing future flood risks, (4) trust in government officials and nongovernmental organizations, (5) deeply held beliefs about relationship between humans and the earth (New Ecological Paradigm), (6) participation in flood recovery processes, and (7) home and personal demographics.

A.3.4.2 Local Official Survey

A second survey focused on local officials with formal responsibilities related to flood disaster recovery took place annually for three years following the floods. The respondents included staff and board members from municipal administration (e.g., city manager), emergency management, public works, planning, transportation, boards, and commissions. In communities with flood recovery task force(s), task force members were included as well. The design and implementation of the survey followed recommendations by Dillman, Smyth, and Christian (2014), beginning with a pilot survey test and multiple survey contacts to encourage higher response rates. The survey sample population was contacted three times via email and once via telephone.

Across the three years of the survey, 248 responses were collected (*n* = 189 individuals). Some individuals filled out the survey in all three years, while most answered the survey once or twice, so data are not treated as panel data in the analysis. Average response rates varied from roughly 35.6 percent (2015) to 21.5 percent (2016), typical of response rates in other local-level public official surveys in policy fields (Brody et al., 2010; Robinson & Eller, 2010). The survey included questions focused on: (1) flood damage severity, (2) resource availability and changes in resources after the floods, (3) involvement in discussion of pre-flood policies with various entities, (4) alterations of policies, or (5) adoption of new policies after the floods.

A.3.4.3 Survey Descriptive Statistics

Descriptive statistics for the resident survey are included in Tables A.4, A.5, and A.6. Table A.3 includes data from both the resident and local official surveys.

Survey questions and summary statistics are listed in the tables to follow. On a scale of one (no damage) to seven (complete loss), the average personal property damage reported was 1.85, with mean neighborhood damage of 2.84, and community damage of 4.83. Survey respondents were asked a series of questions to capture their flood-related beliefs about problem severity ("Flooding in my community is a severe problem.") and causal beliefs (including rainfall, inadequate floodplain regulations, floodplain development, deforestation, land-use changes, and global climate change). Each of these questions

Table A.3. *Survey response rates for both waves of community resident survey and local official survey*

Community	Response rate 2016 (%)	Response rate 2017 (%)	Local official survey
Boulder	16.5	22.2	28
Longmont	11.6	16.6	15
Lyons	19.2	30.0	28
Estes Park	13.2	30.0	12
Loveland	10.4	30.0	7
Evans	6.9	16.8	8
Greeley	N/A	N/A	9

Table A.4. *Summary statistics of demographic survey measures from resident surveys*

Variable	Obs.	%
Male	824	49.8
Republican	790	17.9
Bachelor's degree	831	23.6
Own	903	93.0
House	739	81.8
Flood zone location	848	23.0

was measured on a scale of one to five, with five being the highest level of perceived problem severity or cause of the floods. Mean problem severity was 2.89, slightly lower than a neutral response. Extreme rainfall (mean of 4.64 of 5) was rated the highest of potential causes, with development in the floodplain (mean of 3.44) and global climate change (mean 3.25) as the second and third highest rated causes of flooding. Residents were also asked about levels of trust in government officials (local staff and mayors) in managing floods (Table A.5). The

Table A.5. *Summary statistics of damage, ecological worldview, participation, information acquisition, and sense of being informed*

Variable	Obs.	Mean	Median	SD
Damage personal property	884	1.85	1	1.48
Damage neighborhood	873	2.84	3	1.75
Damage community	870	4.83	5	1.47
Views interfere	824	3.76	4	1.01
Views modify	810	2.66	3	1.08
Views control	802	2.18	2	0.946
Trust in mayor	787	3.22	3	1.01
Trust in local staff	820	3.31	4	0.976
Participation	860	2.03	1	1.34
Information acquisition	896	1.30	1	1.29
Sense of being informed	868	3.65	4	0.962

information acquisition measure was a composite measure of yes/no responses to capture whether the resident sought flood-related information from five sources (community website, State of Colorado, FEMA, Facebook, and Twitter).

A.3.4.4 Survey Analysis Methodological Approach
This section provides an overview of the approach used to analyze survey data and measurements. Specific model results and analytical findings reported in the previous chapters are presented in Appendix B. Several specific survey questions are important to discuss here as they relate to the analysis conducted. These survey measures focused on policy preferences and disaster damage estimates beyond the perceived damage as asked in the survey.

Resident Policy Preferences. The resident survey contained questions designed to capture respondent flood recovery policy preferences. These policies included (1) removal of damaged homes from the 100-year floodplain, (2) removal of commercial buildings from the 100-year floodplain, (3) new building codes for buildings in the floodplain, (4) development bans within the 100-year floodplain, (5) new

Table A.6. *Risk perceptions: mean response of residents and local officials across seven communities about perceptions of future flood risk and severity of the problem*

		Percent chance extreme flood in community	Percent chance extreme flood in Colorado	Risk of flooding in community increased over past twenty years (Scale: 1–5)	Risk of flooding in Colorado increased past twenty years (Scale: 1–5)	Flooding in community is a severe problem (Scale: 1–5)
Boulder	Public (n = 172)	33.1	53.0	3.5	3.5	2.8
	Local officials (n = 28)	36.3	61.8	3.7	3.7	3.9
Longmont	Public (n = 107)	24.8	42.3	3.1	3.2	2.4
	Local officials (n = 15)	37.7	65.8	3.8	3.8	3.4
Lyons	Public (n = 176)	32.9	55.6	3.5	3.6	3.3
	Local officials (n = 28)	32.7	53.8	3.8	3.9	3.9
Estes Park	Public (n = 134)	42.0	57.1	3.5	3.5	3.0
	Local officials (n = 12)	36.6	68.2	3.6	3.8	3.8

Loveland	Public (n = 106)	38.5	57.6	4.3	3.4	2.6
	Local officials (n = 7)	51.4	77.6	3.4	3.4	3.0
Evans	Public (n = 85)	47.4	67.1	3.6	3.6	3.0
	Local officials (n = 8)	50.1	70.4	4.0	4.1	3.4
Greeley	Local officials (n = 9)	25.4	40.8	2.6	2.6	1.9
Overall	Public (n = 787)	35.9	55.1	3.4	3.5	2.9
	Local officials (n = 111)	36.9	61.2	3.6	3.7	3.6

emergency response policies, and (6) decreased impervious surfaces. On average, respondents showed the highest overall support for new building codes for buildings located in the 100-year floodplain. Across all measures, support was weakest for decreasing impervious surfaces, with an overall mean of 3.00 (SD = 1.05), a neutral score.

Appendix B
Models and Analyses

The following tables present modeling for various analyses discussed in Chapters 5, 6, and 10. The tables using survey data collected in six study communities (see Appendix A for methodology) display model results that predict respondents' post-flood information acquisition (Table B.1), trust in local officials (Table B.2), perceptions of problem severity (Table B.2), risk perceptions (Table B.2), and policy preferences (Table B.3). This appendix also includes a description of the survey methodology used to collect data in the Columbia, South Carolina, case described in Chapter 10. Descriptive statistics (Table B.4) and modeling results (Table B.5) from South Carolina are also included.

Chapter 10 includes a discussion of disaster recovery across several disaster contexts outside of Colorado, including flooding from Hurricane Joaquin that struck the U.S. Southeast in October of 2015. The summary statistics in Table B.4 and models in Table B.5 were developed using survey data collected from flood survivors after Hurricane Joaquin damaged many neighborhoods in Columbia, South Carolina. In South Carolina, the community of Columbia was selected for survey recruitment based on (1) the extent of flood damage incurred and (2) the socioeconomics of affected neighborhoods. A mobile behavioral research lab enabled travel to offsite locations, allowing for data collection to occur in proximity to flood survivors. While random selection of research participants is nearly impossible in a post-disaster setting, researchers attempted to include individuals from socioeconomically diverse neighborhoods and to seek variation

Table B.1. *Fixed effects ordinal logistic regression predicting*
information acquisition

Variables	Information acquisition
Year 2017	1.047***
	(0.170)
Male	−0.234
	(0.195)
Bachelor's degree	0.416*
	(0.240)
Republican	−0.606**
	(0.288)
Damage to personal property	0.147***
	(0.0531)
Damage neighborhood	−0.0206
	(0.0423)
Damage community	0.267*
	(0.143)
Trust staff	−0.0969
	(0.154)
Trust mayor	−0.0442
	(0.0939)
Trust county	0.121
	(0.128)
Trust State of Colorado	−0.0112
	(0.176)
Trust federal government	0.126
	(0.0871)
Observations	655
Log pseudolikelihood	−966.68
AIC	1,943.37

Note: Bolded variables were found to be statistically significant at an alpha of 0.05.

Table B.2. *Fixed effects ordinal logistic models predicting (1) trust in local government staff, (2) trust in mayor, and (3) perceptions of problem severity, and (4) fixed effects regression model predicting future flood risk*

Variables	(1) Trust staff	(2) Trust mayor	(3) Problem severity	(4) Perception of future flood risk in Colorado
Year	−0.547***	−0.404**	−0.0445	−1.307
	(0.203)	(0.193)	(0.187)	(1.636)
Male	−0.245	−0.233	−0.0867	−4.410*
	(0.213)	(0.174)	(0.165)	(1.946)
Bachelor's degree	0.547***	0.563***	0.176	0.993
	(0.166)	(0.149)	(0.214)	(0.936)
Republican	−0.141*	−0.0351	−0.184	−1.120
	(0.0910)	(0.184)	(0.204)	(2.051)
Damage personal	−0.100	−0.0539	−0.0307	−2.209***
	(0.129)	(0.0663)	(0.0446)	(0.438)
Damage neighborhood	−0.116***	−0.136**	−0.00371	0.587
	(0.0397)	(0.0593)	(0.0385)	(0.441)
Damage community	−0.0633	0.0337	0.229***	2.358***
	(0.0662)	(0.0857)	(0.0732)	(0.577)
Trust staff			−0.267*	1.294
			(0.140)	(0.948)
Trust mayor			0.0368	−1.957
			(0.0949)	(0.977)
Deep core modify	−0.130***	−0.0745*	−0.182***	−1.682*
	(0.0365)	(0.0520)	(0.0657)	(0.715)
Deep core interfere	−0.0230	0.0317	0.197***	3.736***
	(0.0355)	(0.101)	(0.0594)	(0.785)
Deep core control	0.0412	−0.0319	0.123	−1.866
	(0.130)	(0.0941)	(0.114)	(1.388)

Table B.2. (*cont.*)

Variables	(1) Trust staff	(2) Trust mayor	(3) Problem severity	(4) Perception of future flood risk in Colorado
Information acquisition	−0.0348 (0.0657)	−0.0207 (0.0918)	0.164 (0.120)	2.645*** (0.456)
Informed	0.379*** (0.122)	0.269* (0.142)	0.0483 (0.123)	−0.0355 (1.065)
Participation	0.0556 (0.0924)	−0.00832 (0.127)	0.159** (0.0712)	−0.973 (1.051)
Coefficient				44.21*** (8.055)
Observations	674	647	631	627
Log likelihood	−839.96	−848.86	−886.44	−2,942.45
AIC	1,689.93	1,707.72	1,782.88	5,894.91

Note: Bolded variables were found to be statistically significant at an alpha of 0.05.

Table B.3. *Fixed effects ordered logistic models predicting policy support of (1) no new development in 100-year floodplain, (2) removal of damaged homes from 100-year floodplain, (3) reduced amount of paved area in community, and (4) new emergency response policies*

Variables	(1) Floodplain development	(2) Floodplain damage home removal	(3) Decrease impervious surface	(4) New emergency response
Male	0.407 (0.286)	0.282 (0.439)	−0.130 (0.264)	−0.189 (0.289)

Table B.3. (*cont.*)

Variables	(1) Floodplain development	(2) Floodplain damage home removal	(3) Decrease impervious surface	(4) New emergency response
Bachelor's degree	0.415	0.0681	0.626	0.324
	(0.338)	(0.262)	(0.541)	(0.281)
Republican	−0.529***	−0.0468	−0.0329	0.0669
	(0.191)	(0.218)	(0.296)	(0.241)
Damage personal	−0.0544	0.0194479	0.0350	0.0686
	(0.106)	(0.166)	(0.111)	(0.136)
Damage neighborhood	−0.116	−0.326**	−0.0337	−0.0535
	(0.0919)	(0.141)	(0.121)	(0.147)
Damage community	0.143***	0.107	0.00888	−0.264
	(0.0478)	(0.0837)	(0.0797)	(0.162)
Deep core modify	−0.215	−0.168	0.237	0.0811*
	(0.108)	(0.115)	(0.121)	(0.168)
Deep core interfere	0.217	0.235	0.495***	0.242***
	(0.151)	(0.190)	(0.111)	(0.115)
Deep core control	−0.213***	−0.0178	−0.132	0.242
	(0.0501)	(0.132)	(0.138)	(0.115)
Trust staff	0.0247	0.350	0.0591	0.211
	(0.209)	(0.393)	(0.222)	(0.272)
Trust mayor	−0.0103	−0.168	−0.113	−0.161
	(0.276)	(0.225)	(0.218)	(0.245)
Information total	−0.180*	−0.0855	−0.0703	0.246
	(0.0965)	(0.0872)	(0.0991)	(0.178)
Informed	0.0923	−0.235	−0.0427	−0.459**
	(0.144)	(0.174)	(0.173)	(0.210)
Participation	0.0178	0.117	−0.0415	0.0506
	(0.0755)	(0.123)	(0.0651)	(0.0868)
Problem severity	0.167	0.0922	0.321***	0.460***
	(0.146)	(0.0529)	(0.0954)	(0.139)
Cause: rainfall	−0.0253	0.0903	−0.0376	0.252**
	(0.120)	(0.231)	(0.131)	(0.127)
Cause: Inadequate floodplain regulations	0.421**	0.771***	0.00159	0.627***
	(0.190)	(0.124)	(0.140)	(0.0871)
Cause: floodplain development	0.0869	−0.169	0.111	−0.182**
	(0.218)	(0.159)	(0.162)	(0.0781)

Table B.3. (*cont.*)

Variables	(1) Floodplain development	(2) Floodplain damage home removal	(3) Decrease impervious surface	(4) New emergency response
Cause: deforestation	−0.0477 (0.251)	−0.0217 (0.157)	0.0622 (0.119)	−0.187 (0.142)
Cause: land use	−0.00539 (0.176)	−0.113 (0.143)	0.326 (0.275)	0.298 (0.283)
Cause: global climate change	−0.00163 (0.106)	−0.0478 (0.0831)	0.183 (0.194)	0.0223 (0.239)
Observations	247	246	247	245
Log pseudolikelihood	−347.69	−335.82	−335.53	−273.21
AIC	705.39	681.63	681.06	556.4155

Note: Bolded variables were found to be statistically significant at an alpha of 0.05.

Table B.4. *Summary statistics of demographics of residents surveyed in Columbia, South Carolina*

Variable	Columbia, SC
# Respondents	103
Probability of extreme flood in the next ten years in state	47.6 (31.2)
Belief that respondent themselves will recover	5.2 (1.7)
Belief that respondents' neighborhood will recover	5.0 (1.9)
Belief that respondents' community will recover	5.0 (1.7)
# Respondents	113
% of respondents who own homes	48.1
% owned homes with pre-flood home value <$200,000	81.6
% of respondents <$25,000 annual income	29.3

Table B.4. (*cont.*)

Variable	Columbia, SC
% College graduate	23.9
% Republican Party affiliation	7.60
% African American	56.1
# Respondents	119
Household flood damage (7-point scale of severity)	3.9
	(2.0)
Neighborhood damage (7-point scale of severity)	4.4
	(1.7)
Community damage (7-point scale of severity)	4.8
	(1.5)

Table B.5. *Fixed effects multiple regression models predicting (1) perception of future flood risk in South Carolina and (2) confidence in community-level recovery*

Variable	(1) Future flood risk	(2) Community recovery
Education (bachelor's degree)	1.80	−0.370
	(7.49)	(0.463)
Income	3.72	0.156
	(1.47)**	(0.106)
Republican	−7.02	1.20
	(10.0)	(0.751)
Male	8.99	0.612
	(6.27)	(0.448)
Home ownership	−24.1	−1.13
	(6.83)***	(0.459)
African American	−23.73	0.898
	(7.64)***	(0.532)*
Perception of damages to personal property	−0.518	0.163
	(1.71)	(0.115)
Perception of damages to neighborhood	−2.00	−0.800
	(2.93)	(0.220)
		***

Table B.5. (*cont.*)

Variable	(1) Future flood risk	(2) Community recovery
Perception of damages to community	5.31	0.212
	(2.99)*	(0.213)
Average home value ($K)	−0.101	0.00564
	(0.116)	(0.00839)
Average FEMA damage estimate	−2.72	−0.429
per damaged household ($K)	(7.51)	(0.554)
Percentage of households in zip code	−0.409	0.00510
that were inspected by FEMA	(0.506)	(0.0356)
Constant	75.1	
	(23.0)***	
Wald Chi2	33.35	27.42
N	88	90
AIC	840.91	323.98

$*p < 0.10, **p < 0.05, ***p < 0.01.$

in flood exposure, gender, race, and age. Surveys were conducted in person twelve weeks after the flooding occurred. The models describe the relationship between a set of demographic variables, flood damages experienced, perceptions of flood risks, and confidence in recovery.

Bibliography

9News. (2013, September 16). Colorado flood: Rebuild likely to take more than a year. Retrieved from https://archive.is/20130917013401/http://www.9news.com/news/article/355407/339/Rebuild-likely-to-take-more-than-a-year

Aakre, S., Banaszak, I., Mechler, R., Rübbelke, D., Wreford, A., & Kalirai, H. (2010). Financial adaptation to disaster risk in the European Union. *Mitigation and Adaptation Strategies for Global Change, 15*(7), 721–736.

About Boulder. (2015). The Great Flood of 1894. *About Boulder.* Retrieved from https://aboutboulder.com/blog/history-of-boulder/the-great-flood-of-1894/

About Longmont. (2021). *City of Longmont, Colorado.* Retrieved from www.visitlongmont.org/plan/about-longmont/

Adams, R. M., Prelip, M. L., Glik, D. C., Donatello, I., & Eisenman, D. P. (2018). Facilitating partnerships with community-and faith-based organizations for disaster preparedness and response: Results of a national survey of public health departments. *Disaster Medicine and Public Health Preparedness, 12*(1), 57–66.

Adeola, F. O., & Picou, J. S. (2017). Hurricane Katrina-linked environmental injustice: Race, class, and place differentials in attitudes. *Disasters, 41*(2), 228–257.

Adger, W. N. (2000). Social and ecological resilience: Are they related? *Progress in Human Geography, 24*(3), 347–364.

  (2003). Social aspects of adaptive capacity. In J. B. Smith, R. J. T. Klein, and S. Huq (Eds.), *Climate change, adaptive capacity and development* (pp. 29–49). London: Imperial Press.

Aguilar, J. (2013, September 13). In the mouth of Boulder Canyon: The aftermath of a 100-year flood. *Daily Camera.* Retrieved from www.dailycamera.com/2013/09/13/in-the-mouth-of-boulder-canyon-the-aftermath-of-a-100-year-flood/

  (2014, September 6). Colorado re-emerging from $2.9 billion flood disaster a year later. *Denver Post.* Retrieved from www.denverpost.com/2014/09/06/colorado-re-emerging-from-2-9-billion-flood-disaster-a-year-later/

(2016, September 17). Three years after the great floods of 2013, much work remains to be done in Colorado – The Denver Post. *Denver Post.* Retrieved from www.denverpost.com/2016/09/17/three-years-after-2013-colorado-flood-reconstruction/

(2018, September 9). Colorado's 2013 flood hit the state 5 years ago this week. *Denver Post.* Retrieved from www.denverpost.com/2018/09/09/colorado-floods-2013-recovery/

Albright, E. A. (2009). *Policy change and policy learning in a new democracy: Response to extreme floods in Hungary.* Durham, NC: Duke University.

(2011). Policy change and learning in response to extreme flood events in Hungary: An advocacy coalition approach. *Policy Studies Journal, 39* (3), 485–511.

Albright, E. A., & Crow, D. A. (2015a). Learning in the aftermath of extreme floods: Community damage and stakeholder perceptions of future risk. *Risk, Hazards & Crisis in Public Policy, 6*(3), 308–328.

(2015b). Learning processes, public and stakeholder engagement: Analyzing responses to Colorado's extreme flood events of 2013. *Urban Climate, 14,* 79–93.

(2019a). Beliefs about climate change in the aftermath of extreme flooding. *Climatic Change, 155,* 1–17.

(2019b). Capacity building toward resilience: How communities recover, learn, and change in the aftermath of extreme events. *Policy Studies Journal, 49*(1).

Albright, E. A., Crow, D. A., & Koebele, E. A. (2019). Elite and public narratives in the aftermath of disasters. Paper presented at the American Political Science Association, Washington, DC.

Aldrich, D. P. (2008). The crucial role of civil society in disaster recovery and Japan's preparedness for emergencies. *Japan aktuell, 3*(2008), 81–96.

(2012). *Building resilience: Social capital in post-disaster recovery.* Chicago: University of Chicago Press.

(2019). *Black wave: How networks and governance shaped Japan's 3/11 disasters.* Chicago: University of Chicago Press.

Aldrich, D. P., & Meyer, M. A. (2015). Social capital and community resilience. *American Behavioral Scientist, 59*(2), 254–269.

Aldrich, D. P., & Ono, Y. (2016). Local politicians as linking social capital: An empirical test of political behavior after Japan's 3/11 disasters. *Natural Hazards, 84*(3), 1637–1659.

Anas, B. (2013, September 12). CU-Boulder to remain closed Friday as crews assess safety hazards, water damage. *Daily Camera.* Retrieved from www.dailycamera.com/2013/09/12/cu-boulder-to-remain-closed-friday-as-crews-assess-safety-hazards-water-damage/

Andrews, R., & Boyne, G. A. (2010). Capacity, leadership, and organizational performance: Testing the black box model of public management. *Public Administration Review, 70*(3), 443–454.

Andrews, R., Boyne, G. A., & Enticott, G. (2006). Performance failure in the public sector: Misfortune or mismanagement? *Public Management Review, 8*(2), 273–296.

Ansell, C., & Gash, A. (2008). Collaborative governance in theory and practice. *Journal of Public Administration Research and Theory, 18* (4), 543–571.

Argyris, C. (1976). Single-loop and double-loop models in research on decision making. *Administrative Science Quarterly, 21*(3), 363–375.

(1977). Double loop learning in organizations. *Harvard Business Review, 55*(5), 115–125.

(2000). Double-loop learning. *Wiley encyclopedia of management.*

(2001). 15 Empowerment: The emperor's new clothes. *Creative Management, 195.*

Arnold, J. L. (1988). *The evolution of the 1936 flood control act.* Retrieved from www.publications.usace.army.mil/Portals/76/Publications/EngineerPamphlets/EP_870-1-29.pdf

Auerbach, C. F., & Silverstein, L. B. (2003). *Qualitative data: An introduction to coding and analysis.* New York: New York University Press.

Baker, D., Hamshaw, S. D., & Hamshaw, K. A. (2014). Rapid flood exposure assessment of Vermont mobile home parks following Tropical Storm Irene. *Natural Hazards Review, 15*(1), 27–37.

Barry, J. M. (2007). *Rising tide: The great Mississippi flood of 1927 and how it changed America.* New York: Simon & Schuster.

Bates, F. L., Fogleman, C. W., Parenton, V. J., Pittman, R. H., & Tracy, G. S., & Disaster Research Group, Division of Anthropology and Psychology. (1963). The social and psychological consequences of a natural disaster: A longitudinal study of Hurricane Audrey. *National Academy of Sciences-National Research Council.* https://doi.org/10.1037/14308-000

Baumgartner, F. R., & Jones, B. D. (2009). *Agendas and instability in American politics* (2nd ed.). Chicago: University of Chicago Press.

(2010). *Agendas and instability in American politics.* Chicago: University of Chicago Press.

Baumgartner, F. R., Jones, B. D., & MacLeod, M. C. (2000). The evolution of legislative jurisdictions. *The Journal of Politics, 62*(2), 321–349. Retrieved from www.jstor.org/stable/2647677

Baumgartner, F. R., Jones, B. D., & Mortensen, P. B. (2014). Punctuated equilibrium theory: Explaining stability and change in public policymaking. *Theories of the Policy Process, 8,* 59–103.

Bea, K. (2010 March). Federal Stafford Act disaster assistance: Presidential declarations, Eligible activities, and funding. Library of Congress Washington DC Congressional Research Service.

Beck, T. E., & Plowman, D. A. (2009). Experiencing rare and unusual events richly: The role of middle managers in animating and guiding organizational interpretation. *Organization Science, 20*(5), 909–924.

Becker, C. (2009). Disaster recovery: A local government responsibility. *Public Management, 91*(2), 6–12.

Bennett, C. J., & Howlett, M. (1992). The lessons of learning: Reconciling theories of policy learning and policy change. *Policy Sciences, 25*(3), 275–294.

Berghuijs, W. R., Woods, R. A., Hutton, C. J., & Sivapalan, M. (2016). Dominant flood generating mechanisms across the United States. *Geophysical Research Letters, 43*(9), 4382–4390.

Berke, P. R., & Beatley, T. (1997). *After the hurricane: Linking recovery to sustainable development in the Caribbean.* Baltimore: Johns Hopkins University Press.

Berke, P. R., & Campanella, T. J. (2006). Planning for postdisaster resiliency. *The Annals of the American Academy of Political and Social Science, 604*(1), 192–207.

Berke, P. R., Kartez, J., & Wenger, D. (1993). Recovery after disaster: Achieving sustainable development, mitigation, and equity. *Disasters, 17*(2), 93–109.

Bianchi, C. (2019a, October 19). Colorado weather: State just recorded its hottest September on record. *Denver Post.* Retrieved from www .denverpost.com/2019/10/19/colorado-weather-hottest-september-on-record/

(2019b, September 8). Colorado weather: Whatever happened to September snowfall in Denver? *Denver Post.* Retrieved from www .denverpost.com/2019/09/08/colorado-weather-september-snowfall-denver/

Birkland, T. A. (1997). *After disaster: Agenda setting, public policy and focusing events.* Washington, DC: Georgetown University Press.

(1998). Focusing events, mobilization, and agenda setting. *Journal of Public Policy, 18*(1), 53–74.

(2004). Learning and policy improvement after disaster. *American Behavioral Scientist, 48*(3), 341–364.

(2006). *Lessons of disaster: Policy change after catastrophic events.* Washington, DC: Georgetown University Press.

Birkland, T. A., Burby, R. J., Conrad, D., Cortner, H., & Michener, W. K. (2003). River ecology and flood hazard mitigation. *Natural Hazards Review, 4*(1), 46–54.

Birkland, T. A., & Warnement, M. K. (2014). Focusing events in disasters and development. In N. Kapucu and K. T. Liou (Eds.), *Disaster and Development* (pp. 39–60). London: Springer.

Birkland, T. A., & Waterman, S. (2008). Is federalism the reason for policy failure in Hurricane Katrina? *Publius: The Journal of Federalism, 38*(4), 692–714.

Boin, A., & Lodge, M. (2016). Designing resilient institutions for transboundary crisis management: A time for public administration. *Public Administration, 94*(2), 289–298.

Boin, A., & Rhinard, M. (2008). Managing transboundary crises: What role for the European Union? *International Studies Review, 10*(1), 1–26.

Bolin, B., & Kurtz, L. C. (2018). Race, class, ethnicity, and disaster vulnerability. In H. Rodríguez, W. Donner, & J. E. Trainor (Eds.), *Handbook of disaster research* (pp. 181–203). Cham, Switzerland: Springer.

Borsos, B., & Sendzimir, J. (2018). The Tisza River: Managing a Lowland River in the Carpathian Basin. In S. Schmutz & J. Sendzimir (Eds.), *Riverine ecosystem management* (pp. 541–560). Cham: Springer.

Botzen, W. J. W., Aerts, J. C. J. H., & van den Bergh, J. C. J. M. (2009). Willingness of homeowners to mitigate climate risk through insurance. *Ecological Economics, 68*(8–9), 2265–2277.

Botzen, W. J. W., Kunreuther, H., & Michel-Kerjan, E. (2015). Divergence between individual perceptions and objective indicators of tail risks: Evidence from floodplain residents in New York City. *Judgment and Decision Making, 10*(4), 365–385.

Boulder County Collaborative. (n.d.). Resiliency. Retrieved from www .bccollaborative.org/resiliency.html

Boulder Economic Council. (n.d.). Key industries & companies in Boulder, Colorado. *Boulder Economic Council.* Retrieved from http:// bouldereconomiccouncil.org/boulder-economy/

Boulder County. (2020). Open space and mountain parks. Retrieved from https://bouldercolorado.gov/osmp

(n.d.). 2013 flood recovery. *Boulder County.* Retrieved from www .bouldercounty.org/disasters/flood/2013-flood/

Bovens, M., Hart, P. T., & Gray, P. (1996). Understanding policy fiascos. *Public Administration-Abingdon, 74*(3), 552–552.

Brady, H. E., Verba, S., & Schlozman, K. L. (1995). Beyond SES: A resource model of political participation. *American Political Science Review, 89* (2), 271–294.

Branson-Potts, H. (2020, March 27). The recovery of Paradise was already fragile after the Camp fire. Then came coronavirus. *LA Times.* Retrieved from www.latimes.com/california/story/2020-03-27/corona virus-paradise-california-fire

Brenkert-Smith, H., Champ, P. A., & Flores, N. (2012). Trying not to get burned: Understanding homeowners' wildfire risk–mitigation behaviors. *Environmental Management, 50*(6), 1139–1151.

Brennan, C. (2013, September 12). 100-year-flood: Boulder rainfall records swamped in dueling weather systems. *Daily Camera*. Retrieved from www.dailycamera.com/2013/09/12/100-year-flood-boulder-rainfall-records-swamped-in-dueling-weather-systems/

Brilly, M., & Polic, M. (2005). Public perceptions of flood risks, flood forecasting and mitigation. *Natural Hazards and Earth System Sciences, 5*, 345–355.

Brody, S. D., Highfield, W. E., & Kang, J. E. (2011). *Rising waters: The causes and consequences of flooding in the United States.* Cambridge: Cambridge University Press.

Brody, S. D., Kang, J. E., & Bernhardt, S. (2010). Identifying factors influencing flood mitigation at the local level in Texas and Florida: The role of organizational capacity. *Natural Hazards, 52*(1), 167–184.

Brody, S. D., Zahran, S., Highfield, W. E., Bernhardt, S. P., & Vedlitz, A. (2009). Policy learning from flood mitigation: A longitudinal assessment of the community rating system in Florida. *Risk Analysis, 29*(6), 912–929.

Bubeck, P., Botzen, W. J. W., & Aerts, J. C. J. H. (2012). A review of risk perceptions and other factors that influence flood mitigation behavior. *Risk Analysis: An International Journal, 32*(9), 1481–1495.

Buck, D. A., Trainor, J. E., & Aguirre, B. E. (2006). A critical evaluation of the incident command system and NIMS. *Journal of Homeland Security and Emergency Management, 3*(3), 1–27.

Burby, R. J. (2003). Making plans that matter: Citizen involvement and government action. *Journal of American Planning Association, 69*(1), 33–49.

   (2006). Hurricane Katrina and the paradoxes of government disaster policy: Bringing about wise governmental decisions for hazardous areas. *The Annals of the American Academy of Political and Social Science, 604*(1), 171–191.

Burns, D. (2015). *City of Evans after action report.* Retrieved from www.evanscolorado.gov/sites/default/files/fileattachments/flood/page/1041/evans_flood_2014_aar_final.pdf

Busenberg, G. J. (1999). Collaborative and adversarial analysis in environmental policy. *Policy Sciences, 32*(1), 1–11.

Butte County District Attorney. (2020). *THE CAMP FIRE PUBLIC REPORT: A SUMMARY OF THE CAMP FIRE INVESTIGATION.* Retrieved from www.buttecounty.net/Portals/30/CFReport/PGE-THE-CAMP-FIRE-PUBLIC-REPORT.pdf?ver=2020-06-15-190515-977

Buzogány, A. (2009). Hungary: The tricky path of building environmental governance. In T. A. Börzel (Ed.), *Coping with accession to the European Union* (pp. 123–147). Hampshire: Palgrave.

Calanni, J. C., Siddiki, S. N., Weible, C. M., & Leach, W. D. (2015). Explaining coordination in collaborative partnerships and clarifying the scope of the belief homophily hypothesis. *Journal of Public Administration Research and Theory, 25*(3), 901–927. doi: 10.1093/jopart/mut080

CalFire. (2019). Top 20 largest California wildfires. Retrieved from www .fire.ca.gov/media/5510/top20_acres.pdf

Calkin, D. E., Cohen, J. D., Finney, M. A., & Thompson, M. P. (2014). How risk management can prevent future wildfire disasters in the wildland-urban interface. *Proceedings of the National Academy of Sciences, 111*(2), 746–751.

Caniglia, B. S., Vallée, M., & Frank, B. (2016). *Resilience, environmental justice and the city.* London: Routledge.

Carman, C. J. (1998). Dimensions of environmental policy support in the United States. *Social Science Quarterly, 79,* 717–733.

Cassar, A., Healy, A., & von Kessler, C. (2017). Trust, risk, and time preferences after a natural disaster: Experimental evidence from Thailand. *World Development, 94,* 90–105.

CBS Denver. (2014). Nightly closures for Hwy. 36 At Lyons to repair flood damage. Retrieved from https://denver.cbslocal.com/2014/04/30/ nightly-closures-for-hwy-36-at-lyons-to-repair-flood-damage/

CDP. (2019, October 10). 2019 California wildfires. https:// disasterphilanthropy.org/disaster/2019-california-wildfires/.

Chamlee-Wright, E., & Storr, V. H. (2009). "There's no place like New Orleans": Sense of place and community recovery in the Ninth Ward after Hurricane Katrina. *Journal of Urban Affairs, 31*(5), 615–634.

Chaskin, R. J. (2001). Building community capacity: A definitional framework and case studies from a comprehensive community initiative. *Urban Affairs Review, 36*(3), 291–323.

Chui, C., Feng, J. Y., & Jordan, L. (2014). From good practice to policy formation – The impact of third sector on disaster management in Taiwan. *International Journal of Disaster Risk Reduction, 10,* 28–37.

Coffin v. Left Hand Ditch Co., 6 443 (Colorado Supreme Court 1882).

Collins, M. J. (2009). Evidence for changing flood risk in New England since the late 20th century 1. *JAWRA Journal of the American Water Resources Association, 45*(2), 279–290.

Colorado: An Overview. (2018, June 19). Retrieved from https:// coloradoencyclopedia.org/article/colorado-overview

Colorado Office of Economic Development and International Trade. (2005). Colorado data book. Retrieved from www.state.co.us/OED/business-development/colorado-data-book.cfm

Colorado Department of Local Affairs. (2015a). *Second quarter perform-ance report.* Retrieved from https://cdola.colorado.gov/action-plans-required-reports

(2015b). *Third quarter performance report.* Retrieved from https://cdola
.colorado.gov/action-plans-required-reports

(n.d.). State Demography Office. Colorado Department of Local Affairs. Retrieved from https://demography.dola.colorado.gov/

(2017). Understanding resiliency. Retrieved from www.coresiliency.com/ understanding-resiliency

Colorado Division of Homeland Security and Emergency Management. (2013, September 17). Statewide fatality number revised. Retrieved from www.coemergency.com/2013/09/statewide-fatality-number-revised.html

Colorado Resiliency Office. (2019). Colorado's resiliency story. Colorado Resilience Office. Retrieved from www.coloradoresiliency.com

Columbia, S. C. (2016). Road to recovery annual report: Status of recovery one year after the historic flood even in October 2015. Retrieved from https://columbiasc.gov/depts/flood/final-road_to_recovery_annual_report_print.pdf

Comfort, L. K., Birkland, T. A., Cigler, B. A., & Nance, E. (2010). Retrospectives and prospectives on Hurricane Katrina: Five years and counting. *Public Administration Review, 70*(5), 669–678.

Congressional Research Service. (2007). Federal emergency management policy changes after Hurricane Katrina: A summary of statutory provisions (Congressional Research Service Report No. rl33729).

Conlan, T. J. (2006). From cooperative to opportunistic federalism: Reflections on the half-century anniversary of the commission on inter-governmental relations. *Public Administration Review, 66*(5), 663–676.

Conlan, T. J., Posner, P. L., & Rivlin, A. M. (2009). *Intergovernmental management for the 21st century.* Washington, DC: Brookings Institution Press.

Cooper, C., & Block, R. (2007). *Disaster: Hurricane Katrina and the failure of Homeland Security.* New York: Macmillan.

Crow, D. A. (2010a). Local media and experts: Sources of environmental policy initiation? *Policy Studies Journal, 38*(1), 143–164.

(2010b). Policy entrepreneurs, issue experts, and water rights policy change in Colorado. *Review of Policy Research, 27*(3), 299–315.

(2019). *Resilience planning in Colorado's local governments: A baseline survey report.* Retrieved from www.coresiliency.com/resilience-planning-survey

Crow, D. A., & Albright, E. A. (2019). Intergovernmental relationships after disaster: State and local government learning during flood recovery in

Colorado. *Journal of Environmental Policy & Planning*, 21(3), 257–274.

Crow, D. A., Albright, E. A., Ely, T., Koebele, E. A., & Lawhon, L. A. (2018). Do Disasters lead to learning? Financial policy change in local government. *Review of Policy Research*, 35(4), 564–589.

Crow, D. A., Albright, E. A., & Koebele, E. A. (2017). Evaluating informational inputs in rulemaking processes: A cross-case analysis. *Administration & Society*, 49(9), 1318–1345.

(2021). The role of coalitions in disaster policymaking. *Disasters*, 45(1): 19–45.

Crow, D. A., Berggren, J., Lawhon, L. A., Koebele, E. A., Kroepsch, A., & Huda, J. (2017). Local media coverage of wildfire disasters: An analysis of problems and solutions in policy narratives. *Environment and Planning C: Politics and Space*, 35(5), 849–871.

Crow, D. A., Dixon, L. A., Koebele, E. A., Kroepsch, A., Schild, R., & Huda, J. (2015). Information, resources, and management priorities: Agency outreach and mitigation of wildfire risk in the West. *Risk, Hazards & Crisis in Public Policy*, 6(1), 61–90.

Crow, D. A., Lawhon, L. A., Berggren, J., Huda, J., Koebele, E. A., & Kroepsch, A. (2017). A narrative policy framework analysis of wildfire policy discussions in two Colorado communities. *Politics & Policy*, 45 (4), 626–656.

Cselószki, T. (2006). Civil sector thoughts on the further development of the Vásárhelyi Plan, specifically with respect to changes in land use. Alliance for the Living Tisza Association, Nagyköru, HU.

Cutter, S. L., Barnes, L., Berry, M., Burton, C., Evans, E., Tate, E., & Webb, J. (2008). A place-based model for understanding community resilience to natural disasters. *Global Environmental Change*, 18(4), 598–606.

de Vries, D. H. (2017). Temporal vulnerability and the post-disaster 'Window of Opportunity to Woo': A case study of an African-American floodplain neighborhood after Hurricane Floyd in North Carolina. *Human Ecology*, 45(4), 437–448.

Deets, S. (2009). Constituting interests and identities in a two-level game: Understanding the Gabcikovo-Nagymaros Dam conflict. *Foreign Policy Analysis*, 5(1), 37–56.

Derthick, M. (2007). Where federalism didn't fail. *Public Administration Review*, 67, 36–47.

Dessai, S., & Hulme, M. (2004). Does climate adaptation policy need probabilities? *Climate Policy*, 4(2), 107–128.

Diakakis, M., Deligiannakis, G., Katsetsiadou, K., & Lekkas, E. (2015). Hurricane Sandy mortality in the Caribbean and continental North America. *Disaster Prevention and Management*, 24(1), 132–148.

Diffenbaugh, N. S., Swain, D. L., & Touma, D. (2015). Anthropogenic warming has increased drought risk in California. *Proceedings of the National Academy of Sciences, 112*(13), 3931–3936.

Dillman, D. A., Smyth, J. D., & Christian, L. M. (2014). *Internet, phone, mail, and mixed mode surveys. The tailored design method.* Hoboken, NJ: John Wiley & Sons.

DiPasquale, D., & Glaeser, E. L. (1998). Incentives and social capital. Are homeowners better citizens? *National Bureau of Economic Research, No. w6363.*

Donahue, A. K., Eckel, C. C., & Wilson, R. K. (2014). Ready or not? How citizens and public officials perceive risk and preparedness. *The American Review of Public Administration, 44*(4 suppl), 89S–111S.

Douglas, M. (1970). *Natural symbols.* London: Barrie and Rockliff/The Cresset Press.

(1982). Introduction to grid/group analysis. In M. Douglas (Ed.), *Essays in the Sociology of Perception* (pp. 1–8). London: Routledge & Kegan Paul.

Dunbar, R. G. (1960). The significance of the Colorado agricultural frontier. *Agricultural History, 34*(3), 119–125. Retrieved from http://links.jstor .org/sici?sici=0002-1482%28196007%2934%3A3%3C119% 3ATSOTCA%3E2.0.CO%3B2-A

Dunlap, R. E., van Liere, K. D., Mertig, A. G., & Jones, R. E. (2000). New trends in measuring environmental attitudes: Measuring endorsement of the new ecological paradigm: A revised NEP scale. *Journal of Social Issues, 56*(3), 425–442.

Durman, C., Gregory, J. M., Hassell, D. C., Jones, R., & Murphy, J. (2001). A comparison of extreme European daily precipitation simulated by a global and a regional climate model for present and future climates. *Quarterly Journal of the Royal Meteorological Society, 127*(573), 1005–1015.

Egan, P. J., & Mullin, M. (2017). Climate change: US public opinion. *Annual Review of Political Science, 20,* 209–227.

Elliott, E., Seldon, B. J., & Regens, J. L. (1997). Political and economic determinants of individuals' support for environmental spending. *Journal of Environmental Management, 51*(1), 15–27.

Elliott, J. R., & Pais, J. (2006). Race, class, and Hurricane Katrina: Social differences in human responses to disaster. *Social Science Research, 35*(2), 295–321.

Emergency Management Agency. (2016). The Stafford Act, as amended and Emergency Management-related Provisions of the Homeland Security Act, as amended, FEMA 592.

Etheredge, L. S. (1981). Government learning: And overview. In S. L. Long (Ed.), *The handbook of political behavior* (vol. 2, pp. 73–161). New York: Pergamon.

Farquhar, S., & Dobson, N. (2004). Community and university participation in disaster-relief recovery. *Journal of Community Practice, 12*(3–4), 203–217.

Federal Emergency Management Agency. (2011). A whole community approach to emergency management: Principles, themes, and pathways for action. US Department of Homeland Security, Washington, DC.

(2013). Colorado flooding one month later: Positive signs of recovery. Retrieved from www.fema.gov/news-release/2013/10/11/colorado-flooding-one-month-later-positive-signs-recovery

(2013a, October 7). BOULDER COUNTY DISASTER RECOVERY CENTER OPENS IN LYONS. *FEMA.* Retrieved from www.fema.gov/news-release/2013/10/07/boulder-county-disaster-recovery-center-opens-lyons

(2013b, October 1). Colorado severe storms, flooding, landslides, and mudslides (DR-4145). *FEMA.* Retrieved from www.fema.gov/disaster/4145

(2015). South Carolina severe storms and flooding (DR-4241). Retrieved from www.fema.gov/disaster/4241

(2017). Colorado floods federal assistance fact sheet. Retrieved from www.fema.gov/news-release/2014/09/09/2013-colorado-floods-federal-assistance-fact-sheet

(2018). 2013 Colorado floods: FEMA Individual assistance overview. Retrieved from www.fema.gov/news-release/20200807/2013-colorado-floods-fema-individual-assistance-overview

(2019). FEMA: About the agency. Retrieved from www.fema.gov/about-agencyFederal

(2020). Retrieved from www.fema.gov/public-assistance-local-state-tribal-and-non-profit

Field, C. B., Barros, V., Stocker, T. F., & Dahe, Q. (2012). *Managing the risks of extreme events and disasters to advance climate change adaptation: Special report of the intergovernmental panel on climate change.* Cambridge: Cambridge University Press.

Finch, C., Emrich, C. T., & Cutter, S. L. (2010). Disaster disparities and differential recovery in New Orleans. *Population and Environment, 31* (4), 179–202.

Folke, C. (2006). Resilience: The emergence of a perspective for social–ecological systems analyses. *Global Environmental Change, 16*(3), 253–267.

Fothergill, A., & Peek, L. A. (2004). Poverty and disasters in the United States: A review of recent sociological findings. *Natural Hazards, 32*(1), 89–110.

Freedman, A. (2013). Flood-Ravaged Boulder, Colo., Sets Annual Rainfall Record. *Climate Central.* Retrieved from www.climatecentral.org/news/flood-ravaged-boulder-colorado-sets-annual-rainfall-record-16481

Fung, A. (2006). Varieties of participation in complex governance. *Public Administration Review, 66*(s1), 66–75.

Fussell, E. (2015). The long-term recovery of New Orleans' population after Hurricane Katrina. *American Behavioral Scientist, 59*(10), 1231–1245.

Gabe, T., Falk, E. H., Mason, V. W., & McCarty, M. (2005). *Hurricane Katrina: Social-demographic characteristics of impacted areas.* Washington, DC: Congressional Research Service, Library of Congress, 2005.

Gardner, P. D., Cortner, H. J., & Widaman, K. (1987). The risk perceptions and policy response toward wildland fire hazards by urban homeowners. *Landscape and Urban Planning, 14*, 163–172.

Garnett, J. D., & Moore, M. (2010). Enhancing disaster recovery: Lessons from exemplary international disaster management practices. *Journal of Homeland Security and Emergency Management, 7*(1), 1–20.

Garrett, T. A., & Sobel, R. S. (2003). The political economy of FEMA disaster payments. *Economic Inquiry, 41*(3), 496–509.

Gerber, B. J. (2007). Disaster management in the United States: Examining key political and policy challenges. *Policy Studies Journal, 35*(2), 227–238.

Godschalk, D. R., Brody, S. D., & Burby, R. J. (2003). Public participation in natural hazard mitigation policy formation: Challenges for comprehensive planning. *Journal of Environmental Planning and Management, 46*(5), 733–754.

Gormley Jr, W. T. (1986). Regulatory issue networks in a federal system. *Polity, 18*(4), 595–620.

Gotham, K. F. (2015). Limitations, legacies, and lessons: Post-Katrina rebuilding in retrospect and prospect. *American Behavioral Scientist, 59*(10), 1314–1326.

   (2017). *The elusive recovery: Post-hurricane Katrina rebuilding during the first decade, 2005–2015.* Los Angeles, CA: Sage.

Goyer, Elita. 2020. Paradise rebuilding and recovery: 1,000 building permits secured. Retrieved from: www.actionnewsnow.com/content/news/Paradise-Rebuilding-and-Recovery-1000-building-permits-secured-570815351.html

Green, C. H., Tunstall, S., & Fordham, M. (1991). The risks from flooding: Which risks and whose perception? *Disasters, 15*(3), 227–236.

Greenberg, M. R., Weiner, M. D., Noland, R., Herb, J., Kaplan, M., & Broccoli, A. J. (2014). Public support for policies to reduce risk after Hurricane Sandy. *Risk Analysis, 34*(6), 997–1012.

Grundfest, E. C., White, G. F., & Downing, T. C. (1978). Big Thompson flood exposes need for better flood reaction system to save lives. *Civil Engineering – ASCE, 48*(2), 72–73.

Haddow, G. D., Bullock, J. A., & Coppola, D. P. (2010). The historical context of emergency management. In G. D. Haddow & J. A. Bullock (Eds.), *Introduction to emergency management*. Burlington, MA: Butterworth-Heinemann.

Hagerty, C. (2019, October 16). The survivors. *Vox*. Retrieved from www .vox.com/the-highlight/2019/10/16/20908291/camp-fire-wildfire-cali fornia-paradise-survivors

Hall, P. A. (1993). Policy paradigms, social learning, and the state: The case of economic policymaking in Britain. *Comparative Politics, 25*(3), 275–296.

Hammer, R. B., Stewart, S. I., & Radeloff, V. C. (2009). Demographic trends, the wildland–urban interface, and wildfire management. *Society & Natural Resources, 22*(8), 777–782.

Han, Z., Hu, X., & Nigg, J. (2011). How does disaster relief works affect the trust in local government? A study of the Wenchuan earthquake. *Risk, Hazards & Crisis in Public Policy, 2*(4), 1–20.

Handmer, J. (1996). Policy design and local attributes for flood hazard management. *Journal of Contingencies and Crisis Management, 4*(4), 189–197.

Hartmann, T., & Spit, T. (2016a). Implementing the European flood risk management plan. *Journal of Environmental Planning and Management, 59*(2), 360–377.

(2016b). Legitimizing differentiated flood protection levels–Consequences of the European flood risk management plan. *Environmental Science & Policy, 55*, 361–367.

Hartman, C. W., Squires, G., & Squires, G. D. (Eds.). (2006). *There is no such thing as a natural disaster: Race, class, and Hurricane Katrina*. New York: Taylor & Francis.

Heikkila, T., & Gerlak, A. K. (2013). Building a conceptual approach to collective learning: Lessons for public policy scholars. *Policy Studies Journal, 41*(3), 484–512.

Heitz, C., Spaeter, S., Auzet, A.-V., & Glatron, S. (2009). Local stakeholders' perception of muddy flood risk and implications for management approaches: A case study in Alsace (France). *Land Use Policy, 26*(2), 443–451.

Helmer, M., & Hilhorst, D. (2006). Natural disasters and climate change. *Disasters, 30*(1), 1–4.

Hennessy, K., Gregory, J. M., & Mitchell, J. (1997). Changes in daily precipitation under enhanced greenhouse conditions. *Climate Dynamics, 13*(9), 667–680.

Henry, A. D., Lubell, M., & McCoy, M. (2010). Belief systems and social capital as drivers of policy network structure: The case of California regional planning. *Journal of Public Administration Research and Theory*, 21(3), 419–444.

Herweg, N., Zahariadis, N., & Zohlnhofer, R. (2017). The multiple streams framework: Foundations, refinements, and empirical applications. In C. M. Weible and P. A. Sabatier (Eds.), *Theories of the policy process* (4th ed., pp. 17–52). Boulder, CO: Westview Press.

Hess, R. H. (1916). The Colorado water right. *Columbia Law Review*, 16 (8), 649–664.

Ho, M.-C., Shaw, D., Lin, S., & Chiu, Y.-C. (2008). How do disaster characteristics influence risk perception? *Risk Analysis*, 28(3), 635–643.

Hooghe, L., Marks, G., & Marks, G. W. (2001). *Multi-level governance and European integration*. Boulder, CO: Rowman & Littlefield.

Huber, G. P. (1991). Organizational learning: The contributing processes and the literatures. *Organization Science*, 2(1), 88–115.

Ingraham, P. W., Joyce, P. G., & Donahue, A. K. (2003). *Government performance: Why management matters*. Baltimore: Taylor & Francis.

Ingram, J. C., Franco, G., Rumbaitis-del Rio, C., & Khazai, B. (2006). Post-disaster recovery dilemmas: Challenges in balancing short-term and long-term needs for vulnerability reduction. *Environmental Science & Policy*, 9(7–8), 607–613.

Jenkins-Smith, H., Nohrstedt, D., Weible, C. M., & Ingold, K. (2018). The advocacy coalition framework: An overview of the research program. In C. M. Weible and P. A. Sabatier (Eds.), *Theories of the policy process* (4th ed., pp. 135–171). Boulder, CO: Westview Press.

Jenkins-Smith, H. C., & Sabatier, P. A. (1999). The advocacy coalition framework: An assessment. *Theories of the Policy Process*, 118, 117–166.

Jensen, J. (2011). The current NIMS implementation behavior of United States counties. *Journal of Homeland Security and Emergency Management*, 8(1).

Jensen, S. E. (2006). Policy tools for wildland fire management: Principles, incentives, and conflicts. *Natural Resources Journal*, 46, 959–1003.

Johansen, C., Horney, J., & Tien, I. (2017). Metrics for evaluating and improving community resilience. *Journal of Infrastructure Systems*, 23 (2), 04016032.

Johnson, C. L., Tunstall, S. M., & Penning-Rowsell, E. C. (2005). Floods as catalysts for policy change: Historical lessons from England and Wales. *International Journal of Water Resources Development*, 21(4), 561–575.

Jones, B. D., & Baumgartner, F. R. (2005). *The politics of attention: How government prioritizes problems*. Chicago: University of Chicago Press.

Jones, M. D., & Crow, D. A. (2017). How can we use the 'science of stories' to produce persuasive scientific stories? *Palgrave Communications*, 3(1), 53.

Kaenel, C. v. (2020, February 19). Work continues on Building Resiliency Center in Paradise. Retrieved from www.chicoer.com/2019/11/09/work-continues-on-building-resiliency-center-in-paradise/

Kahan, D. M. (2008). Cultural cognition as a conception of the cultural theory of risk. In S. Roeser (Ed.), *Handbook of risk theory.* Springer.

Kahneman, D. (2011). *Thinking, fast and slow.* New York: Farrar, Straus, and Giroux.

Kahneman, D., Slovic, S. P., Slovic, P., & Tversky, A. (1982). *Judgment under uncertainty: Heuristics and biases.* Cambridge: Cambridge University Press.

Kaniasty, K., & Norris, F. (1999). The experience of disaster: Individuals and communities sharing trauma. In *Response to disaster: Psychosocial, community, and ecological approaches* (pp. 25–61).

Kapucu, N., & Garayev, V. (2012). Designing, managing, and sustaining functionally collaborative emergency management networks. *The American Review of Public Administration, 43*(3), 312–330.

Kellens, W., Terpstra, T., & de Maeyer, P. (2013). Perception and communication of flood risks: A systematic review of empirical research. *Risk Analysis, 33*(1), 24–49.

Kennedy, C. S., Weise, E., & Maschke, A. (2017, October 13). California fires: With growth comes risk of living near wildfire-prone areas. *Reno Gazette Journal.* Retrieved from www.rgj.com/story/news/2017/10/13/california-fires-growth-comes-risk-living-near-wildfire-prone-areas/763361001/

Kennedy, P., Ressler, E., Rodriguez, H., Quarantelli, E. L., & Dynes, R. (2009). *Handbook of disaster research.* Cham, Switzerland: Springer Science & Business Media.

Kincaid, J., & Stenberg, C. W. (2011). "Big Questions" about intergovernmental relations and management: Who will address them? *Public Administration Review, 71*(2), 196–202.

Kindelspire, T., & Rochat, S. (2013, September 12). 500-year flood nearly cuts Longmont in two, forces evacuations. *Longmont Times-Call.* Retrieved from www.timescall.com/2013/09/12/500-year-flood-nearly-cuts-longmont-in-two-forces-evacuations/

Kingdon, J. (2003). *Agendas, alternatives, and public policies* (2nd ed.). New York: Pearson.

Klinenberg, E. (2003). Review of heat wave: Social autopsy of disaster in Chicago. *New England Journal of Medicine, 348*(7), 666–667.

Knight, O. (1956). Correcting nature's error: The Colorado-Big Thompson project. *Agricultural History, 30*(4), 157–169. Retrieved from http://links.jstor.org/sici?sici=0002-1482%28195610%2930%3A4%3C157%3ACNETCT%3E2.0.CO%3B2-S

Koebele, E. A. (2015). Assessing outputs, outcomes, and barriers in collaborative water governance: A case study. *Journal of Contemporary Water Research & Education, 155*(1), 63–72.

(2019). Cross-coalition coordination in collaborative environmental governance processes. *Policy Studies Journal, 48*(3), 727–753. doi: 10 .1111/psj.12306

Koebele, E. A., Crow, D. A., Dixon, L., Schild, R., Kroepsch, A., & Clifford, K. (2015). Wildfire outreach and citizen entrepreneurs in the wildland-urban interface: A cross-case analysis in Colorado. *Society & Natural Resources, 28*(8), 918–923.

Konisky, D. M., Hughes, L., & Kaylor, C. H. (2016). Extreme weather events and climate change concern. *Climatic Change, 134*(4), 533–547.

Konisky, D. M., Milyo, J., & Richardson, L. E. (2008). Environmental policy attitudes: Issues, geographical scale, and political trust. *Social Science Quarterly, 89*(5), 1066–1085.

Koontz, T. M., & Johnson, E. M. (2004). One size does not fit all: Matching breadth of stakeholder participation to watershed group accomplishments. *Policy Sciences, 37*(2), 185–204.

Koontz, T. M., & Thomas, C. W. (2006). What do we know and need to know about the environmental outcomes of collaborative management? *Public Administration Review, 66*, 111–121.

Kothavala, Z. (1997). Extreme precipitation events and the applicability of global climate models to the study of floods and droughts. *Mathematics and Computers in Simulation, 43*(3–6), 261–268.

Krause, R. M. (2011). Policy innovation, intergovernmental relations, and the adoption of climate protection initiatives by US cities. *Journal of Urban Affairs, 33*(1), 45–60.

Kundzewicz, Z. W., Kanae, S., Seneviratne, S. I., Handmer, J., Nicholls, N., Peduzzi, P., . . . Mach, K. (2014). Flood risk and climate change: Global and regional perspectives. *Hydrological Sciences Journal, 59*(1), 1–28.

Kuz, M., & D'Orio, W. (2020, April 20). Fighting 'invisible fire': Why Paradise is ready for coronavirus. *Christian Science Monitor.* Retrieved from www.csmonitor.com/USA/Society/2020/0420/Fighting-invisible-fire-Why-Paradise-is-ready-for-coronavirus

Kweit, M. G., & Kweit, R. W. (2004). Citizen participation and citizen evaluation in disaster recovery. *The American Review of Public Administration, 34*(4), 354–373.

Laws, M. B., Yeh, Y., Reisner, E., Stone, K., Wang, T., & Brugge, D. (2015). Gender, ethnicity and environmental risk perception revisited: The importance of residential location. *Journal of Community Health, 40* (5), 948–955.

Leach, W. D. (2002). Surveying diverse stakeholder groups. *Society & Natural Resources, 15*(7), 641–649.

Leach, W. D., & Sabatier, P. A. (2005a). Are trust and social capital the keys to success? In P. A. Sabatier (Ed.), *Swimming upstream: Collaborative approaches to watershed management* (pp. 233–258). Cambridge, MA: MIT Press.

(2005b). To trust an adversary: Integrating rational and psychological models of collaborative policymaking. *American Political Science Review, 99*(04), 491–503.

Leavitt, H. J. (1965). Applied organizational change in industry, structural, technological and humanistic approaches. *Handbook of Organizations, 264.*

Lee, T., & van de Meene, S. (2012). Who teaches and who learns? Policy learning through the C40 cities climate network. *Policy Sciences, 45*(3), 199–220.

Lein, L., Angel, R., Bell, H., & Beausoleil, J. (2009). The state and civil society response to disaster: The challenge of coordination. *Organization & Environment, 22*(4), 448–457.

Leiserowitz, A. A. (2005). American risk perceptions: Is climate change dangerous? *Risk Analysis: An International Journal, 25*(6), 1433–1442.

Liesbet, H., & Gary, M. (2003). Unraveling the central state, but how? Types of multi-level governance. *American Political Science Review, 97*(2), 233–243.

Lin, S., Shaw, D., & Ho, M.-C. (2008). Why are floods and landslide victims less willing to take mitigation measures than the public? *Natural Hazards, 44*(2), 305–314.

Lindell, M. K., & Hwang, S. N. (2008). Households' perceived personal risk and responses in a multihazard environment. *Risk Analysis: An International Journal, 28*(2), 539–556.

Lindell, M. K., & Prater, C. S. (2000). Household adoption of seismic hazard adjustments: A comparison of residents in two states. *International Journal of Mass Emergencies and Disasters, 18*(2), 317–338.

Linnerooth-Bayer, J., & Sjostedt, G. (2010). *Transboundary risk management.* London: Routledge.

Lord, C., Ross, L., & Lepper, M. (1979). Biased assimilation and attitude polarization: The effects of prior theories on subsequently considered evidence. *Journal of Personality and Social Psychology, 37*(11), 2098–2109.

Lounsberry, S. (2018, September 18). Five years after flood, recovery nears $500M. *Daily Camera.* Retrieved from www.dailycamera.com/2018/09/01/five-years-after-flood-recovery-nears-500m/

Lubell, M. (2004). Collaborative environmental institutions: All talk and no action? *Journal of Policy Analysis and Management, 23*(3), 549–573.

Lyles, W., & Stevens, M. (2014). Plan quality evaluation 1994–2012: Growth and contributions, limitations, and new directions. *Journal of Planning Education and Research, 34*(4), 433–450.

Mackey, M. (2020, January 27). Town of Paradise opens Building Resiliency Center to help residents with rebuilding. *KRCR News*. Retrieved from https://krcrtv.com/news/local/town-of-paradise-opens-building-resili ency-center-to-help-residents-with-rebuilding

Magis, K. (2010). Community resilience: An indicator of social sustainability. *Society & Natural Resources, 23*(5), 401–416.

Majchrzak, A., Jarvenpaa, S. L., & Hollingshead, A. B. (2007). Coordinating expertise among emergent groups responding to disasters. *Organization Science, 18*(1), 147–161.

Margerum, R. D. (2008). A typology of collaboration efforts in environmental management. *Environmental Management, 41*(4), 487–500.

Marks, G., & Hooghe, L. (2004). Contrasting visions of multi-level governance. In I. Bache & M. Flinders (Eds.), *Multi-level governance* (pp. 15–30). Oxford: Oxford University Press.

Marks, G., Hooghe, L., & Blank, K. (1996). European integration from the 1980s: State-centric v. multi-level governance. *JCMS: Journal of Common Market Studies, 34*(3), 341–378.

Marlowe, J. (2012). Fiscal slack, reserves, and rainy-day funds. In H. L. J. Justice, and E. Scorscone (Eds.), *Local government fiscal health* (pp. 321–342). Burlington, MA: Jones and Bartlett.

Matczak, P., Flachner, Z., & Werners, S. E. (2008). Institutions for adapting to climate change in the Tisza river basin. *Klimá 21" Füzetek, 55*, 87–100.

May, P. J. (1992). Policy learning and failure. *Journal of Public Policy, 12*, 331–354.

May, P. J., & Burby, R. J. (1996). Coercive versus cooperative policies: Comparing intergovernmental mandate performance. *Journal of Policy Analysis and Management, 15*(2), 171–201.

May, P. J., & Jochim, A. E. (2013). Policy regime perspectives: Policies, politics, and governing. *Policy Studies Journal, 41*(3), 426–452.

McCaffrey, S. M. (2015). Community wildfire preparedness: A global state-of-the-knowledge summary of social science research. *Current Forestry Reports, 1*(2), 81–90.

McCaffrey, S. M., Toman, E., Stidham, M., & Shindler, B. (2013). Social science research related to wildlife management: An overview of recent findings and future research needs. *International Journal of Wildland Fire, 22*(1), 15–24.

McCallum, D. B., Hammond, S. L., & Covello, V. T. (1991). Communicating about environmental risks: How the public uses and perceives information sources. *Health Education Quarterly, 18*(3), 349–361.

McCann, H. (2019, October 14). New laws help prepare communities for wildfire – Public Policy Institute of California. Retrieved from www .ppic.org/blog/new-laws-help-prepare-communities-for-wildfire/

McCarthy, F. X. (2010). *FEMA's disaster declaration process: A primer.* Washington, DC: DIANE Publishing.

McDonnell, S., Ghorbani, P., Desai, S., Wolf, C., & Burgy, D. M. (2018). Potential challenges to targeting low-and moderate-income communities in a time of urgent need: The case of CDBG-DR in New York State after superstorm sandy. *Housing Policy Debate, 28*(3), 466–487.

McGee, T. K., McFarlane, B. L., & Varghese, J. (2009). An examination of the influence of hazard experience on wildfire risk perceptions and adoption of mitigation measures. *Society & Natural Resources, 22*(4), 308–323.

McGhee, T. (2013, September 12). Colorado flood: No relief in sight as record rain falls – The Denver Post. *Denver Post.* Retrieved from www .denverpost.com/2013/09/12/colorado-flood-no-relief-in-sight-as-record-rain-falls/

McGuire, M. (2006). Intergovernmental management: A view from the bottom. *Public Administration Review, 66*(5), 677–679.

McGuire, M., & Silvia, C. (2010). The effect of problem severity, managerial and organizational capacity, and agency structure on intergovernmental collaboration: Evidence from local emergency management. *Public Administration Review, 70*(2), 279–288.

McMahon, X. (2018, October 18). Climate change means more rainfall and flooding, but not less drought. Here's Why | Colorado Public Radio. *Colorado Public Radio.*

Meletti, D. S., & O'Brien, P. W. (1992). Warnings during disaster: Normalizing communicated risk. *Social Problems, 39*(1), 40–57.

Menzel, D. C. (2006). The Katrina aftermath: A failure of federalism or leadership? *Public Administration Review, 66*(6), 808–812.

Merzdorf, J. (2019, July 9). A drier future sets the stage for more wildfires – Climate change: Vital signs of the planet. *Global Climate Change.* Retrieved from https://climate.nasa.gov/news/2891/a-drier-future-sets-the-stage-for-more-wildfires/

Miles, B., & Morse, S. (2007). The role of news media in natural disaster risk and recovery. *Ecological Economics, 63*(2–3), 365–373.

Miles, M. B., Huberman, A. M., & Saldaña, J. (2013). *Qualitative data analysis: A methods sourcebook.* Thousand Oaks, CA: Sage.

Miller, S. A. (1959). Flood control problems in the South Platte River Basin, Colorado. *CER; 59–71.*

Milly, P. C. D., Wetherald, R. T., Dunne, K., & Delworth, T. L. (2002). Increasing risk of great floods in a changing climate. *Nature, 415*(6871), 514–517.

Mintrom, M. (1997). Policy entrepreneurs and the diffusion of innovation. *American Journal of Political Science, 41*(3), 738–770.

Mintrom, M., & Normal, P. (2009). Policy entrepreneurship and policy change. *Policy Studies Journal, 37*(4), 649–667.

Moore, E. A., & Koontz, T. M. (2003). Research note a typology of collaborative watershed groups: Citizen-based, agency-based, and mixed partnerships. *Society & Natural Resources, 16*(5), 451–460.

Moss, M., Schellhamer, C., & Berman, D. A. (2009). The Stafford Act and priorities for reform. *Journal of Homeland Security and Emergency Management, 6*(1), 1–21.

Moyson, S., Scholten, P., & Weible, C. M. (2017). Policy learning and policy change: Theorizing their relations from different perspectives. *Policy and Society, 36*(2), 161–177.

Muñoz, C. E., & Tate, E. (2016). Unequal recovery? Federal resource distribution after a Midwest flood disaster. *International Journal of Environmental Research and Public Health, 13*(5), 507.

Musselman, K. N., Lehner, F., Ikeda, K., Clark, M. P., Prein, A. F., Liu, C., ... Rasmussen, R. (2018). Projected increases and shifts in rain-on-snow flood risk over western North America. *Nature Climate Change, 8*(9), 808–812.

Myers, C. A., Slack, T., & Singelmann, J. (2008). Social vulnerability and migration in the wake of disaster: The case of Hurricanes Katrina and Rita. *Population and Environment, 29*(6), 271–291.

Nakagawa, Y., & Shaw, R. (2004). Social capital: A missing link to disaster recovery. *International Journal of Mass Emergencies and Disasters, 22*(1), 5–34.

National Oceanic and Atmospheric Administration. (2000, 2007). The Great Galveston Hurricane of 1900.

National Weather Service. (n.d.). NWS Boulder Denver Weather History. National Weather Service. Retrieved from www.weather.gov/bou/wxhistory

Nickerson, R. S. (1998). Confirmation bias: A ubiquitous phenomenon in many guises. *Review of General Psychology, 2*(2), 175–220.

Nohrstedt, D., & Nyberg, L. (2015). Do floods drive hazard mitigation policy? Evidence from Swedish municipalities. *Geografiska Annaler: Series A, Physical Geography, 97*(1), 109–122.

Nohrstedt, D., & Weible, C. M. (2010). The logic of policy change after crisis: Proximity and subsystem interaction. *Risk, Hazards & Crisis, 1* (2), 1–32.

O'Donovan, K. (2017). Policy failure and policy learning: Examining the conditions of learning after disaster. *Review of Policy Research, 34,* 537–558.

O'Toole Jr, L. J., & Hanf, K. (1998). Hungary: Political transformation and environmental challenge. *Environmental Politics,* 7(1), 93–112.

Oaks, S. D. (1982). Floods in Boulder County, Colorado. Retrieved from https://udfcd.org/FWP/F2P2_Reports/BoulderCountyHistory/Floods%20in%20Boulder%20County,%20Colorado%20%20%20%20Sherry%20Oaks.pdf

Oetzel, J., & Oh, C. H. (2015). Managing nonmarket risk. In T. C. Lawton & T. S. Rajwani (Eds.), *The Routledge companion to non-market strategy* (pp. 263–278). New York: Routledge.

Oh, C. H., & Oetzel, J. (2011). Multinationals' response to major disasters: How does subsidiary investment vary in response to the type of disaster and the quality of country governance? *Strategic Management Journal, 32*(6), 658–681.

Oh, C. H., Oetzel, J., Rivera, J., & Lien, D. (2020). Natural disasters and MNC sub-national investments in China. *Multinational Business Review, 28*(2), 245–274.

Page, S. (2016). A strategic framework for building civic capacity. *Urban Affairs Review, 52*(4), 439–470.

Pagneux, E., Gisladottir, G., & Jonsdottir, S. (2011). Public perception of flood hazard and flood risk in Iceland: A case study in a watershed prone to ice-jam floods. *Natural Hazards,* 58(1), 269–287.

Palm, R. I. (2019). *Earthquake insurance in California: Environmental policy and individual decision-making.* New York: Westview Press.

Palm, R., Palm, R. I., & Hodgson, M. E. (1992). *After a California earthquake: Attitude and behavior change.* Chicago: University of Chicago Press.

Pantti, M., Wahl-Jorgensen, K., & Cottle, S. (2012). *Disasters and the media.* New York: Peter Lang.

Paudel, Y., Botzen, W. J. W., & Aerts, J. C. J. H. (2015). Influence of climate change and socio-economic development on catastrophe insurance: A case study of flood risk scenarios in the Netherlands. *Regional Environmental Change, 15*(8), 1717–1729.

Peacock, W. G., Dash, N., & Zhang, Y. (2007). Sheltering and housing recovery following disaster. In H. Rodriguez, E. L. Quarentelli, & R. R. Dynes (Eds.), *Handbook of disaster research* (pp. 258–274). New York: Springer.

Peek, L. (2012). They call it 'Katrina fatigue': Displaced families and dis-
   crimination in Colorado. In L. Weber & L. A. Peek (Eds.), *Displaced:*
   Life in the Katrina diaspora (pp. 31–46). Austin: University of Texas
   Press.
Penn, I. (2020, May 18). PG&E says wildfire victims back settlement in
   bankruptcy. Retrieved from www.nytimes.com/2020/05/18/business/
   energy-environment/pge-bankruptcy-wildfire-victims.html
Perry, R. W. (2007). What is a disaster? In H. Rodriguez, E. L. Quarentelli,
   & R. R. Dynes (Eds.), *Handbook of disaster research* (vol. 463,
   pp. 1–15). New York: Springer.
Persons, D. (2014, March 10). Estes Park is all about tourism – Estes Park Trail-
   Gazette. *Estes Park Trail Gazette.* Retrieved from www.eptrail.com/
Petak, W. J. (1985). Emergency management: A challenge for public administration. *Public Administration Review, 45,* 3–7.
Pierce, J. J. (2016). Advocacy coalition resources and strategies in Colorado
   hydraulic fracturing politics. *Society & Natural Resources, 29,*
   1154–1168.
Provan, K. G., & Milward, H. B. (1995). A preliminary theory of interorga-
   nizational network effectiveness: A comparative study of four community mental health systems. *Administrative Science Quarterly, 40*(1),
   1–33.
Quarantelli, E. L. (1988). Disaster crisis management: A summary of
   research findings. *Journal of Management Studies, 25*(4), 373–385.
Quattrone, G. A., & Tversky, A. (1988). Contrasting rational and psychological analyses of political choice. *American Political Science Review,*
   82(3), 719–736. Retrieved from www.jstor.org/stable/1962487
Raaijmakers, R., Krywkow, J., & van der Veen, A. (2008). Flood risk
   perceptions and spatial multi-criteria analysis: An exploratory research
   for hazard mitigation. *Natural Hazards, 46*(3), 307–322.
Reporter-Herald Staff. (2018, September 8). The 2013 Flood: A timeline.
   Loveland Reporter-Herald. Retrieved from www.reporterherald.com
Rivera, J. (2010). *Business and public policy: Responses to environmental &*
   social protection processes. Cambridge: Cambridge University Press.
Rivera, J. D. (2018). Reliance on faith-based organizations for tangible
   assistance in times of disaster: Exploring the influence of bonding social
   capital. *Sociological Spectrum, 38*(1), 39–50.
Rivera, J. D., & Nickels, A. E. (2014). Social capital, community resilience,
   and faith-based organizations in disaster recovery: A case study of Mary
   Queen of Vietnam Catholic Church. *Risk, Hazards & Crisis in Public*
   Policy, 5(2), 178–211.
Robert T. Stafford Act. (2000). Robert T. *Stafford Disaster Relief and*
   Emergency Assistance Act, as amended by Public Law, 106–390.

Robert T. Stafford Disaster Relief and Emergency Assistance Act, P.L. 93-288 as amended. (2003). [Washington, DC]: Federal Emergency Management Agency, [2003].

Roberts, N. C., & King, P. J. (1991). Policy entrepreneurs: Their activity structure and function in the policy process. *Journal of Public Administration Research and Theory: J-PART, 1*(2), 147–175. Retrieved from http://links.jstor.org/sici?sici=1053-1858%28199104% 291%3A2%3C147%3APETASA%3E2.0.CO%3B2-1

Robinson, S. E., & Eller, W. S. (2010). Participation in policy streams: Testing the separation of problems and solutions in subnational policy systems. *Policy Studies Journal, 38*(2), 199–216.

Robinson, S. E., Eller, W. S., Gall, M., & Gerber, B. J. (2013). The core and periphery of emergency management networks. *Public Management Review, 15*(3), 344–362.

Rogers, R. W., & Prentice-Dunn, S. (1997). Protection motivation theory. In D. Gochman (Ed.), *Handbook of health behavior research I: Personal and social determinants* (pp. 113–132). New York: Plenum Press.

Romano, A. (2013, September 15). Hundreds of Greeley, Evans residents displaced by historic flood. Retrieved from www.greeleytribune.com/ news/local/hundreds-of-greeley-evans-residents-displaced-by-historic-flood/

Rose, A., Porter, K., Dash, N., Bouabid, J., Huyck, C., Whitehead, J., ... West, C. T. (2007). Benefit-cost analysis of FEMA hazard mitigation grants. *Natural Hazards Review, 8*(4), 97–111. Retrieved from http:// ascelibrary.org/doi/abs/10.1061/(ASCE)1527-6988(2007)8:4(97)

Rose, R. (1991). What is lesson-drawing? *Journal of Public Policy, 11*(1), 3–30.

Rubin, C. B., & Barbee, D. G. (1985). Disaster recovery and hazard mitigation: Bridging the intergovernmental gap. *Public Administration Review, 45*, 57–63.

Rubin, C. B., Saperstein, M. D., & Berbee, D. G. (1985). Community recovery from a major natural disaster. *FMHI Publications, Paper 87.* Retrieved from http://scholarcommons.usf.edu/fmhi_pub/87?utm_ source=scholarcommons.usf.edu%2Ffmhi_pub%2F87&utm_medium= PDF&utm_campaign=PDFCoverPages

Rubin, H. J., & Rubin, I. S. (2005). *Qualitative interviewing: The art of hearing data.* Thousand Oaks, CA: Sage.

Ruin, I., Gaillard, J.-C., & Lutoff, C. (2007). How to get there? Assessing motorists' flash flood risk perception on daily itineraries. *Environmental Hazards, 7*, 235–244.

Ruiz-Grossman, S. (2019). California's camp fire was the most expensive natural disaster worldwide in 2018. *HuffPost.* Retrieved from www

.huffpost.com/entry/california-camp-fire-costliest-disaster-2018_n_
5c37b1b4e4b045f6768a484f

Rumbach, A., Sullivan, E., & Makarewicz, C. (2020). Mobile home parks
and disasters: Understanding risk to the third housing type in the United
States. *Natural Hazards Review, 21*(2), 05020001.

Runyan, R. C. (2006). Small business in the face of crisis: Identifying barriers
to recovery from a natural disaster. *Journal of Contingencies and Crisis
Management, 14*(1), 12–26.

Russell, G. E., Boyd, A., Lederer, S., Zeus, C., Langer, L., Engraving, C., &
Camera, S. (1923). *The Berkeley fire: Dedicated to the people of
Berkeley who have proved themselves great hearted in giving, courage-
ous in losing, and clear eyed in building toward a safer future.* [San
Francisco] Berkeley: Published by George E. Russell, Aero-
Photographer, San Francisco and the Camera Shop, Berkeley Lederer,
Street & Zeus Co., Printers.

Russell, L. A., Goltz, J. D., & Bourque, L. B. (1995). Preparedness and
hazard mitigation actions before and after two earthquakes.
Environment and Behavior, 27(6), 744–770.

Sabatier, P. A. (1988). An advocacy coalition framework of policy change
and the role of policy-oriented learning therein. *Policy Sciences, 21*
(2–3), 129–168.

(1999). *Theories of the policy process.* Boulder, CO: Westview Press.

Sabatier, P. A., Focht, W., Lubell, M., Trachtenberg, Z., Vedlitz, A.,
Matlock, M., ... Kamieniecki, S. (2005). *Swimming upstream:
Collaborative approaches to watershed management.* Cambridge, MA:
MIT Press.

Sabatier, P. A., & Jenkins-Smith, H. C. (1993a). The advocacy coalition
framework: Assessments, revisions, and implications for scholars and
practitioners. In P. A. Sabatier & H. Jenkins-Smith (Eds.), *Policy change
and learning: An advocacy coalition approach* (pp. 211–236). Boulder,
CO: Westview Press.

(1993b). *Policy change and learning: An advocacy coalition approach.*
Boulder, CO: Westview Press.

(1999). The advocacy coalition framework. In P. A. Sabatier (Ed.), *Theories
of the policy process* (pp. 117–168). Boulder, CO: Westview Press.

Sabatier, P. A., & Weible, C. M. (2007a). The advocacy coalition framework. *Theories of the policy process, 2,* 189–220.

(2007b). The advocacy coalition framework: Innovations and clarifica-
tions. In P. A. Sabatier (Ed.), *Theories of the policy process* (2nd ed.,
pp. 189–200). Boulder, CO: Westview Press.

Saegert, S. (2006). Building civic capacity in urban neighborhoods: An empirically grounded anatomy. *Journal of Urban Affairs, 28*(3), 275–294.

Schattschneider, E. E. (1975). *The semisovereign people*. Hinsdale, IL: The Dryden Press.

Schneider, M., & Teske, P. (1992). Toward a theory of the political entrepreneur: Evidence from local government. *American Political Science Review*, 86(3), 737–747. Retrieved from http://links.jstor.org/sici?sici= 0003-0554%28199209%2986%3A3%3C737%3ATATOTP%3E2.0 .CO%3B2-D

Schwartz, R., & Sulitzeanu-Kenan, R. (2004). Managerial values and accountability pressures: Challenges of crisis and disaster. *Journal of Public Administration Research and Theory*, 14(1), 79–102.

Shaw, R., & Izumi, T. (2016). *Civil society organization and disaster risk reduction*. Japan: Springer.

Shrader-Frechette, K. S. (1991). *Risk and rationality: Philosophical foundations for populist reforms*. Berkeley: University of California Press.

Siegrist, M., & Gutscher, H. (2006). Flooding risks: A comparison of lay people's perceptions and expert's assessments in Switzerland. *Risk Analysis*, 26(4), 971–979.

Sjöberg, L. (1999). Risk perception by the public and by experts: A dilemma in risk management. *Human Ecology Review*, 6(2), 1–9.

Slimak, M. W., & Dietz, T. (2006). Personal values, beliefs, and ecological risk perception. *Risk Analysis*, 26(6), 1689–1705.

Slovic, P. (1987). Perception of risk. *Science*, 236(4799), 280–285.

Small Business Administration (SBA). (2015). Colorado Grant B-13-DS-08-0001, April 1, 2015 thru June 30, 2015. Performance Report Community Development Systems, Disaster Recovery Grant Reporting System (DRGR).

Smith, G. P. (2012). *Planning for post-disaster recovery: A review of the United States disaster assistance framework*. Washington, DC: Island Press.

Smith, G. P., Martin, A., & Wenger, D. E. (2018). Disaster recovery in an era of climate change: The unrealized promise of institutional resilience. In H. Rodríguez, W. Donner, & J. E. Trainor (Eds.), *Handbook of disaster research* (pp. 595–619). Cham, Switzerland: Springer.

Smith, G. P., & Wenger, D. E. (2007). Sustainable disaster recovery: Operationalizing an existing agenda. In H. Rodriguez, E. L. Quarentelli, & R. R. Dynes (Eds.), *Handbook of disaster research* (pp. 234–257). New York: Springer.

Smith, M., & Hennen, D. (2013, September 20). Record rain, steep canyons fueled Colorado floods. *CNN*. Retrieved from www.cnn.com

Spader, J., & Turnham, J. (2014). CDBG disaster recovery assistance and homeowners' rebuilding outcomes following Hurricanes Katrina and Rita. *Housing Policy Debate*, 24(1), 213–237.

Staff. (2013, September 12). Closures: Host of area roads closed, as well as CU, Naropa, Boulder Valley, St. Vrain school. *Daily Camera*. Retrieved from www.dailycamera.com/2013/09/12/closures-host-of-area-roads-closed-as-well-as-cu-naropa-boulder-valley-st-vrain-schools/

(2014, March 14). Colorado gets another $199 million to spend on flood recovery. *Times Call*. Retrieved from www.timescall.com

Stallings, R. A., & Quarentelli, E. L. (1985). Emergent citizen groups and emergency management. *Public Administration Review*, 45(Special Issue: Emergency Management: A Challenge for Public Administration), 93–100.

State of Colorado. (2020). *COLORADO: Action plan for disaster recovery.* Retrieved from http://hermes.cde.state.co.us/drupal/islandora/object/co:13168/datastream/OBJ/view

Steelman, T. A., McCaffrey, S. M., Velez, A.-L. K., & Briefel, J. A. (2015). What information do people use, trust, and find useful during a disaster? Evidence from five large wildfires. *Natural Hazards*, 76(1), 615–634.

Stevens, M. R., Lyles, W., & Berke, P. R. (2014). Measuring and reporting intercoder reliability in plan quality evaluation research. *Journal of Planning Education and Research*, 34(1), 77–93.

Stone, D. (2011). *Policy paradox: The art of political decision making* (3rd ed.). New York: Norton.

Surminski, S., Aerts, J. C. J. H., Botzen, W. J. W., Hudson, P., Mysiak, J., & Pérez-Blanco, C. D. (2015). Reflections on the current debate on how to link flood insurance and disaster risk reduction in the European Union. *Natural Hazards*, 79(3), 1451–1479.

Szlávik, L. (2003). The development policy of flood control in Hungary. Department of Water Management and Informatics, Budapest: Water Resources Research Centre (VITUKI).

Tabachnik, S. (2018, December 24). With 80,000 new residents, Colorado is the seventh-fastest growing state in the U.S. *Denver Post*. Retrieved from www.denverpost.com/2018/12/24/colorado-population-growth/

Tate, E., Strong, A., Kraus, T., & Xiong, H. (2016). Flood recovery and property acquisition in Cedar Rapids, Iowa. *Natural Hazards*, 80(3), 2055–2079.

Teske, P., & Schneider, M. (1994). The bureaucratic entrepreneur: The case of city managers. *Public Administration Review*, 54(4), 331–340. Retrieved from http://links.jstor.org/sici?sici=0033-3352%28199407%2F08%2954%3A4%3C331%3ATBETCO%3E2.0.CO%3B2-A

The Blog. (2012, July 31). Big Thompson flood of 1976. *Denver Post*. Retrieved from http://blogs.denverpost.com/library/2012/07/31/big-thompson-flood-disaster-colorado-1976/2795/

Thomas, D., Butry, D., Gilbert, S., Webb, D., & Fung, J. (2017). The costs and losses of wildfires. *Spec. Publ. NIST SP-1215.*

Tierney, K. J. (2007). Businesses and disasters: Vulnerability, impacts, and recovery. In H. Rodriguez, E. L. Quarentelli, & R. R. Dynes (Eds.), *Handbook of disaster research* (vol. 643, pp. 275–296). New York: Springer.

Tierney, K. (2014). *The social roots of risk: Producing disasters, promoting resilience.* Palo Alto, CA: Stanford University Press.

Traylor, P. (2017, September 14). PHOTOS: Colorado's massive floods of 2013 – The Denver Post. *Denver Post.* Retrieved from www.denverpost .com

Tversky, A., & Kahneman, D. (1974). Judgment Under Uncertainty: Heuristics and Biases. *Science, 185*(4157), 1124–1134.

Tyler, D. (2017, January 23). Front range. *Colorado encyclopedia.* Retrieved from https://coloradoencyclopedia.org/taxonomy/term/1655/all

United Nations Environment Programme. (2020). Why Australia's 2019–2020 bushfire season was not normal, in three graphs. Retrieved from www.unenvironment.org/news-and-stories/story/why-australias-2019-2020-bushfire-season-was-not-normal-three-graphs

United Nations General Assembly. (2016). Report of the open-ended inter-governmental expert working group on indicators and terminology relating to disaster risk reduction. New York: United Nations General Assembly, 41.

United Nations Intergovernmental Panel on Climate Change. (2012). *Managing the risks of extreme events and disasters to advance climate change adaptation: Special report of the intergovernmental panel on climate change* (C. B. Field Ed.). Cambridge: Cambridge University Press.

United Nations Intergovernmental Panel on Climate Change, Houghton, J. T., Ding, Y., Griggs, D. J., Noguer, M., Linden, P. J. v. d., ... Johnson, C. A. (Eds.). (2001). *Climate Change 2001: The scientific basis. Contribution of working group I to the third assessment report of the intergovernmental panel on climate change.* Cambridge and New York: Cambridge University Press.

Urban Design Associates. (2019). *Town of paradise long-term community recovery plan.* Retrieved from https://issuu.com/makeitparadise/docs/2350rptbook_final190624/1

Urban Land Institute. (2015). Ten years after Katrina, ULI Louisiana members reflect on progress in New Orleans. Retrieved from https://americas.uli.org/uli-connect/ten-years-katrina-uli-louisiana-members-reflect-progress-new-orleans/

U.S. Department of Homeland Security. (2006). A performance review of FEMA's disaster management activities in response to Hurricane

Katrina. Washington, DC: DHS (Department of Homeland Security), Office of Inspector General, Office of Inspections and Special Reviews.

U.S. Department of the Interior & US Department of Agriculture. (2001). *Urban wildland interface communities within vicinity of federal lands that are at high risk from wildfire.* Retrieved from www.federalregister.gov/articles/2001/01/04/01-52/urban-wildland-interface-communities-within-the-vicinity-of-federal-lands-that-are-at-high-risk-from#h-24.

United States Senate. (2006). Hurricane Katrina: A nation still unprepared. Report to the Committee on Homeland Security and Government Affairs, Washington, DC.

Vanlandingham, K. E. (1968). Municipal home rule in the United States. *William & Mary Law Review, 10,* 269.

Vari, A., Linnerooth-Bayer, J., & Ferencz, Z. (2003). Stakeholder views on flood risk management in Hungary's Upper Tisza Basin. *Risk Analysis: An International Journal, 23*(3), 585–600.

Velez, A.-L. K., Diaz, J. M., & Wall, T. U. (2017). Public information seeking, place-based risk messaging and wildfire preparedness in southern California. *International Journal of Wildland Fire, 26*(6), 469–477.

Verisk. (2019). *Wildfire risk analysis.* Retrieved from www.verisk.com/insurance/campaigns/location-fireline-state-risk-report/

Wachinger, G., Renn, O., Begg, C., & Kuhlicke, C. (2013). Risk perception paradox-implications for governance and communication of natural hazards. *Risk Analysis, 33*(6), 1049–1065.

Webb, G. R., Tierney, K. J., & Dahlhamer, J. M. (2000). Businesses and disasters: Empirical patterns and unanswered questions. *Natural Hazards Review, 1*(2), 83–90.

Weeks, J. D., & Hardy, P. T. (1984). The legal aspects of local government. *Small cities and counties: A guide to managing.* Washington, DC: International City Management Association.

Weible, C. M. (2005). Beliefs and policy influence: An advocacy coalition approach to policy networks. *Political Research Quarterly, 58*(3), 461–477.

Weible, C. M., & Sabatier, P. A. (2005). Comparing policy networks: Marine protected areas in California. *Policy Studies Journal, 33*(2), 181–199.

(2007). A guide to the advocacy coalition framework. In *Handbook of public policy analysis: Theory, politics, and methods* (pp. 123–136). New York: Routledge.

Weible, C. M., Sabatier, P. A., & Lubell, M. (2004). A comparison of a collaborative and top down approach to the use of science in policy: Establishing marine protected areas in California. *Policy Studies Journal, 32*(2), 187–207.

Weible, C. M., Sabatier, P. A., & McQueen, K. (2009). Themes and variations: Taking stock of the advocacy coalition framework. *Policy Studies Journal, 37*(1), 121–140.

Welz, A. (2020). Fire fallout: How ash and debris are choking Australia's rivers. Retrieved from https://e360.yale.edu/features/fire-fallout-how-ash-and-debris-are-choking-australias-rivers

Weston, C., Gandell, T., Beauchamp, J., McAlpine, L., Wiseman, C., & Beauchamp, C. (2001). Analyzing interview data: The development and evolution of a coding system. *Qualitative Sociology, 24*(3), 381–400.

Whipple, K. (2011, September 16). Colorado's 300 days of sunshine claim: It's a myth, and state's climatologist tells us why. Retrieved from www.westword.com/news/colorados-300-days-of-sunshine-claim-its-a-myth-and-states-climatologist-tells-us-why-5875821

White, G. F., Kates, R. W., & Burton, I. (2001). Knowing better and losing even more: The use of knowledge in hazards management. *Global Environmental Change Part B: Environmental Hazards, 3*(3), 81–92.

Wildavsky, A., & Dake, K. (1990). Theories of risk perception: Who fears what and why? *Daedalus, 119*, 41–60.

Wilson, P. A. (2009). Deliberative planning for disaster recovery: Remembering New Orleans. *Journal of Public Deliberation, 5*(1), 1–23.

Wolensky, R. P., & Miller, E. J. (1981). The everyday versus the disaster role of local officials: Citizen and official definitions. *Urban Affairs Quarterly, 16*(4), 483–504.

Wolfe, R. A., & Pulter, D. S. (2002). How tight are the ties that bind stakeholder groups? *Organization Science, 13*(1), 64–80.

Wong, S. D., Broader, J. C., Walker, J. L., & Shaheen, S. A. (2020). *Understanding California wildfire evacuee behavior and joint choice-making.* UC Berkeley: Transportation Sustainability Research Center. Retrieved from https://escholarship.org/uc/item/4fm7d34j

Yin, R. K. (2003). *Case study research: Design and methods.* Thousand Oaks, CA: Sage.

(2013). *Case study research: Design and methods.* Thousand Oaks, CA: Sage.

Yonetani, T., & Gordon, H. B. (2001). Simulated changes in the frequency of extremes and regional features of seasonal/annual temperature and precipitation when atmospheric CO2 is doubled. *Journal of Climate, 14*(8), 1765–1779.

Index

Printed in the United States
by Baker & Taylor Publisher Services